JOHN EVERETT MILLAIS

JOHN EVERETT MILLAIS

A BIOGRAPHY

G.H. Fleming

Constable · London

First published in Great Britain 1998 by
Constable and Company Limited
3 The Lanchesters, 162 Fulham Palace Road
London W6 9ER
Copyright © G.H. Fleming 1998
ISBN 0 094 78560 0
The right of G.H. Fleming to be identified as the author of this work
has been asserted by him in accordance
with the Copyright, Designs and Patents Act 1988
Set in Monotype Garamond 12pt
by Servis Filmsetting Ltd
Printed in Great Britain
by St Edmundsbury Press Ltd
Bury St Edmunds, Suffolk

A CIP catalogue record for this book
is available from the British Library

For Beata and Clare

Contents

CONTENTS

Illustrations

Preface

This book was conceived more than thirty-five years ago when I began the first of my two books on those daring young Victorian artistic rebels who called themselves the Pre-Raphaelite Brotherhood. I was drawn to them primarily because of that engaging rascal Dante Gabriel Rossetti, who I assumed was the leading pre-Raphaelite. I was quickly disabused of that notion. Not only was Rossetti not the most important Pre-Raphaelite, he was not even, except briefly, a Pre-Raphaelite at all. Far and away the most notable of the Brothers was John Everett Millais.

When the Brotherhood was created, in 1848, Millais, nineteen years old, was Great Britain's most promising young artist. As for his colleagues, none of them had any professional standing at all. (Rossetti had not yet exhibited a picture or published a poem.) Without Millais there would have been no Brotherhood. He alone gave it stature. Indeed the organising meeting was held in his home.

Because of his reputation, Millais was the Pre-Raphaelite who got the most attention, and when the press aimed its heavy guns at the Brothers, he was the one who suffered the most vilification. Late in the century, James Whistler would sue John Ruskin for libel because of a negative comment on one of his paintings, but Ruskin's remark was the epitome of gentleness when contrasted with what was said about Millais's pictures.

Millais managed to survive the assault and enjoyed a career that went far beyond Pre-Raphaelitism. In 1872, twenty years after the Brotherhood had disbanded, *The Times* called him 'beyond all question the greatest painting power of our time'. Twenty years later, the *Academy*, England's most influential literary weekly of the 'nineties, characterised his artistic career as 'among the national glories of English art'. This career began in 1846, when Millais was not yet seventeen, and ended with his death fifty years later. During this half century he turned out some 350 easel paintings, a total exceeded by only one British painter of note, Turner, and his versatility ranged from historical, mythological, Biblical, and literary subjects to contemporary scenes, landscapes, and portraits of men, women, children, and animals. Gainsborough's comment on Reynolds – 'Damn him, how various he is!' – is singularly suited to John Millais.

For forty years Millais was his nation's most popular creative artist. During the height of his fame the prestigious *Saturday Review* observed, 'The Millais of the year so soon becomes everybody's talk that there is no need to describe it. Hardly any book approaches it in the speed and vividness of its impression. The diffusion of Mr Dickens's tales, at their best, or of a new volume by Mr Tennyson, perhaps come the nearest.' Unlike many popular artists, Millais was highly honoured by his peers. He was the youngest ever Associate of the Royal Academy, one of the youngest full Academicians, the first painter to be awarded a hereditary title and, finally, president of the Royal Academy.

One would expect Millais, like Rossetti, should be the subject of numerous biographies. Six or seven books deal with his art, but, amazingly, until now there has been only one book-length biography, the two-volume *Life and Letters of Sir John Millais*, by his fourth son, John Guille Millais, which appeared in 1899. This has been a valuable source, but its many omissions and inaccuracies rule it out as a reliable life story and its highly biased point of view makes it less a biography than a hagiography. This long-standing neglect of Millais has therefore enabled me to produce a volume in which about three-quarters of its contents appear for the first time within the covers of a book.

Millais was a prolific correspondent, and I have made much use of his letters which, among other things, reveal the inner drama of his creative life. I have also drawn a great deal from contemporary reviews of his work, which played an important role in shaping his career, for he read them closely. In going over these critiques now it is intriguing to see just how wrongheaded art critics can be. The critical commentaries, moreover, assisted me in placing Millais within the context of his era.

This book could have been longer, much longer. If I had included everything in my files, I could have created a 'chronicle biography' with well over a thousand pages. But that did not interest me. The great jazz trumpet player Miles Davis once said, 'I always listen to what I can leave out.' For my part, I looked for what I could leave out. I preferred to be selective rather than exhaustive (and exhausting).

The reader will note the absence of footnotes and superscripts in the body of the work. At the end a section of notes provides the source of every quotation.

Acknowledgments

Many persons – students, colleagues, scholars, librarians, curators, research assistants, typists, friends, and acquaintances – have been helpful in one way or another. To list all of them would be impossible and pretentious. I must, however, name two persons: my research assistant Beata Duncan, and my literary agent, Clare Pearson, whose assistance has gone well beyond what anyone could reasonably have anticipated. It is easier to cite helpful libraries. I have spent many weeks at the Pierpont Morgan Library in New York City, the principal repository of materials relating to John Everett Millais. Its staff members have been knowledgeable, courteous, and co-operative. I have also enjoyed customary privileges at other libraries: the Bodleian Library, Oxford; the British Library, London; the British Newspaper Library, Colindale; the University of British Columbia Library, Special Collections; the library of the Chicago Art Institute; the Fitzwilliam Museum, Department of Manuscripts, Cambridge; the Guildhall Library, London; the Houghton Library, Harvard University; the Huntington Library, San Marino, California; the Library of Congress, Manuscript Division, Washington; the New York Public Library, New York City; the Princeton University Library; the library of the Royal Academy of Arts, London; the John Rylands University Library of Manchester, Special Collections; the library of the Victoria and Albert Museum, London; the Beinecke Rare Book Room and Manuscript Library, Yale University.

My home base of operations, for the third time, has been Chicago's Newberry Library. Everyone there knows that I appreciate what they have done for me.

CHAPTER 1

1829—37

WHEN he was a young man, John Millais observed, 'A few years ago the scion of a respectable family felt it infra dig to follow art as a profession; there was a feeling of uncertainty as to the artist's place in society, and doubts entertained as to whether it was the fitting occupation of a *gentleman*; the relatives of such an aspirant looked upon it as a disgrace that one of their blood should choose such a calling as a means of gaining a livelihood . . . Art was never thought otherwise than ennobling in itself . . . but to be a practical worker therein was considered a degradation, to be classed with those who labour with their hands.'

Luckily his parents were atypical. Holman Hunt, who became Millais's closest friend, once said, 'It amazed me that his family was actually delighted at the prospect of his becoming an artist.' Mr and Mrs Millais didn't just consent to their son's vocational choice. They *encouraged* him. This was the first sign of his living under a lucky star.

John Everett Millais, his parents' eldest child, was born on 8 June 1829. He spent most of his first nine years on the island of Jersey, where his paternal ancestors had settled before 1066 and had been landholders at least since 1331. At one time the family must have had some local celebrity; a range of hills north-east of the capital, St Helier, is called Les Monts Millais. John Everett's father, John William, married Mary Evamy, daughter of a prosperous commercial fisherman. Their marriage was the first for him, the second for her, a widow with two small boys. They had three children, John Everett and, soon thereafter, William Henry and Emily Mary.

The family lived comfortably on the edge of St Helier, overlooking the sea. John William was a genial, handsome man. Years later, Emily Mary, writing to her brother, would refer to their father as 'a fine healthy man, so free from any excess'. He was a gentleman of leisure who loved music. He played the flute, his wife was a violinist, and their house was often the scene of chamber music recitals. John Everett never took up an instrument, but he would always enjoy listening to music.

Johnny's general education began routinely in the local grammar school, but he wasn't there for long. His only previous biographer, his fourth son, John G. Millais, maintained that on his first day he earned a paddling for disobedience. Before the schoolmaster could strike, Johnny allegedly bit his hand and was sent home, never to return. This story sounds apocryphal; nothing else in his childhood may be fairly seen as an act of defiance. But for whatever reason Johnny did eventually stop going to school, and he began receiving instruction from his mother at home.

Reflecting her background, Mrs Millais's teaching was strong in history and literature, weak in science and mathematics. Within these limits, she was apparently a gifted teacher. For many years the subjects of her son's paintings would come from British and European history, English literature, foreign literature in translation, mythology, and the Bible, all of which formed the core of her teaching.

Mrs Millais's lessons might be seen as groundwork for a future painter at a time when the subject of a picture was all-important. But she could not have had this in mind in becoming her son's teacher. To be sure, he constantly sketched with a pencil or crayon, but millions of other youngsters have done this. His earliest drawings must have been good, but he was not regarded as a *Wunderkind*. Perhaps because they themselves were artistically talented, Johnny's parents did not seem to find anything remarkable in his work.

* * *

A favourite resort of Jerseyans was the picturesque Breton town of Dinan. Steam packets crossed over to St Malo; river boats then carried the passengers up to Dinan. In the autumn of 1836 the Millais family took this excursion and young Johnny naturally took out his pencils. Since they were staying near a military post, he sketched soldiers performing everyday activities. One afternoon a couple of officers stopped to look at his work.

'They uttered loud ejaculations of astonishment,' his brother related. 'They patted him on the back, and asked where we lived. Our house was only a stone's throw off, so we took them up into the drawing room, where they urged my father and mother to send the child to Paris to be educated in the arts.

'The officers showed this sketchbook to their brothers in arms. They could not believe that it was the work of a boy of seven, so one of them fetched little Johnny. In fear and trembling he came and made a still more excellent sketch – of the colonel smoking a cigar.'

This was the first turning point in the life of John Everett Millais. His parents realised that if he was uncommonly talented, he needed guidance. Upon returning home, they arranged for drawing lessons.

* * *

Johnny's teacher was a Mr Bissel. Their relationship was no reprise of the schoolroom experience. The self-motivated drawer of pictures at once became a diligent follower of instructions. He was told to 'draw from the flat', by copying drawings and engravings, mostly from the eighteenth century. Again and again. Art teachers believed that mastering the work of predecessors would provide a painter with a storehouse of material to draw upon, thereby stimulating one's own originality.

Johnny copied painstakingly, always indoors. He probably didn't call into question this procedure by asking for permission to draw directly from nature. Bissel would not have mentioned landscape art. It was not part of the classical tradition. Studio work was everything. A Victorian fine arts magazine referred to Jersey, with its hills and valleys, trees and flowers, cliffs and ocean views, as 'emphatically a painter's paradise . . . the epitome of all that is beautiful in scenery and embracing every element that appeals to the artistic eye'. None of this greatly affected John Millais, who lacked an innate feeling for nature. He was like Wordsworth's Peter Bell:

A primrose by a river's brim
A yellow primrose was to him
And it was nothing more.

Actually his first landscape work was done when he was twenty, and then only as background. His first pure landscape came when he was forty-one.

After about a year, Bissel told Mr and Mrs Millais that Johnny was extraordinarily talented and was now ready for the next level, copying from antique statues. For lack of equipment, it couldn't be done in Jersey. He advised sending the boy to London, where he could utilise his gifts.

Johnny's parents might have placed him with friends or relatives in London. Or he and his mother might have stayed there together. Either of these actions would have constituted a remarkable upheaval. But they went much further, deciding that the whole family – Mr and Mrs Millais, their three children, and the two boys from her first marriage – would move to the metropolis, abandoning home, friends, a centuries-old heritage in response to a suggestion by a provincial drawing master. Thus was John Everett Millais's lifework determined at the age of eight.

CHAPTER 2

1838–43

ON their arrival in London the Millais family stopped at the moderately priced Adam Street Hotel between the Strand and the river, and the next morning Johnny and his mother walked over to Trafalgar Square, as yet a 'square' in name only, just a vacant space. Apart from the church of St Martin-in-the-Fields, nothing was there but the National Gallery building. Its 166 pictures had lately been put in place, but Mrs Millais and her son had not come for them. Until 1869, the Gallery would share space with the nation's foremost visual arts organisation, the Royal Academy of Arts. It was the Academy that had drawn Johnny and his mother to Trafalgar Square.

After ascending to the portico and passing into the entrance hall, they were directed to a staircase. They walked down one flight to the ground floor office of Britain's pre-eminent arts official, the president of the Royal Academy.

The president, since 1830, was a sixty-eight-old Irishman, Sir Martin Archer Shee. A moderately good portraitist, he had gained his post less for professional achievements than appearance, personality, and character. He was classically educated, fluent in French, handsome and affable, with an eloquent voice and impeccable manners. He had written two published novels, numerous poems, and a tragedy. In his satirical poem 'English Bards and Scotch Reviewers', Lord Byron referred to him as 'The poet's rival, but the painter's friend.'

After handing him a letter of introduction from Bissel, Mrs Millais told Shee why they were in London and asked for guidance on Johnny's future. According to her, this exchange occurred:

'Madam, do you want my honest advice?'

'Yes, Sir Martin, that is why we are here.'

'I think your son would be better employed sweeping chimneys than studying to become a painter.'

Mary Millais kept insisting that he had said this, so there must be some basis to her story. But it is inconceivable that he could have been quite so brusque. The general tenor of his response is however understandable. The profession was hazardously overcrowded. The 1841 census would disclose the presence of 3500 artists in Britain, far more than needed! Few painters earned a tolerable income. Shee himself had struggled to eke out a bare living; for a time he augmented his professional earnings by writing exhibition reviews. So in good conscience he could not encourage an unknown youngster to enter this domain.

Mrs Millais, however, was undaunted. She handed over a folio of drawings, which Shee politely received, probably expecting to spend less than five minutes with them. But as he looked them over, his attitude changed. Like the French army officers, he was incredulous.

'Madam,' he asked, 'did your son do these drawings by himself?'

'Yes, Sir Martin, this is entirely his work.'

He then gave Johnny a pencil and a sheet of paper attached to a board and asked him to copy a nearby statue. After a few minutes, pencil and paper were returned. Martin Shee was convinced. He apologised to Mrs Millais. Her son was extraordinarily gifted and definitely should plan on a career in painting. But he was too young for art school. He should enroll in a grammar school and spend his free time drawing in the British Museum.

* * *

Bloomsbury, the district north-east of Oxford Street, was where the Millais family would live. Many of its residents were involved in the arts – writers, musicians, and painters – and living accommodation was mostly comfortable and reasonably priced. They chose a house near Fitzroy Square in Charlotte Street.

Various painters had lived and worked in Charlotte Street, most notably John Constable, from 1822 until his death in 1837. Others would come later, but according to London's postal directories none were there during the Millais tenancy. The street had become highly commercial, with shops for at least fifty-four tradesmen: a shoemaker, a tobacconist, two pawnbrokers, three bakers, an undertaker, a hair dresser, two cabinet makers, a corset maker, a pork butcher, a plumber, two tailors, a patent medicine vendor, three upholsterers, etc. The directory for 1839 shows just one Charlotte Street resident whose name is followed by 'Esq.' – John William Millais.

As soon as they had settled, Emily Mary enrolled at a grammar school, and William registered with a tutor. Johnny would continue to take lessons from his mother. Complementing his home instruction were almost daily visits to the British Museum, where he copied classical antiquities, and frequent trips to the National Gallery, where he learned by heart most of the paintings.

While walking about, he enjoyed the sights and sounds of early Dickensian London, but not as a painter. The streets, buildings, parks, and river would not draw forth from him even one picture. His subjects would always come from other sources.

* * *

Around the corner from the Adam Street Hotel, in John Street, a building housed London's oldest art organisation, the Society for the Encouragement of Arts, Manufactures, and Commerce, popularly known as the Society of Arts. One way of carrying out its mandate was to hold an annual open drawing competition. Johnny, who perhaps had seen the building when he stopped at the hotel, entered the 1839 contest, unconcerned that he would be competing against adults. He submitted a large imagined scene from the Battle of Bannockburn. On a Saturday in June, prizes were presented in the society's auditorium.

I shall never forget that day [William Millais recalled long afterwards]. My brother wore a white plaid tunic, with black belt and buckle; short white frilled trousers, showing bare legs, with white socks and patent leather shoes; a large white collar, a bright necktie, and his hair in golden curls.

When the Secretary called out [as winner of the silver medal] 'Mr John Everett Millais', the little lad walked up unseen by the Duke of

[13]

Sussex, who was giving the prizes, and sat at a raised desk. After a time the Duke observed that 'the gentleman is a long time coming up,' to which the Secretary replied, 'He *is* here, your Royal Highness.' The Duke stood up and saw the boy, and giving him his stool to stand upon, the pretty little golden head appeared about the desk.

The Duke, having weak eyesight, could make nothing of the drawing when it was held up, in spite of trying several glasses, but was assured it was a marvellous performance. He patted my brother's head, wished him success, and handed him his medal.

Johnny was now ready for art school.

* * *

In nineteenth-century Britain, the usual goal of aspiring male artists was acceptance by the schools of the Royal Academy. (Females were not prohibited from enrolling, but in fact all students were male until 1860, when the Academy approved an application, accompanied by requisite drawings, from 'L.A. Herford'. Apparently no one on the admissions committee knew that 'L.A.' stood for Laura Ann.)

The schools of the Royal Academy were London's equivalent to Paris's École des Beaux-Arts. But unlike Paris, where various ateliers prepared pupils for the École, London in 1839 had only two similar establishments. One of them was in Margaret Street, Cavendish Square, directed by a Spanish master, Don Vollaloros, but it was only a year old, too new for Mr and Mrs Millais. They chose the simply named School of Art, which had flourished at 6 Streatham Street, in the heart of Bloomsbury, since 1820. Because of its founder-proprietor, Henry Sass, it was called Sass's Academy.

Sass, forty-nine years old in 1839, is a case in point for George Bernard Shaw's dictum, 'He who can does. He who cannot, teaches.' Sass was a portrait painter, diligent, methodical and mediocre. As a Royal Academy student, he had been noted for never being absent. Constable called him 'the inexorable Sass, who set an excellent example for regularity of attendance at school. I presume not to hold him up as an example in any other respect.' Sass wasn't much of a painter, but he was a good teacher. One of his pupils, who had left just before Millais came, was the popular creator of crowd scenes, William Frith, who said, 'I feel that I owe everything to Sass and his teaching. Many of my brother artists, I feel sure, would endorse my verdict on our dear old teacher.'

When Frith arrived, he didn't regard Sass as 'dear'. He had a portfolio of drawings, which the master acknowledged: 'Ah, copies from Dutch prints! Shouldn't wonder if you eventually take to engraving. What induced you to spend time on such things? Terrible waste. But can't have done you much harm if you forget all about them.'

Sass's veneration of the antique governed his agenda. A student began by laboriously copying an outline. He continued day after day, week after week, month after month, until finally the magic word *'Bene'* appeared on a drawing, signifying promotion to the next echelon, the study of light and shade. In the second class, Frith recalled, 'A huge white plaster ball standing on a pedestal was my first object of attention, by the representation of which in Italian chalk I was initiated into the principles of light, shadow, and rotundity . . . I spent six weeks copying that awful ball.' Then, after more weeks of copying other objects, Frith advanced to the final stratum, the study of tonal differences.

John Millais appeared in Streatham Street soon after his tenth birthday, the youngest ever 'Sassite'. His age didn't create problems. He got on with the others and adapted quickly to the routine. He was regular in attendance, and no one worked harder. Sass had no prescribed period of study. His programme was aimed at the semi-annual qualifying examination for the Royal Academy Schools. Every Sassite waited for the master to say, 'You should try for the Academy.' Frith and John Calcott Horsley, future Academicians, stayed for two years, the norm for good students. Dante Gabriel Rossetti lingered on for four years.

Just ten months after arriving, John Millais was advised to 'try for the Academy'. He was not yet eleven years old.

* * *

In the nineteenth century, the Royal Academy of Arts was internationally known for its annual Summer Exhibition which, along with Paris's Salon, was one of the world's most prestigious art shows. But when the Academy was founded in 1768, the Exhibition was not its raison d'être. The original Instrument, signed by George III, stated that the principal object was 'the maintenance of schools' of painting, sculpture, and architecture, in which everything – masters, professors models, a library – would be free. The Exhibition was an afterthought to provide, through entrance fees and catalogue sales, support for the schools.

When John Millais applied for admission, the qualifying examination was in two parts. First, an applicant had to submit a chalk drawing, not less than two feet high, of an undraped antique figure, and two anatomised figure drawings, with bones and muscles properly labelled. Also required was a letter from a responsible person attesting to the aspirant's character. The deadlines in 1840 were the 28th of June and December.

On 25 June, the Keeper of the Academy, George Jones, received this letter:

Not having any of the printed forms used on this occasion, I beg leave to recommend John Everett Millais as a candidate to become a Probationer in the Royal Academy. His age and aspect will I think justify me in bearing favourable testimony to his *moral* character, and combined with his talents will I am sure interest you in his favour.

Should this mode of recommendation be in your opinion informal, I shall supply one more regular if you will have the goodness to send me a printed form.

Believe me, my dear sir,
very faithfully yours,
Martin Archer Shee.

This informal recommendation was acceptable, as were Johnny's drawings. On Friday, 17 July, the name of John Millais was added to the roll of probationers. Within a few months he would have to show that he had not been helped with his drawings by duplicating them in a Royal Academy studio. This was part two of the entrance examination. He spent the probationary period preparing for it.

He now lived at 6 Caroline Street, below Bedford Square, his family's third London residence. They had left Charlotte Street at the start of the year and spent several months above Bedford Square at 23 Alfred Street. None of the houses had a studio.

In December Trafalgar Square was starting to take shape. Workers were paving the ground and laying a foundation for the Nelson column. And in this month, on the 12th, John Millais passed his examination and became a bona fide Royal Academy student. He received a circular ivory ticket certifying that for ten years he was 'entitled to study daily in the Academy and to have access to models, paintings, books, etc., and to receive instruction, attend lectures, and have all other privileges, with no payment'. His age was eleven years, six months, and six days. No other student, before or since, has been as young as he.

* * *

Painting students were enrolled in three divisions of instruction. The first was the Antique School, at the rear of the ground floor in the sculpture gallery (no longer existing as such). The class sat in two semi-circular rows of seats copying casts of ancient statues and groups. They could stay from ten until three and from five until seven.

The nominal instructor was the administrative head of the schools, George Jones, RA, noted for battle paintings and a physical resemblance to the Duke of Wellington. Polite and friendly, he was popular with the students, but other duties kept him from spending much time with them. He 'taught' by offering conventional advice during daily half-hour rounds. This routine was frequently disparaged. *Blackwood's Magazine* editorialised that 'the students are taught for nothing, and the instruction is of commensurate value.' George Dunlop Leslie, a future Academician, called the procedure 'wasted time'. Leslie stayed long enough to reach the next level, but George Frederick Watts dropped out and worked alone at home.

John Millais, however, didn't complain. He was delighted to be there. Frith, twenty-one years old and still in the Antique School, witnessed Johnny's arrival. He recalled 'the amusement of students – some of whom were almost middle-aged – when a handsome little boy, dressed in a long coat confined at the waist by a black leather band, walked in and gravely took his place amongst us'. His gravity was not long-lasting. An eventual Academician, Frederick Goodall, seven years older, called him 'the most animated and most excitable boy I ever met'.

Another subsequent RA contributed to his development.

'One day,' Millais recounted, 'when I was drawing from the Antique, a young man tapped me on the shoulder and asked if I would sit to him as a model for a page to Robert the Bruce. He was painting the Battle of Bannockburn. I assented and went to his studio.'

The man was John Phillip, a twenty-three-old student in the second painting school, who would become famous for his Spanish pictures. Johnny visited Phillip's studio, in Fitzroy Square, not just to sit. Encouraged by his host, he tried his hand with a paint brush. The result was his first oil painting, *Cupid Crowned with Flowers*, showing the boy god, aged seven or eight, looking angelic as his mother crowns him with a wreath. Could the young artist have seen himself in that celestial boy? Venus, resembling a Victorian housewife, may have symbolised Johnny's mother, who certainly looked upon her son as a little god and had already invested him with the success that she was convinced would be his. This may be farfetched, but it is intriguing that among all the incidents from ancient mythology, he chose this particular one.

In the spring of 1841, Philip returned to his home in Aberdeen for a prolonged stay. *Cupid Crowned with Flowers* thus was completed before John Millais's twelfth birthday. (It is reproduced in volume one, page 24, of John G. Millais's *Life and Letters*.)

*   *   *

In November 1843, Admiral Nelson's statue took its place as the showpiece of Trafalgar Square, and John Everett Millais moved up a notch.

The Academy's Laws and Regulations provided that to be pro-moted, an Antique student had to 'deliver to the Keeper a finished Drawing of a Statue or a Group, accompanied by a finished drawing as large as Nature of a Hand and Foot. He also shall make a Drawing in twelve consecutive sittings of two hours each from a Statue espe-cially placed for that purpose.' Johnny did what was required, his work was accepted, and he advanced to the Life School.

A couple of weeks later, the Academy awarded its biennial prizes. Victorian Britain's premier fine arts publication, the *Art Journal*, reported on the affair:

On Saturday, the 9th of December, a general meeting was held in Trafalgar Square 'for the election of officers and other business,' the principal being the delivery of student prizes before a large assembly of Academicians, guests, and students.

The distribution of medals was a very imposing ceremony. A high degree of enthusiasm was manifested by cheers as each student received his reward. It was not difficult to ascertain, by the extent of greeting, the estimate in which each was held . . . Mr Millais, who wore a boy-shirt collar and seemed to be no more than fourteen or fifteen years old, was hailed with long continued cheers when he received the prize for the best drawing from the antique.

One member of the audience, with a guest ticket, was a sixteen-year-old independent art student, William Holman Hunt. This was his recollection:

When it came the turn of the antique school, attention was breathless as the preliminary words were uttered slowly, and the name of John Everett Millais was given as winner of the first prize. A slim lad with curly hair and a white collar arose eagerly and was handed from seat to seat till he descended into the arena, where, remembering his manners, he bowed and approached the desk. The applause was boisterous . . .

Of all the students, no name was so often mentioned as that of Millais. I had not until now seen the boy of whom I had heard so much. I had formed so exalted an idea of him that it would have been painful had he fallen short of my standard. It was not so; he was exactly what I had pictured.

CHAPTER 3

1844–46

In the Life School, students faced real teachers. Every month a different Royal Academician appeared as a Visitor to 'set the figures, examine the performances of students, advise and instruct'. The class met under the dome five times a week from six until eight in the evening. During the day, Life students were usually free to do as they pleased. Millais frequently went to his 'home away from home', the British Museum. On one visit a chance encounter was the most significant event of his early life. It happened in June 1844. The other party recalled the incident:

One day when absorbed in my work of copying in the Sculpture Gallery, a boy stood for a few moments behind me. After a close scrutiny, he went off suddenly. Observing his black velvet tunic, belt, and shining bright hair curling over a white turned-down collar, I recognised Millais.

Later I went into the Elgin Room and saw him drawing Illysus. As I approached, he suddenly turned and said, 'I say, aren't you the fellow who was doing that drawing in Room XIII?'

'Yes, that was me.'

'That's a good drawing. You ought to be in the Academy.'

'That's exactly my opinion. Unfortunately, the Council twice decided the other way.'

'You just send that drawing, and you will be in like a shot. Take my word for it. I ought to know. I got the first medal last year in the Antique, and it wasn't the first one I have received, I can tell you. Now, remember, your drawing will get you in the Academy.'

Thus did John Millais and Holman Hunt – he went by his middle name – have their first conversation. Hunt again reacted favourably to the Academy's star pupil. Millais's conceit was too ingenuous to be objectionable. Besides, it was dissolved by a disarmingly warm smile. Three weeks later Hunt gained probationary status at the Academy.

* * *

The son of a modestly compensated warehouse manager, Holman Hunt grew up in the drab north-eastern suburb of Haggerston, amidst factories, gas works, and almshouses. Like Millais, he loved drawing, but, unlike Millais he did not receive much parental encouragement. His father didn't object to this pastime, but when, late in 1839, the boy spoke of becoming a painter, his father removed him from school, intending to place him at a twelve-hour-a-day job in his warehouse. Hunt forestalled his father by going to work for an estate agent. His employer, an amateur painter, encouraged him to attend an evening drawing class. He did so for a year. Then his boss retired, and his job evaporated.

Again Mr Hunt mentioned the warehouse. Again his son found something better, designing patterns for a calico concern. Now fifteen, he went for the first time to the National Gallery. The visit energised him. Some of the pictures, he thought, might have been done by his drawing master. He was more than ever confident about a career as a painter, quit his job and threw down a gauntlet. If he couldn't become an artist, he would join the army. Reluctantly his father yielded, and Hunt began preparing for the Royal Academy Schools. But not at Sass's. To preserve his individuality, he trained solitarily. Twice he applied to the Academy; twice he was rejected. He then told his father that if he failed again, he would forget about painting as a profession. As we have seen, the third time was the charm. After passing the second part of the entrance test, he was enrolled in the Antique School late in 1844.

* * *

Soon after Hunt arrived at the Academy, he and Millais began a mutually beneficial friendship. 'We talked about our views on art,' Hunt said, 'and our ideals. We revealed our innermost thoughts and formed ardent resolves for the future.' Alike in many ways, in one respect they were notably dissimilar.

Hunt was an outspoken iconoclast. At the Antique School, he related, his 'denunciation of the gods of the art world became a password with the other students, who sometimes doubted my sincerity. How could anyone be in earnest who said Murillo's *Holy Family* was rubbish?' Hunt's classmates were right to doubt his sincerity because he really didn't believe this himself. He just wanted to shock them. Also, he was 'trying to find a path for my feet, and mine only'. He believed that most contemporary English painters had chosen a road that was banal and platitudinous, and he was unequivocally determined not to join them.

Well-travelled paths were good enough for Millais, who was in no way unorthodox. Hunt noted that he always dressed conventionally. His ideas were just as uncontroversial. One day Millais called Hunt an agitator. Jesus, he was reminded, was denounced as an agitator.

'Yes, and he got stoned! Quite right, too, from the point of view of the people, who saw nothing of his divinity, only his agitation. If I had been there, I'm afraid I would have thrown stones, too.'

Although historically inaccurate, he made his point. As a disturber of the British art universe, Holman Hunt couldn't count on support from John Millais.

*   *   *

In the biography of his father, John G. Millais wrote the following:

In 1845 Millais became acquainted with Serjeant Thomas, a retired lawyer who traded in works of art. Recognising his genius and knowing that he was very poor, Thomas offered him £100 a year to come to his house every Saturday and paint small pictures. A contract was drawn up and duly signed, binding Millais to serve for two years. Little did he know of the galling yoke that hung upon his neck. Thomas, who as a picture dealer, got a profit out of his work, worried him beyond measure by his constant interference, restrictive rules, and general insolence of manner. At last – long before the two years were over – things came to a crisis. One Saturday morning Millais came to work ten minutes late, and Thomas attacked him furiously, winding up a long harangue with a personal remark that stung him to the quick. He had just arranged his palette with fresh colours, and in a moment it was sent flying at Thomas's head . . . A violent smashing of the door announced Millais's departure and his determination never to enter the house again.

Because of passages like this I have been less than enthusiastic about John G. Millais's book. This is a piece of almost total fiction. Millais did not become acquainted with Ralph Thomas in 1845. Their families had been friends for a number of years. Thomas did not become a serjeant-at-law until 1852. Far from being retired, he was active until his death in 1862. They didn't sign a contract, which would have been illegal because Millais was a minor. They had a friendly verbal agreement. Thomas did not strike a hard bargain because Millais was 'very poor'. He was never poor. He worked for Thomas not for the compensation but for the opportunity to paint.

For years he had been drawing, but except for one picture in John Phillip's studio, he had done no painting. Too impatient to wait for advancement to the Academy Painting School, he eagerly accepted Thomas's offer. They parted in 1846, but not because of a fight. There was no fight. Millais left because his family had moved again, into a new house with a studio. Now, John Everett could paint at home.

* * *

The Millais address was 83 Gower Street (number 7 today). Gower Street, running from Bedford Square to the Euston Road, lined with late eighteenth-century three- and four-storey brown brick houses, has not received much applause. John Ruskin thought it marked the depth of ugliness in street architecture, and in his *London Handbook* of 1849 Peter Cunningham called it a 'monotonous street with dull, third-rate houses'. In one sense the houses were third-rate because, for rating purposes, they were taxed in the third category. Yet, like Sloane Street, in Knightsbridge, which Cunningham also called third-rate, Gower Street was a socially correct address. When Millais arrived, the residents included six surgeons, three physicians, four clergymen, two barristers, three architects, three solicitors, two dentists, two professors, and no tradesmen or artisans. In the postal directory, 'Esq.' followed the names of thirty-six Gower Street house-holders.

The Millais family lived in one of four flats in the second building from Bedford Square on the western side. It has a narrow front, three storeys and an attic. Brown bricks are above the ground floor, white stucco below. In the rear there is a small garden.

The most recent occupant had been George Clint, a painter known for theatrical pictures – scenes from plays and portraits of actors. In 1821, aged fifty-one, he became an Associate of the Royal Academy. Fifteen years later, because he had not become a full Academician, he resigned his associateship. When a Parliamentary committee investigated complaints relating to the Royal Academy, the principal prosecutorial witness was George Clint. Controversy was no stranger to 83 Gower Street.

* * *

The Millais probably made their move because of a room, nineteen feet six inches by twenty feet, at the rear of the ground floor, Clint's studio. John Millais didn't wait long to get started. Early in 1846 he began a type of painting then in vogue, a multi-figured historical action scene. He was prompted by a book of history and by an engraving. The book was John Luffman's popular *Elements of Universal History and Chronology*. The relevant passage deals with the ruthlessness of Francisco Pizarro when he invaded the Inca empire: 'Pizarro himself advanced towards the emperor, whom he took prisoner; while his soldiers, incited by Vincent de Valverde, massacred all that surrounded the monarch.' The engraving was a picture by lately deceased Henry Briggs, RA, of *The First Interview between the Spaniards and Peruvians* showing Pizarro's duplicity, professing friendship while planning a massacre. Millais carried the narrative forward and depicted the slaughter, a sixteen-year-old student finishing off a story that an Academician had started.

Millais's models were friends, neighbours, and relatives, including his father, who was always happy to assist his son in whatever way he could. Mrs Millais was also helpful, researching for him in the British Museum and reading aloud while he worked. He wasn't always properly appreciative. Nine-year-old Florence Thomas, daughter of the man for whom he had briefly worked, visited his studio while the picture was in progress. She reported that 'when his father, ready to do anything to help, proffered a mild suggestion, Johnny replied, "By George, my dear fellow, you know nothing about it." After a similar suggestion from his mother, he said, "My good woman, what are you talking about?"'

But note how he treated young Florence. Mr Millais asked her if she wanted to watch Johnny or would rather draw her own picture. 'I was very shy,' she related, 'and I said very softly, "draw". I was provided with paper and pencils and placed opposite a little cast of a cupid with wings, suspended from the ceiling.' It wasn't easy. Johnny saw her struggling, and several times without prompting he left his own work. Gently, without condescension, he showed her what to do and how to do it.

* * *

Millais began with a bang. His picture measures fifty by sixty-eight inches and contains some thirty figures. The conquistador is seizing the emperor while his men assault the courtiers. In the foreground, arms raised, a priest holds a cross and blesses the atrocities. Most of the figures are shadowy, but four are individualised: Pizarro, the emperor, an officer, lower left, and a cringing woman, lower right, awaiting her doom. This was not the kind of picture that would make Millais famous; nevertheless it foreshadowed the future.

A story is told with clarity, immediacy and dramatic impact, a Millais hallmark. The priest exemplifies the artist's abhorrence of the hypocrisy of organised religion. The pleading, touchingly ingenuous woman was his first expressively beautiful female. He had a trick – I don't use the word pejoratively – of manipulating a woman's eyes and mouth to give her expression a softened beauty and he was already doing this at the age of sixteen.

This beautiful victim illustrates a strong early influence, that of William Etty, RA.

* * *

Etty, fifty-nine years old in 1846, personally and professionally was highly individualistic. As a Royal Academy student he had won a gold medal, entitling him to use the facilities for life. He was almost the only person who ever fully exercised this privilege. He lived in Buckingham Street, off the Strand. Every evening he would walk over to the National Gallery building and climb a flight of one hundred steps to the Life School, arriving promptly at six o'clock. Sitting among students with his brushes and pigments, he was a legendary figure. To the other Academicians he was an embarrassment. Some of them had remonstrated with him because of what they called unprofessional behaviour. He ignored their protests. The Life School, he said, 'fills up a couple of hours in the evening, which I should be at a loss how else to employ'.

Etty maintained a good rapport with the students. Frederick Goodall, who entered the Life School just ahead of Millais, said that Etty 'had the greatest voice and manners of any one I ever knew and was kindness itself in giving instructions to young artists'.

Millais must have talked to Etty and examined his work. His own early pictures clearly show the Etty influence. One obvious point of contact was in the use of colours. Etty was a great colourist, and so was Millais. And yet despite his reputation as a colourist, Etty repeatedly emphasised the importance of form. 'Let your principal attention be to Form,' he said, 'for without *that*, the best colouring is but chance.' Sounding like Ingres, he asserted, '*Drawing* is the soul of art.' It is more than likely that Millais heard him say something like this, and he, too, would always recognise the priority of form.

The Ettyean influence also appeared in the content of Millais's work. Etty's subjects, mostly from the past and usually classical or mythological, permitted him to portray what he did better than anyone else, female nudes. 'I found,' he once said, 'that all great painters of antiquity painted the Human Form. I resolved to paint nothing else, finding that God's most glorious work to be Woman, and that human beauty had been concentrated in her.' Again and again he painted nude women. It became a passion. (Ironically, he was a lifelong bachelor.)

Occasionally Etty invited students to his flat for conversation and light refreshments. One can readily imagine Millais inspecting whatever pictures were there. Although he would not paint a total nude until 1870, he was permanently won over by the female creations of the Life School's perpetual student.

* * *

'I accept an exhibition as a necessary artistic arena, where as a rule the best works are found out. I am bound to admit it is often cruel and unfair. The immediate neighbourhood of conflicting subject and colouring, life size beside camera work . . . is never contemplated by the artist, and a delicate, refined work might be entirely lost hung between a crude snowstorm and a violent sunset.'

This was how Millais at the height of his career looked upon exhibitions, an integral part of his life for fifty-one years. It all began in February of 1846, when the Royal Academy sent out the customary notice for its annual show. Artists were invited to send in their 'performances' – a curious word in this context – on Monday, 6 April, or Tuesday, the 7th. Since they hadn't ever exhibited anything, Hunt and Millais did not receive a copy of the announcement. But they knew of the deadline and were hurrying to finish their paintings. Conforming to convention, Millais gave his picture a fully descriptive title: *Pizarro Seizing the Inca of Peru*. Leaving nothing to the viewer's imagination, he also included for the catalogue the applicable sentence from Luffman. Hunt's picture was a small one of a little girl holding a watch to her ear. Its title was simply *Hark!*.

There was no doubt about where the pictures would go. London had numerous exhibitions but only one Exhibition, opening at noon on the first Monday in May at the galleries of the Royal Academy. John Millais and Holman Hunt did not think of going elsewhere. On 7 April their paintings were en route to Trafalgar Square.

Two weeks later they would learn if they were in or out. Since well over half of all submissions were habitually rejected, it was a long fortnight.

It is not clear how Millais passed the time, but for Hunt this was a period of extraordinary significance. Unable to concentrate on work, he borrowed a book of art criticism, volume two of *Modern Painters*. He devoured it in less than two days. 'Of all its readers,' he said, 'none could have felt more strongly than I that it was written for him.' At once he sought out, and absorbed, the first volume. According to the title page of volume one, the author was 'A Graduate of Oxford'. Because of his youth, he withheld his name. With volume two, he came out of the closet. He was twenty-seven-year-old John Ruskin.

The impact of *Modern Painters* on Hunt was due in part to its forceful style. But more important was its content. Hunt believed that contemporary British art was governed by 'hackneyed conventionality', with 'pictured waxworks playing the part of human beings'. No one at the Academy supported him. Then Ruskin entered his life and put his thoughts into proper focus. Hitherto his approach had been mostly negative. He knew what he didn't like, but he hadn't developed positive standards. Ruskin provided a key to affirmation. Young artists 'should go to Nature in all singleness of heart and walk with her laboriously and trustingly, having no other thoughts but how best to penetrate her meaning'. Their 'duty' was 'to be humble and earnest in following the steps of Nature'. If also they wanted to study paintings, they should bypass Old Masters in favour of early Italians, forerunners of Raphael, whose work showed 'a loving fidelity of the thing studied'.

Modern Painters had a great psychological effect on Hunt. 'Up to that time,' he said, 'I had thought that the world regarded art as a vagabondish cleverness, and that it was almost a disgrace to have a passion for it.' After reading *Modern Painters*, he was proud to be an artist. 'By Jove!' he said to a friend. 'Ruskin feels the power and responsibility of art more than any author I have read.'

He tried to convert his companion, but Millais wouldn't read one sentence of *Modern Painters*. He thought only of his *Pizarro*.

* * *

Until 1875, the Royal Academy's hopeful exhibitors appeared in person at the entrance to learn of their fate. They would identify themselves to the porter, who, after looking into a book, might loudly exclaim, 'Mr S, your paintings, all of them, have been chucked!' Holman Hunt and John Millais had to feel apprehensive as they joined the queue and inched their way forward until they reached the uniformed functionary with a black book. They gave their names. Each received the same response: 'Mr Hunt (Mr Millais) your picture has been accepted. Please sign for your season ticket to the Exhibition.'

For a colourful description of the summer show, here is the prolific Victorian writer Margaret Oliphant's view of proceedings:

No public event creates so much interest throughout all classes as the opening of the Royal Academy Exhibition. From all corners of the country, people rich enough to pay a yearly visit to London reckon this one of their inducements, and even the hastiest excursionist must take a hurried glance at 'the pictures'. No book receives the discussion, the attention, the public notice which the Exhibition does. At every dinner table, at every summer assembly . . . it is in everybody's mouth. From ten o'clock till six the rooms are thronged with an eager crowd, enduring dust, heat, and fatigue . . . It could scarcely be possible to find a more thoroughly representative crowd. Fashion in wondrous appeal; fine young men about town, and uncouth striplings from school; country people, city people; men from clubs, women with schoolroom parties; connoisseurs and speculators . . . make up a crowd which is more instructive than the art itself. To almost all of these the Exhibition is an article of faith. To miss it for a year would be worse than many a little moral peccadillo. Even to delay the first visit to the Academy shows an indifference which few persons claiming to be refined or educated would like to be accused of. A certain latitude may be allowed about going to church, but about going to the Academy none is possible.

On the Friday before the formal Monday opening a private view was held for participants and privileged guests in and out of the art world. When John Millais arrived and saw *Pizarro* hanging with paintings by eminent Academicians, it was a glorious moment. What if his picture was twenty feet from the floor, near the ceiling, where it may have seemed invisible without opera glasses? It was better to be skied in Trafalgar Square than to hang at eye level anywhere else.

The seventy-eighth annual Summer Show of the Royal Academy of Arts opened on 4 May 1846. 'The present exhibition,' the *Art Journal* affirmed, 'is considered by artists, connoisseurs, and public alike to be the best since the removal to Trafalgar Square [from Somerset House, in 1838].' Because of many fine pictures by established exhibitors, a sixteen-year-old student might not expect anyone to notice his maiden endeavour under the roof. Yet it *was* seen, and by critics for major publications. The weekly *Literary Gazette* called *Pizarro* 'a spirited picture . . . in which everything harmonises into the striking composition'. The *Art Journal* lamented that 'the position of this excellent picture deprives us of the opportunity of inspecting its details'. It was, the writer said, 'more worthy of a favourable place than many that are better hung'.

Then there was *The Times*, read by everybody who was anybody. A favourable notice in *The Times* almost guaranteed a sale. In 1846, *The Times*'s reviewer mentioned about one-tenth of the works, including this one: '"Pizarro," by J.E. Millais, a youth of sixteen, is worth recording because we can see enough of it to declare that the knowledge of composition and effect is highly creditable, considering the early age of the artist, though the height at which it is hung forbids judgment as to detail.'

Henry Hodgkinson, Millais's half-brother, now settled in Oxford, had bought *Pizarro* prior to the opening, though thanks to *The Times*, it would have sold without this brotherly intervention. Expressing interest in the painting was John Miller of Liverpool who just happened to be one of Britain's most prominent, and most discriminating, patrons of art.

CHAPTER 4

1846—48

In the eight years since Mary Millais conferred with Martin Shee, financial expectations for artists had improved dramatically. 'There never has been a period when British art had brighter prospects,' the *Art Journal*'s reviewer of the 1846 Exhibition wrote. 'There is no lack of private patronage. The middle class in England – the class with wealth to expend upon luxuries – has learned to appreciate the practical utility and true enjoyment to be derived from Art. Let the supply increase; we have no fear but the demand will increase with it.' One sign of these new conditions was the sale of a picture currently hanging in Trafalgar Square, the veteran painter William Macready's *Choosing the Wedding Gown*, a simple scene from *The Vicar of Wakefield*, which fetched an almost unheard-of price, £1000 (equal to $5000 at the time).

Earlier I noted that the railroad did more than introduce a new means of transportation. It opened up markets for industrialists of the Midlands and the North. They now had more money for luxury items, including paintings. And they could get down to London easily and see for themselves.

John Millais might have echoed Wordsworth:

> Blessed was it that dawn to be alive,
> But to be young was very heaven!

* * *

During the summer and autumn of 1846, Millais was pre-occupied with a project unrelated to the Academy, an early instance of something that would characterise his career, his remarkable versatility.

After the Houses of Parliament had burned down in 1834, a Commission was created to obtain works of art for the new buildings. It set up four competitions, one of which, announced in 1844, invited artists to submit oil paintings 'within the general classes of religion, history, and poetry'. Nine prizes would be awarded: three of £500, three of £300, and three of £200. The deadline was June 1847.

Late in the summer of 1846, Millais became an entrant with *A Widow's Mite*, illustrating a familiar story in the Gospels of Mark and Luke. He used Mark's account: 'And Jesus sat over against the treasury and beheld how the people cast money into the treasure; and many that were rich cast in much: and there came a certain poor widow, and she threw in two mites, which make a farthing. And he called unto his disciples and saith unto them, "Verily this poor widow hath cast in more than all they which have cast into the treasure, for all they did cast in of their abundance, but she of her want did cast in all she had."'

The work was of heroic dimensions, ten by sixteen feet, his largest ever. Probably because he was unsure of himself, he waited until he was almost finished before mentioning it to Hunt. Then he could barely contain his excitement: 'Look here, I'm painting a picture as big as Raphael's cartoons, and that's no end of a job, I can tell you. More than twenty figures, all the size of life. It's "A Widow's Mite" – a splendid subject, isn't it? With the old, frowning Pharisees, the reverential disciples, the poor woman, and of course the Saviour. Doesn't it afford grand opportunities?'

One opportunity was the chance, as in *Pizarro*, to give the story a personal interpretation. His widow is young, attractive, sexual. She is accompanied by a small boy, apparently her son, who, curiously, is naked. Since it wasn't due until June, he put it aside in February to begin his entry for the Royal Academy Exhibition.

* * *

Millais's submission for the 1847 Summer Show would be another multi-figured assault, almost a replication of 1846, with time, place, and gender changed. Now he dipped into Anglo-Saxon history and lit upon mid-tenth-century events involving Edwy, King of the English; his wife, Elgiva; Odo, Archbishop of Canterbury; and Dunstan, Abbot of Glastonbury (later St Dunstan). Supposedly after Edwy gained the throne, Elgiva persuaded him to banish Dunstan from the kingdom. A year later, in a perhaps related action, Odo accused Edwy and Elgiva of being blood related and dissolved their marriage. Then, according to one version of the narrative, Odo ordered his soldiers to seize and disfigure Elgiva.

In Millais's picture, *Elgiva*, the queen is the central figure. While her retainers are being slaughtered, Odo's men brand her face, 'in order,' a note for the catalogue explains, 'to destroy that fatal beauty which had seduced Edwy'. Again Millais was aroused by an incident of cruelty and injustice, with organised religion coming out badly. This time the clerical figure was responsible for the brutality. And he was the Archbishop of Canterbury.

Elgiva, Hunt thought, was even better than *Pizarro*, 'perhaps because it afforded Millais the opportunity of painting a woman [as the central figure]'.

Elgiva was accepted but dreadfully positioned, in the infamous Octagon Room, a tiny, badly lighted gallery that had been an office. One writer called it 'a condemned cell into which works are thrust and forgotten'. *Elgiva* consequently was overlooked by almost everyone but the *Art Journal*'s reviewer, who called it 'powerfully conceived ... forcible and original'. Millais meanwhile was busily completing *A Widow's Mite*.

* * *

On 4 June 1847, he sent off his gargantuan canvas to the competition site, Westminster Hall. On the next day, the most important Victorian literary weekly, the *Athenaeum*, got around to *Elgiva*: 'A very promising composition by J.E. Millais, who, if he study and be not led away by mistaken encomiums of friends, may do well.' Any doubts about the implication of this sentence would have vanished a month later. The same writer, reviewing the Westminster show, said, 'If the author of *A Widow's Mite*, Mr J. Millain [sic] – a very young artist, we understand – be not spoilt by over-praise, there is enough in this picture to show that with proper training he may deserve all which they claim for him.

[33]

That word 'genius' – which we have heard with reference to him – is one which has not yet had the signification definitely settled – at least in Art.'

Perhaps, although it is doubtful, the misspelled name was a printing error, but the interposed observation on his youth was surely meant to be deflating and the general tone suggests John Millais may have become insufferably conceited. If he needed to be brought down to size, it might have been done by the prize announcement. *A Widow's Mite* was not a winner. But he was probably not disappointed. Pictures of this size would never be his forte. Besides, he had heard that he may have lost out because of the nude boy.

The time spent on *A Widow's Mite* hadn't been wasted. It led to his first major commission. A wealthy resident of Leeds, John Atkinson, was having his house renovated with six ground floor lunettes to be decorated. Atkinson asked his friend Charles Cope, an Associate of the Royal Academy, to recommend someone for the job and, after seeing *A Widow's Mite*, Cope suggested Millais. He was engaged for the undertaking, and during July and August spent six weeks living and working in the Atkinson house. His canvases illustrated four stages of life – Childhood, Youth, Manhood, and Age – as well as two representations of Art and Music. John Atkinson was highly pleased with the finished product; his enthusiasm could have done nothing to deflate the artist's feelings of self-admiration.

Upon returning to London, Millais entered another competition, the Royal Academy's biennial contest for a historical picture in oils on a given topic. This year, the subject, from the Book of Judges, was 'The Tribe of Benjamin seizing the Virgins who danced at Shiloh'. In a spectacular scene, reminiscent of Rubens's *Rape of the Sabine Women*, he showed a couple of dozen men about to grasp semi-nude dancing women.

The prize ceremony was on 10 December. When Millais was proclaimed the gold medal winner, no one was surprised, least of all the winner himself. 'His habitual success,' Hunt reported, 'gave this new triumph only the character of an ordinary step forward. His priority, however, did provoke captious feeling on the part of his less brilliant compeers.' And also some critics. Thus the *Art Journal* informed its readers that 'a student named Millais was reported to have gained the gold medal.' There was no doubt about who had won the medal, and anybody who wrote for the *Art Journal* knew who Millais was. He must really have seemed impossibly self-satisfied.

* * *

Three depicted seizures were enough. For the next Academy Exhibition, Millais would do a quiet scene, his first 'literary' painting. He was inspired by an unlikely triumvirate: Holman Hunt, Boccaccio, and Sir Joshua Reynolds.

In 1847, Hunt had exhibited *his* first picture with a literary source, one of Sir Walter Scott's lesser known novels, *Woodstock*. A group scene whose topic was explicit in the title, *Dr Rochecliffe performing Divine Service in the cottage of Joceline Joliffe*, it was well enough received for Hunt to decide on another literary painting for 1848. From a popular novelist, Hunt turned to someone who, dead for twenty-seven years, was still an obscure poet, John Keats. In 1845 or 1846, Hunt had accidentally come upon and was excited by a volume of Keats's poetry, which led him, in the autumn of 1847, to begin a picture based on 'The Eve of St Agnes', which he maintained was the first painting inspired by Keats. (Not one biography of the poet had yet been published.)

Millais couldn't be persuaded by Hunt to read Keats, but he liked the idea of a literary painting. His source would be Boccaccio's *Decameron*. He chose the first story of the fifth day of the *Decameron* which deals with Cymon, a wealthy young Cypriot living temporarily in the country. One day, walking in the woods, he comes upon a young woman asleep, 'the fairest thing he had ever seen'. She is wearing 'so thin a garment that it hid well nigh nothing of her snowy flesh, covered only from the waist down'. Cymon stands admiringly until the woman, Iphigenia, awakens. Recognising the son of a rich man, she lets him walk her home. Millais would show the couple walking together. (The rest of the story tells of how, after overcoming numerous obstacles, Iphigenia and Cymon, whose 'life has changed because of his love', marry and 'live long and happily'.)

How did he meet up with the *Decameron*? His mother could hardly have included it in her lessons. This is where Sir Joshua Reynolds comes in. One of his last paintings was *Cymon and Iphigenia*, showing

Cymon gazing upon the sleeping Iphigenia, and well enough known through an engraving to have introduced Cymon and Iphigenia to Millais.

In his picture, Millais presents a vacant-eyed, wide-grinning rustic and his topless companion holding hands as they walk toward the viewer. The hand-holding is not part of the tale, but this was the least of the modifications to Boccaccio's original work. Obsessed with multi-figure work, Millais surrounded the pair with nine scantily clad nymphs, three of whom are bare-breasted. They were the artist's invention, as was a large, excellently painted dog walking with the couple. In its final form, the picture shows a detailed foreground and background of foliage, trees, and clouds, added several years later.

* * *

When *Cymon and Iphigenia* was nearly done, Hunt visited the Gower Street studio.

As always [he recollected] the street door was opened by the servant, but there was no time to make an enquiry because the parlour door suddenly opened and revealed Mrs Millais, who was full of fire and conjured me to listen.

'Johnnie is behaving abominably,' she said. 'You would not believe it. He shuts us out of the studio altogether. For twelve days neither his father nor I have been allowed to enter. I ask you, Hunt, is that the way to treat parents? Isn't it disgraceful?'

I then saw the studio at the end of the passage open, and Johnnie called out, 'Don't mind her. Come here.'

Assuring her that there must be some important reason for his conduct, I joined the provoker of the discontent.

As he shut the door, he said, 'I'm sorry for my dear old mother, but the time has come when I cannot have my studio made into a general sitting room, and there's no way of making the change gradually. It must be done abruptly and firmly.'

They began to talk. Their conversation was interrupted by a knock on the door.

'Who's there?' asked Millais.

'I have brought you the tea myself,' his mother said.

Usually it was brought by a servant. Hunt rose to open the door, but Millais stopped him with his hand and a silent shake of the head.

'I really can't let you in, Mama,' he said. 'Please put the tray down, and I'll take it in myself.'

'I call upon you, Hunt,' she said, 'to witness this behaviour to his mother.'

His only reply was, 'You'll see in time how right I am.'

He was convinced that *Cymon and Iphigenia* justified his conduct. He was certain that it was his best picture yet. Studio visitors, including Hunt, concurred. Everyone who had viewed it, however, was a friend or family member. And naturally it had been standing alone.

'Every picture in its studio,' he remarked some years later, 'is seen in a favourable light. Thus the artist surrounded by flattering friends is apt to take too elevated an opinion of his performance. If he is worth much, a warning whisper will say in his ear, "Don't believe in it."'

But in 1848 Millais was too young and too self-satisfied to hear warning whispers, and *Cymon and Iphigenia* wasn't really as good as he thought. There are fine things in it. The figures were his best thus far. The dog shows that he could have become an outstanding animal painter. The overall pattern is well proportioned, firmly controlled. Technically the picture surpasses anything he had yet done. But there are flaws.

The painting doesn't show much inventiveness. A young couple is walking in the woods, and that is it. There is no dramatic interest or excitement. And some details are of questionable relevance. Why is the dog present? To show that he could paint an animal? Are the nymphs there just because of William Etty? How else can one explain three women with gratuitously naked breasts? Finally, unlike *Pizarro*, *Elgiva*, and *A Widow's Mite*, the picture does not reveal a personal involvement in the subject.

Clearly Millais had not thought much, if at all, about a theory of art or principles of painting. He was just a highly skilled craftsman. There was, however, no reason to doubt its acceptance for the Exhibition. It was well above minimal standards for approval.

As usual, Millais and Hunt sent off their entries together. Unlike Millais, Hunt *had* been working with a system of principles. They governed his choice of subject and its treatment. He was attracted to 'The Eve of St Agnes' because it 'illustrates the sacredness of honest responsible love and the weakness of proud intemperance'. His subject was the final scene, Madeline and Porphyro preparing to leave the castle during the drunken revelry. The contrast between the young couple and the carousers exemplified for Hunt the appeal of the poem. Also, the last lines are brimming with particularised details. A true devotee of Ruskin, Hunt depicted with absolute veracity the porter 'lying in uneasy sprawl', the 'wakeful bloodhound', the 'chains silent on the footworn stone', the doorkey leading to everlasting happiness. All of Keats's details are there, and nothing else. Hunt's last pre-Pre-Raphaelite painting, *The Eve of St Agnes*, was easily the best thing he had done.

* * *

Following the usual two-week wait, Hunt and Millais casually sauntered down to Trafalgar Square to collect their season tickets. After giving his name, Hunt received his ticket and was asked to sign for it. After giving *his* name, Millais got the shock of his life. *Cymon and Iphigenia* had been 'chucked'!

He couldn't understand it. Nor could anyone else who had seen the painting in his studio. Yet for several coalescing reasons, the Academy's decision is understandable. In the first place, by doing a continuation of a celebrated work by Reynolds, he was asking for trouble. He seemed to be courting comparison with the saintlike Sir Joshua. Also the selection committee could not have been pleased with the liberties taken with Boccaccio. In all areas of life, youngsters were expected to be respectful of their elders. Finally there was the obvious, even ostentatious, influence of Etty.

Etty's influence on young artists had been of concern to the Royal Academicians. When Millais won the gold medal, his main rival had been an Etty disciple. At the prize ceremony, Hunt recalled, George Jones, RA 'commented with instructive frankness' on Etty.

'He cautioned the young,' Hunt said, 'against imitating the unequalled colourist of the English school, pointing out that Etty reached his pre-eminence by a course of struggles to overcome difficulties, and that young artists emulating him could only acquire a superficial dexterity – a handful of tricks doomed to failure and disappointment.'

Now, two months later, the Academy's star pupil was flaunting his Ettyism. The four semi-nudes, three of them unnecessary, and the singularly garish colours, appeared like Ettyism thrown into the viewer's face. All of this fitted into a pattern, the spoiled brat syndrome, which was probably a worrisome matter at the Academy. Perhaps it was thought this young man needed a setback to straighten him out. In any event, John Millais now knew how it felt to experience 'failure and disappointment'.

CHAPTER 5

1848–49

The Eve of St Agnes, Hunt's first painting to be really noticed, was sold for its asking price, £70. Now he could rent a studio, at 7 (now 46) Cleveland Street, at the corner of Howland Street, where he was joined by another art student, Dante Gabriel Rossetti. The two of them had entered the Antique School together but had been only chance acquaintances. Because Rossetti was flamboyant and casual about classwork, Hunt considered him a dilettante. Then at the 1848 Exhibition, Rossetti approached Hunt and loudly proclaimed his picture to be the best in the show. They began a conversation which was continued in a coffee house and ended with an agreement to share a studio.

The son of an Italian political exile who taught at King's College in the Strand, Rossetti was a poet-painter who had not published a poem or exhibited a picture. His enthusiasm for Hunt's painting was largely due to its source. He too had picked up and enjoyed a book of poems by Keats and so he was delighted to see *The Eve of St Agnes*. But for John Keats, the two men might never have come together.

Their studio was nothing to brag about. 'This gaunt chamber could not be more depressing,' a friend said. 'One approached it by a half-lighted staircase, up which the fuss and clatter of a boys' school frequently rose. Add to these unseemly elements a dimly lighted, musty hall, and a shabby, out-at-elbows doorway on a street that was rapidly "going down in the world".' But Hunt and Rossetti didn't mind. They had a place of their own.

Millais was then visiting his half-brother Henry Hodgkinson in

Oxford. Upon his return, early in August, he frequently spent evenings with Hunt and Rossetti, usually in Gower Street. When he felt like it, Rossetti could be the epitome of charm. Now on his best behaviour, he favourably impressed Millais, who had known him only slightly. Their conversations usually dealt with contemporary British painting. Hunt and Rossetti, displeased with what was being done, expressed their opinions forcefully. Largely because of his recent rejection, Millais was a sympathetic listener.

A few years earlier, Hunt had been an almost solitary complainer. Now mainstream critics were dissatisfied with much that appeared on gallery walls. 'Year after year,' one of them wrote, 'there has been the same pictorial skills, the same all-pervading prettiness, the same brilliancy of effect, produced in the same conventional manner, with the same absence of lofty aim or original thought. Talent has not been wanting, or even genius. The fault is with the system.'

The three youths – aged nineteen (Millais), twenty (Rossetti), and twenty-one (Hunt) – endorsed lofty aims and original thoughts, and each of them – even Millais at that moment – was ready to challenge the system. But they lacked a guide, other than Ruskin, and Ruskin was a writer. They needed a visual touchstone.

* * *

One night when Hunt and Rossetti entered Millais's studio, he pointed to a large borrowed book. It was called *Pisa. Campo Santo*, subtitled *Pitture a fresco del Campo di Pisa*. Early Italian art, thanks to Hunt, had often been part of their conversations, but they had never seen a pre-Raphael painting. Even the National Gallery didn't own one. And so when Millais saw this book, he seized the chance to borrow it. (It is not clear from whom it came. Perhaps it belonged to the Royal Academy library.)

Published twenty years earlier, the volume contained Carlo Lasinio's engravings of the frescoes at Campo Santo, next to Pisa's cathedral. Campo Santo is a twelfth-century burial ground surrounded by a thirteenth-century building with fourteenth- and early fifteenth-century frescoes. The artists were Giotto and such lesser lights as Benozzo Gozzoli, Spineto Aretino, Simone Memmi, Pietro Laurati, and Andrea Orcagna.

Three years earlier, Ruskin had visited Campo Santo. He wrote to his father, 'I never believed the patriarchal story before, but I do now. You cannot conceive the vividness and fullness of conception of these men. In spite of every violation of the rules of art, Abraham, Adam, Cain, Rachel, Rebekah are there, real, visible, substantial, such as they must have been.' Ruskin was referring to the originals. The engravings he called 'execrable'. Lasinio, to be sure, was an amateur. But it was he who led the Gower Street trio to early Italian art. He was all they had.

They saw naive depictions of the expulsion from paradise, Noah's entrance into the ark, the building of the tower of Babel, Abraham's near-sacrifice of Isaac, the destruction of the walls of Jericho, and the meeting of Solomon and the Queen of Sheba.

'We did not curb our amusement,' Hunt related, 'at the immature perspective, the undeveloped drawing, the feebleness of light and shade,' but these flaws were glossed over because 'there was no trace of conventionality. The whole spirit was simple and sincere. It appealed to us almost with the force of a revelation.'

Of the three, Millais felt this revelation most strongly. Rossetti was enthusiastic for a time, but eventually he would go off on his own and forget about Giotto and his friends. Hunt was excited mainly because the book had enhanced his self-confidence, reinforcing his belief in the path he was following. But for Millais, it was the opening of a new vista.

I am reminded of a discovery three decades earlier by the man who had been a catalyst for them. These mediocre engravings affected Millais in much the same way that George Chapman's pedestrian translation of *The Iliad* had stirred John Keats. Neither duplication is comparable to its prototype, but this is irrelevant. When Keats read Chapman, he was twenty. When Millais looked at Lasinio, he was nineteen. Each was ready to be galvanised by *something*. And each was galvanised. Keats wrote 'On First Looking into Chapman's Homer', infinitely superior to his earlier poems. Millais would paint a picture light years ahead of anything that he had done. Keats's real discovery – literally overnight – was of himself as a poet. Millais also found himself. Heretofore, he had turned out pictures without much of a focus. Now he would be guided by a controlling principle. A third-rate translator had uncovered the genius of Keats. A third-rate engraver would do the same for Millais.

* * *

If Hunt and Millais had been alone, the Campo Santo episode would have affected only themselves, and we might never have heard of it. Because of their companion, this evening was a night to remember. Gabriel Rossetti – like Hunt, he went by his middle name – would attract acolytes for most of his life. Lasino gave him his first organising opportunity. For him the book was a rallying cry. To challenge the British art structure, he felt, they would need allies. Two or three days after seeing the engravings, he made his move. He suggested that they form a society.

Hunt was moderately amused by the idea of an organised diffusion of his views, but Millais was sceptical. Because of his absorption in his own work, he would not ordinarily have shown much interest in a group endeavour, but probably because of *Cymon and Iphigenia*, he was open-minded. When Rossetti saw that his friends would contemplate his proposal, he rattled off names of prospective colleagues: Thomas Woolner, James Collinson, and his own younger brother, William.

Woolner was a twenty-three-year-old sculpture student at the Academy who had exhibited four pieces at RA shows. Collinson, also a twenty-three-year-old student, had had two paintings at Academy Exhibitions, one of which, *The Charity Boy's Debut*, was an 1847 success. William Rossetti was a likeable fellow, nineteen years old, with a government job in Somerset House. His only apparent qualification for membership in a body of artists was his enrolment in a Maddox Street drawing school. Gabriel Rossetti may have wanted a society of seven because he regarded seven as a mystical number. If so, Hunt quickly put forward the name of a nineteen-year-old student in the Antique School, Frederick George Stephens. At least Rossetti wouldn't totally dominate the prospective organisation.

* * *

Much has been written and said about the origin of the term Pre-Raphaelite Brotherhood. Everyone agrees that 'Brotherhood' came from Rossetti. He was also, I believe, responsible for 'Pre-Raphaelite'.

In July, while *The Eve of St Agnes* hung in Trafalgar Square, the publisher Edward Moxon brought out a pioneering biography, Richard
Moncton Milnes's two-volume *Life, Letters, and Literary Remains of John
Keats*. Milnes was a minor literary figure whose interest in Keats had
started at Cambridge, as a member of the Apostles, an informal group
that met frequently for literary and philosophical discussions. One of
the Apostles, Alfred Tennyson, introduced the others to Keats.
Milnes became a Keats devotee and spent many years on his book,
which helped to bring about a recognition of Keats's place in the
history of English poetry.

On 12 August, the *Athenaeum* ran a rave review of the work. Gabriel
Rossetti at once bought it. On 20 August he wrote to his brother, on
holiday in Brighton, 'I have not had time to get through the first
volume of *Keats*, which is exceedingly interesting. Keats was a glorious
fellow and says in one place (to my glorious delight) that, having
looked over a folio of the first and second schools of Italian painting,
he has come to the conclusion that the early men surpassed Raphael
himself.'

The relevant passage is part of a letter from Keats to his brother
and sister: 'I just looked over a book of prints . . . specimens of the
first and second age of Art in Italy. I do not think I ever had a greater
treat out of Shakespeare; full of romance and tender feeling;
magnificence of drapery beyond everything I ever saw, not excepting
Raphael's; grotesque but making up a fine whole, finer to me than
more accomplished works, as there was left so much room for
imagination.'

When the threesome talked about forming an organisation, the
biography was fresh on Rossetti's mind. It is unlikely that Millais or
Hunt would have proposed a name for a society that they hadn't yet
sanctioned. But for Rossetti, having just read about Keats's response
to painters preceding Raphael, it would have been natural to suggest
'Pre-Raphaelite'. And so, provisionally, the Pre-Raphaelite
Brotherhood came into existence.

All that was now needed was a stamp of approval from Millais.
Because of his stature, this was essential. Without him, the
Brotherhood would die stillborn. And he was dubious. He spoke
frankly to Hunt about their intended colleagues: 'I can quite see that

Gabriel Rossetti, if he can paint, should join us, but I didn't know his brother was a painter. And there's Woolner. We can expect great pictures from him, can't we? And won't Collinson make a great leader of a rebellion? Stephens, too! Does he paint? Are we really going through with this?'

There were sound reasons for his doubts. Woolner was a good sculptor, but sculpture didn't fit into their plans. Collinson was lazy and indecisive. Stephens and William Rossetti had never shown any artistic talent. Millais nevertheless agreed to a meeting of the seven. If the others could win him over, he would go along with the idea. Otherwise the Pre-Raphaelite Brotherhood would be just a Rossettian pipe dream.

The gathering took place on 20 September at 83 Gower Street. Holman Hunt, whom Millais would call 'President of the PRB', was the informal chairman. Hunt summarised the conversations which had led to the possible formation of a society to be called the Pre-Raphaelite Brotherhood. The name, he emphasised, did not imply an intention to imitate early Italians. They would simply share their forerunners' motivation. They would work independently of dogma. They would seek, inspiration in nature and paint what they saw. As Stephens said later, perhaps echoing Hunt, 'Pre-Raphaelitism is neither more nor less than a protest of sincerity against the fatuousness of conventional art. It owes nothing but the example of sincerity to foreign or ancient artists.'

If they had met a few years later, Hunt might have quoted from the words of one of the best Italian Pre-Raphaelites, as expressed in Browning's dramatic monologue 'Fra Lippo Lippi':

> . . . you've seen the world
> – The beauty and the wonder and the power,
> The shapes of things, their colours, lights and shades,
> Changes, surprises – and God made it all!
> – For what? Do you feel thankful, ay or no
> For this fair town's face, yonder river's line,
> The mountain round it and sky above,
> Much more the figures of man, woman, child,
> These are frame to? What's it all about?

To be passed over, despised? or dwelt upon,
Wondered at? oh, this last, of course! – you say.
But why not do as well as say, – paint these
Just as they are . . .?

Even without 'Fra Lippo Lippi', Hunt struck a responsive chord in his auditors. Their enthusiastic response overcame Millais's reservations. He needed no more convincing. The Pre-Raphaelite Brotherhood was a fait accompli, born in his studio at 83 Gower Street, perhaps only because of *Cymon and Iphigenia's* rejection.

*   *   *

The Brothers agreed to include 'PRB' on their works of art. They also pledged not to reveal the meaning of the initials because of the universal attitude toward Raphael, exemplified in this excerpt from a magazine article of 1845: 'Raffaele maintains the first rank among painters because none other has united so many excellences and is so free from faults. His genius was tempered by never-failing judgment. He excelled all other artists in his combination of powers, and what he possessed he displayed without offence; taste is never violated in his works.'

Actually the Brotherhood did not totally devalue Raphael. Soon after its formation, they drew up and signed a 'List of Immortals', beginning with a preamble: 'We the undersigned declare that the following list of Immortals constitutes the whole of our Creed, and that there exists no other Immortality than what is centred in their names.' The eighty-four names were divided into five groups, in a descending order of greatness. This rather bizarre assemblage was drawn up without much forethought. The Brothers called out whatever names they thought of at the moment. At the insistence of Hunt, Jesus Christ was alone at the top. Then came Shakespeare and the author of the Book of Job. The third group consisted of Homer, Dante, Chaucer, Leonardo da Vinci, Goethe, Keats, Shelley, King Alfred, Landor, Thackeray, Washington, and Browning. Washington's prominent presence may seem surprising since people were still alive who had lived through the American revolution. He was high on the list because of William Rossetti, who had strong republican sympathies.

The foregoing names were followed by five, four, and three stars. Among those in the two-star category were Boccaccio, Tennyson, and Raphael. (Raphael's contemporary, Titian, and two immediate followers, Tintoretto and Veronese, were honoured with one star, but the only Italian Pre-Raphaelite on the list was Fra Angelico. A curious omission is that of Giotto.)

Hunt regarded Raphael as 'an artist of the most independent and daring course'. His followers, however, were something else: 'They accentuated his poses into pictures; caricatured the turns of his heads and the lines of his limbs so that figures were drawn in patterns; twisted companies of men into pyramids, and placed them like pieces on a chessboard in the foreground.' Certainly Raphael deserved a higher rating, but his mere presence shows that the Brothers were not unappreciative of his work.

As for Millais, some years later he called Raphael's Sistine Madonna 'a picture painted on earth directed by a mind in Heaven, high in this sense that it has sealed on canvas for all time the nobility which may and does at times breathe through us mortals . . . This exaltation of a face, glorified for the moment by the holiness of pure thought is what makes this work High Art, the combination of the human and the divine.'

*　　*　　*

The Brothers inevitably split into two groups, a Big Three and a Little Four. (Woolner would become a Royal Academician, but as a sculptor he was never a Pre-Raphaelite artist. The Brotherhood's ideals could be realised only by applying colours onto a single-plane surface.) If anything was to be done, it would be done by Hunt, Rossetti, and Millais, who planned on a joint assault in the summer of '49 at Trafalgar Square. They would each exhibit one painting. Millais, however, could not get started at once. First, he had to fulfill a portrait commission from someone in Hampstead. Meanwhile, Hunt and Rossetti worked on pictures already begun.

The formation of the Brotherhood was not directly related to outside events, but these men had to have been affected by the Continental uprising and Chartist demonstrations at home. Hunt had been 'stirred by the spirit of freedom in the air', and his current picture, *Rienzi*, reflected his feelings. It depicts a scene from the first chapter of Edward Bulwer-Lytton's *Rienzi*, a popular novel of 1835. (The book had already inspired Wagner's opera of the same name.) A fourteenth-century Italian freedom fighter, Rienzi hadn't intended to be a patriot. He became an activist only after the assassination of his younger brother. 'But for that event,' Bulwer-Lytton wrote in a passage Hunt inserted in the catalogue, 'the future liberator of Rome might have been a dreamer, a scholar, a poet. But from that time all his faculties, energies, fancies, genius became concentrated to a single point; and patriotism leaped into the life and vigour of a passion.' The uncompromisingly realistic scene shows the hero kneeling by his brother's body, arm lifted high, crying out, 'Justice! Justice!'

Contrasting with *Rienzi*, Rossetti's picture was *The Girlhood of Mary Virgin*, an imagined scene from the domestic life of the seventeen-year-old Mary. Supervised by her mother, she embroiders a lily, copying from a flower in a vase. Seen through a window, Mary's father, on a balcony, prunes an overhanging, fruit-laden vine. Like Hunt, Rossetti was visualising a scene as it might have occurred.

In the second week of November, Millais finally began his picture. While doing *The Eve of St Agnes*, Hunt had tried to interest Millais in Keats: 'I took "Isabella" from my pocket, and I read some favourite stanzas, but after half a dozen stanzas, he burst out, "It's like a parson."'

'Although nettled, I laughed, "I'll leave the volume here with you."'

Eventually Millais looked into it and, as Hunt had hoped, he revised his opinion. The poem indeed inspired his initial Pre-Raphaelite painting.

Based on a Boccaccio tale, Keats's 'Isabella' is set in fourteenth-century Florence. The title character is a beautiful young unmarried woman in an elite family. She and a resident employee, Lorenzo, are secretly in love. Her two brothers, planning a 'proper' marriage for their sister, are enraged when they discover the affair. They lure Lorenzo from the house, kill him and bury his body. In a dream Lorenzo appears to Isabella and tells her of his murder and burial. She finds the body, severs the head, takes it home, and places it in a flower pot, covered by a basil plant. Because of her concern for the plant, the brothers steal the pot and find the head. Conscience-striken, they go into exile. Isabella wastes away and dies.

Millais recognised the dramatic importance of the moment when the brothers became aware of the liaison. But Keats isn't specific about this. He merely says that they had:

> found by many signs
> What love Lorenzo for their sister had
> And how she loved him too.

One of the 'signs' is mentioned early:

> They could not sit at meals but feel how well
> It soothed each to be the other by.

The moment of realisation, Millais concluded in a flash of insight, came at a family dinner. This would be his subject. Twelve people, seen mostly in profile, would sit at a long table, with Isabella and Lorenzo in the foreground side by side. A servant and the family dog, lying alongside Isabella, would complete the picture. The couple would gaze at each other in a way to leave no doubt about their feelings. The brothers would be opposite them, one smiling sardonically and the other angrily kicking the dog.

The painting would be exactingly detailed, a replica of what might have been. Millais carefully researched everything from water glasses to earrings. To insure accuracy in clothing, for example, he followed illustrations in a book borrowed by Rossetti's father from the King's College library, Camillo Bonnard's *Costumi dei Secoli XIII, XIV, e XV*. Not just the clothing would individualise the human figures. More than ever before, Millais concentrated on facial expressions and gestures, showing human beings as they are, irrespective of time and place. They would be eating, drinking, talking and gesticulating.

His models, as usual, were mostly people he knew, carefully chosen. For the first time in his portraits he aimed at psychological accuracy. Consider his use of the Rossetti brothers. Gabriel sat for the man in the rear, who alone is drinking. Film-makers would call this type casting. William was the original of Isabella's lover, an unassuming, unpretentious, decent human being, just like William himself.

William's portrait was the only one not scrupulously true to life. His thinning black hair was transformed into a full head of golden brown hair. This was done because of artistic propriety. Millais could adhere to a system and still maintain his freedom, recognising that a gap can separate a set of rules from the application thereof. This was something that often would seem beyond the perception of Holman Hunt.

Millais's painting, *Isabella*, would have been an ambitious undertaking for any artist, let alone a nineteen-year-old student with five months for the job. (Hunt and Rossetti, with far fewer figures, had a five-month head start.) He was confident, however, that he could do it. Once he was under way, everyone was astonished by his speed. As Hunt said, he could work 'at a pace beyond all calculation'. One explanation of his rapidity lay in his mastery of the fundamentals of drawing. The hours, days, weeks, and months in Jersey, in Streatham Street and in the Antique School had not been wasted.

* * *

Millais did not spend every waking moment on *Isabella*. He found time for physical activities, indoors if necessary. Stephens recalled how 'he was wont, when time did not allow of outdoor exercise, to surprising feats of agility. He was great in leaping. In his studio he would clear my arm outstretched from the shoulder – that is about five feet from the ground – at one spring, with not more than a fourteen-foot run.'

He also did some socialising, often with his Brothers who gathered once a month for an evening of conversation. But at least twice Millais missed a meeting at Stephens's house. The first absence, he told Hunt, had been due to 'excessive fatigue from a dancing party till four in the morning'. The second time, he explained to Hunt, he had been 'roaming about the streets for want of an object'.

This seemingly innocuous sentence is intriguing. Millais was nineteen years old, with a normal sex drive. He was 'roaming about', perhaps on nearby Tottenham Court Road, probably to find female companionship. Victorians were not often explicit about such matters in their correspondence, but Hunt, a sometime wanderer himself, would have comprehended.

Because of pressures of work, Millais avoided commitments, which may explain his seeking out a lady of the evening. It certainly wasn't necessary with his looks. One woman with numerous male friends called him 'the handsomest man I ever saw'. Hunt said that he 'had the face of an angel'. William Rossetti recalled 'a beautiful youth' with a 'face nearer to being angelic than any other male visage I have seen'. He had fair skin, blue eyes, and bronze-coloured, curling hair. He was six feet tall and weighed ten and a half stone (147 pounds). In temperament he was nearly always serene and cheerful, rarely angry. His gait reflected his personality: he walked firmly with a spring in his step.

In many ways his opposite, Gabriel Rossetti was 'a young man of foreign aspect', Hunt reported, 'about five feet seven inches tall with long brown hair touching his shoulders, seldom walking erect, but rolling carelessly as he slouched along, staring with dreaming eyes. He was lightly built and altogether unaffected by athletic exercise. He was careless in his dress and would allow spots of mud to remain dry on his legs for several days. He was courteous and generous in compliment but had an uncontrollable temper under the trials of studio work.'

The third part of the trinity, a friend recorded in her diary, was 'a very genial creature with blue laughing eyes and a nose with a merry little upward turn in it, dimples in the cheek, and the whole expression sunny and full of boyish happiness'. And everyone who knew him seems to have agreed that Hunt was genial and unaffected.

* * *

Millais's *Isabella* is truly remarkable, with much to applaud: the vitality of the scene; the directness with which the story is told; the dramatic interest; the almost Shakespearean mixture of the lighthearted and potentially tragic; the remarkable unity despite thirteen figures and numerous accessories; the individualised, expressive portraits; the meticulous details. The eminent American art critic Clement Greenberg wrote, 'The simplest way almost of accounting for a great work of art is to say that it is a thing possessing simultaneously the maximum of diversity and the maximum of unity possible to that diversity.' By this criterion, *Isabella* is unquestionably a great work.

No one could doubt that *this* would be accepted. Since Hunt and Rossetti had completed their paintings, the trio was presumably ready for the joint assault. But on 10 April, only two of their pictures went to Trafalgar Square. *The Girlhood of Mary Virgin* hung elsewhere.

* * *

On the eve of the battle, the most militant of the soldiers abandoned his comrades. In mid-March, Rossetti surreptitiously carried his painting to the Chinese Gallery, at Hyde Park Corner, site of the third annual show of the Association to Promote the Free Exhibition of Modern Art. The Free Exhibition, as it was popularly known, was free neither to visitors, charged one shilling for admission, nor to artists, who paid an entrance fee (unlike virtually every other show in town). It was 'free' in that anyone could buy wall space. It was London's lowliest art show. For this the principal founder of the PRB deserted his friends!

Why did he do it? Because, I think, of a fear from which he would always suffer, the fear of failure. He recognised his technical shortcomings, and he knew how many Royal Academy entries were routinely rejected. A year earlier it had happened to Millais. And so he played safe and went where he knew he would be accepted. Hunt and Millais were furious, but they couldn't talk to the renegade. He carefully avoided Gower Street and Cleveland Street.

The Free Exhibition opened on 26 March. In this assemblage of mediocrity, a good picture would stand out. The *Girlhood*, a fine painting, which almost certainly would have been taken by the Academy, was the reviewers' most frequently cited work. Before his friends' pictures had left their studios, Rossetti received favourable notices in the *Morning Chronicle*, *The Observer*, the *Literary Gazette*, and the *Athenaeum*. The reporter for the *Athenaeum* found it 'pleasant to turn from the mass of commonplace . . . to a work which would be creditable to any exhibition . . . a picture with much of that sacred mysticism inseparable from the works of the early masters.' Its 'sincerity and earnestness' reminded the writer 'of the feeling with which the early Florentine monastic painters wrought'. Although still angry, Rossetti's associates saw this response as a favourable portent for *them*.

* * *

At the Academy private view, Hunt and Millais were delighted to see their pictures 'on the line' for the first time. This phrase eventually came to denote a position at eye level, but at Trafalgar Square it had a more precise meaning. A narrow wooden ledge at a height of eight feet eight inches extended around the walls of each gallery. When the top of a frame reached this ledge, the picture was 'on the line'. In its distinctive manner, *Punch* explained what this meant to an exhibitor: 'The line is the front seat at the theatre; the corner place, out of the draught, in a railway carriage; the grand stand at the Derby . . . Painters are as anxious to be hung "on the line" as convicts are to escape the same fate.'

Hunt and Millais were exhibited side by side, the hanging committee apparently recognising similar motivations. Many reviewers also seemed aware of their objectives. This is understandable. Six of the seven Brothers were students at the Academy where their obsession with early art had to be known to classmates and to some of the Academicians, and because of the art world's insularity, this knowledge would have spread to the critics.

The press dealt favourably with both major Pre-Raphaelites, especially Millais. The weekly *John Bull* noted how *Isabella* 'carries one back into early Italian times' and how 'not only are the costumes and accessories carefully studied, the physiognomies and mode of life are characteristic.' The *Literary Gazette* called the picture 'a very clever copy of that ancient style in almost every feature.' The *Art Journal* was ecstatic: 'This is a pure aspiration in the feeling of the early Florentine school. The figures are crowded, but that was characteristic of the period. The picture is an example of rare excellence and learning, perhaps the most remarkable work in the whole Exhibition.'

And so it went, one favourable notice after another. Only one detail in Millais's painting went unnoticed, or was thought not worth mentioning, three small letters at the bottom of Isabella's chair: 'PRB'.

CHAPTER 6

1849–50

In 1847 and 1848 Millais had spent summer holidays in Oxford with his half-brother, Henry Hodgkinson and his wife, who had sat for Isabella. He enjoyed this venerable city. The towers, domes, steeples, and gateways; the meadows and groves of trees; the gownsmen on the High Street and the skiffs on the river – all of this provided a pleasant contrast to Gower Street and Tottenham Court Road. On these visits he had embraced the city. Late in May of 1849 he returned there; now he had come to work. To avoid socialising, he did not stay with the Hodgkinsons. He was the guest of a rich old man named Drury, who treated him like a grandson.

Millais appreciated what it meant to be 'on the line'. *Isabella* had been sold on opening day for the asking price, £150. The buyers, three Bond Street tailors who hung it in their shop, liked it enough to provide the artist with lagniappe, a suit of clothes.

Hunt and Rossetti also sold their paintings. Rossetti's, the last to go, went to a wealthy art patron. When Millais heard about it, he wrote to Hunt, 'I am stunningly delighted he has sold it and to such a nobby person. The success of the PRB is now *quite certain.*' (Rossetti's apostasy had been written off.) The Pre-Raphaelites' favourite words of approval were 'stunner' and 'stunning', the ultimate commendation.

Now no one could have been more enthusiastic than Millais about their organisation. His letters to Hunt began 'My dear Brother' and ended 'Your sincere PRB,' 'Your affectionate PRB,' or 'Your sincere Brother.'

With the money realised from their sales, Hunt and Rossetti

leisurely toured France and the Low Countries. (They did not go to Italy. Rossetti would visit the Continent several times but would never set foot in the home country of his father and the original Pre-Raphaelites.) Millais did not join them because he was eager to follow up on his success. 'Work,' he once told a friend, 'is the great panacea.' Already he was adhering to this credo. His entire summer of 1849 would be devoted to work.

* * *

On 15 May 1849, William Rossetti started a chronicle of the Brotherhood, *The PRB Journal*. The first entry begins, 'At Millais's, Stephens, Collinson, Gabriel, and myself . . . Millais has continued painting the beard of Ferdinand listening to Ariel.' This refers to his coming rendition of an episode in Act I of Shakespeare's *The Tempest*, Ferdinand hearing Ariel's song and asking, 'Where should this music be? I' the air or the earth?' Millais's Ferdinand would face the viewer, a hand to his ear. Ariel would be visible, along with bat-like spirits, which Millais called 'half human, half like birds'. The painting would interpret rather than illustrate.

Now in Oxford he was doing his first Pre-Raphaelite background. According to Rossetti's *Journal*, he had 'thoughts of painting a hedge to the closest point of imitation – a thing which has never been attempted'. For the first time, he worked entirely out-of-doors. He almost achieved his goal. After a few weeks, he told Hunt, 'My land-scape is *ridiculously elaborate*. I think you will find it very minute yet not near enough for nature. To do it as it ought to be would take a month a weed. As it is, I have done every blade of grass and leaf distinct.'

He was singlemindedly tenacious about the job at hand. He had an offer, William Rossetti reported, 'to paint a copy of a portrait by Holbein, which as he does not feel disposed to accept, he offered to Stephens'. After sundown, he usually relaxed by reading. He read randomly, delving into whatever looked interesting. Writing to Hunt, he mentioned one selection: 'I have been reading "Don Juan" at night in bed and do not hesitate to pronounce that it is a common work without the slightest regard or feeling for nature. To think of that beast Byron being compared to Keats!'

Millais finished his background late in September. He then moved to the house of James Wyatt, picture dealer, frame-maker, and former mayor of the city. He had agreed to do a full-length portrait of Wyatt and his six-year-old granddaughter. Millais was a fine portrait painter, which he proved in *Isabella*. But those portraits were parts of a subject. He had little interest in straight portraits. The one in Hampstead had been a favour to a friend and potential patron, as was the current Oxford picture, which was painted in a parlour, with Wyatt sitting in a high-backed chair and his granddaughter leaning against him. Millais was as conscientious and painstaking as he had been with his landscape. Everything was replicated – furniture, pictures on the wall, dishes of china in a cabinet, reading glasses lying on an open book, flowers and shrubs beyond a French window, even a lamp post at the garden gate. Nothing was left to the imagination. It was a 'Pre-Raphaelite' portrait. To Millais's credit, the accessories do not overwhelm the figures. James Wyatt has character and individuality, the very model of an ex-mayor of Oxford. His granddaughter is less satisfactory. She can't be compared to her creator's later great portraits of children, but at only twenty years old, he couldn't reasonably be expected to do *everything* well.

When he was done, he returned to London. Fred Stephens stood for the human figure in his Shakespearean picture, which he called *Ferdinand Lured by Ariel*. Before this was finished, early in December, he had decided on the third of three paintings to be sent to the Academy. It would be the most controversial British painting of the nineteenth century.

* * *

On 24 May, when Millais was still in London, William Rossetti wrote in his *Journal*, 'Collinson says he is about to make a Christian art design of Zachariah reading the Scriptures to the Holy Family.' At the same time Gabriel Rossetti was talking about doing a Passover seder of Jesus's family when he was a boy. Neither of these pictures was painted, but they may very well have planted a seed in Millais's mind. Instead of applying a 'Pre-Raphaelite' treatment to a conventional scene, as his Brothers were planning to do, why not go all the way and paint an earthily realistic New Testament picture? With a brand new vision, a totally fresh viewpoint, he would be the first person to present Jesus as a boy in a Nazareth carpenter's shop. In the true sense of the term, this would be a work of modern art.

He would show Jesus about eight years old in his father's shop. Having cut his hand with a nail, he would be seeking sympathy from his mother, kneeling and kissing his cheek. Standing by solicitously would be Joseph, Joseph's helper, the elderly St Anne, and young John the Baptist. This would be a commonplace occurrence, nearly two thousand years old, presented as it might have taken place.

In mid-December he got started. He visited an Oxford Street carpenter's shop, and not just briefly. He spent nearly three weeks in the place. Sometimes he even slept there, in order to begin work early on the following morning. He studied and copied everything – tools, work table, shavings on the floor. Not least important was the artisan himself. 'I was determined,' he told Hunt, 'to choose a man whose frame and muscles had been formed by the exact exercise of the man in my painting.'

Never had he been so excited. 'As week by week flowed by,' Hunt recalled, 'his enthusiasm grew. "I declare to you," he once exclaimed, "when I finished the body of the little St John and turned my eyes from the boy who was sitting and then back to my painting, I could not tell which was which."'

He worked right up until sending-in day, 11 April, when, along with *Ferdinand* and the Wyatt portrait, it went to the Academy. It came to be known as *The Carpenter's Shop* but was exhibited without a title. The catalogue entry was a passage from the Book of Zechariah: 'And one shall say unto him, What are these wounds in thy hands? Then shall he answer, Those with which I was wounded in the house of my friends.'

One wonders why Millais chose this particular verse from a difficult section of an extremely difficult book. One thing is certain: the passage has nothing to do with Jesus. It deals with the response of someone accused of false prophecy because he has what may be a wound self-inflicted in a frenzied fit. At that time almost the only dissenter from this explication was Oxford's Regius Professor of History, a leader in the Oxford Movement, Edward Pusey, who saw the sentences as foreshadowing the crucifixion wound. This interpretation had some currency in Oxford, where Millais probably picked it up.

On 8 April, three days before the Royal Academy sending-in day, the summer art season was again ushered in by the Free Exhibition, in a new gallery with a new name. Now in the four-storey Portland Gallery in Regent Street, its higher-sounding name was the exhibition of the National Institute of Fine Arts. Still 'free' to whoever paid the entrance fee, the exhibitors again included Dante Gabriel Rossetti, with a pendant to his 1849 picture called *Ecce Ancilla Domini* (Behold the Handmaid of the Lord). It showed the angel Gabriel informing Mary of her impending childbirth.

Hunt and Millais did not try to dissuade Rossetti from passing up the Academy. Despite his role in the formation of the Brotherhood, they knew that he wasn't, philosophically, a Pre-Raphaelite. Some years later, writing to Millais, Hunt said, 'Rossetti never did understand what Pre-Raphaelitism meant, but believed that instead of being a real attempt to go back to healthy nature, as you and I did, it was an attempt to revive gothicism, as Herbert, Dyce, and others, including Ford Madox Brown, were doing, and as Rossetti, in his own sensuous, not to say sensual, manner did – as far as he was able, for he was only an amateur.'

Hunt was partly right. Rossetti's paintings, mainly imaginative flights of fancy, had little to do with Pre-Raphaelitism. But even though he was basically a poet who also painted pictures, it doesn't seem fair to call him an amateur.

At the Portland Gallery, Rossetti was joined by a close associate of the Brothers, Walter Deverell, with a scene from *Twelfth Night*. The first review of the show appeared on 20 April in the *Athenaeum*. The critic who had eulogised *The Girlhood of Mary Virgin* now dealt with the *Girlhood*'s companion piece:

What shall we say of a work which we notice . . . as an example of the perversion of talent which has recently been making too much way in our school of Art? . . . Ignoring all that has made art great in the works of the greatest masters, the school to which Mr Rossetti belongs would begin anew and accompany the faltering steps of its earliest explorers. This is archaeology turned from its legitimate uses and made into a mere pedant. These men are slavish imitators of artistic inefficiency . . . Do these crotchet-mongers propose that

Art should begin and end with the early masters? The world will not be led to that deduction by such puerilities as this one, thrust by the artist into the eye of the spectator, an unintelligent imitation of the mere technicalities of old Art.

Rossetti fell into a state of shock. He dashed off a scathing letter to the *Athenaeum*, judged too venomous for publication. (It has not survived.) He vowed that never again would he exhibit anything anywhere at any time, a vow that would not be repudiated.

Actually the real object of the writer's wrath was the group to which Rossetti belonged. Even their friends suffered from guilt by association. On 27 April, the *Spectator* referred to Walter Deverell as an 'absurd . . . nonsensical . . . practical joker, a self-burlesquer aping the imperfections of art on its revival after the middle ages'. As yet the Brotherhood had not been mentioned by name. Then on Saturday, 4 May, two days before the opening of the Royal Academy Exhibition, everything was out in the open.

The popular weekly *Illustrated London News* had a regular column of chitchat, unsigned but in fact written by a Scotsman, Angus Reach. In his 4 May column, Reach reminisced on Wordsworth, who had just died; he noted signs of approaching spring; and he repeated rumours concerning the Government. The column ended with a revelation: 'Has any casual reader of art criticism been puzzled by three mysterious letters, denoting a new-fashioned school of painting? The hieroglyphics are "PRB", the initials of "Pre-Raffaelite Brotherhood." To this league belong ingenious gentlemen who . . . setting aside the Raffaelles, Guidos, Titians, and all such small-beer daubers, devote their energies to reproductions of saints squeezed out perfectly flat . . . their appearance being further improved by limbs being stuck akimbo, so as to produce a most interesting series of angles and finely-developed elbows . . . The "PRBs" would, if they could, make men and women like artfully-shaped and coloured pancakes.'

Many years later Holman Hunt said that Gabriel Rossetti had revealed their secret to the Scottish sculptor Alexander Munro, who then informed Reach. According to Hunt, this paragraph in the *Illustrated London News* let the cat out of the bag. Historians of the Pre-Raphaelite Brotherhood have restated this allegation, but as we have seen, at least two earlier reviewers knew about the society. And on the day of Reach's column, the *Literary Gazette*, commenting upon the Portland Gallery show, said that Deverell's painting 'belongs to a somewhat novel phase in our fine arts, which has been designated the *Pre-Raphael School*'. Speaking of Rossetti, the *Gazette* reckoned that 'if the other be *Pre-Raphael*, this one is *Pre-Pre*, or ancient Byzantine.' On the same day the now notorious 'P-R' word also appeared in *John Bull*.

As I have suggested, it would have been surprising if the news had not got out. The members worked closely with several others who knew about their Brotherhood. As the privileged circle widened, more and more people would be in on the secret. An unveiling of the name was almost guaranteed. Indeed the Brothers themselves were uneasy: none of their pictures of 1850 bore the fraternal initials.

Millais and Hunt had to feel uncomfortable when, on 3 May, they went to the Academy private view. But they couldn't complain about the positioning of their pictures. All but *Ferdinand* were well placed. Seeing *The Carpenter's Shop* for the first time, Hunt said, 'My dear fellow, it is truly marvellous, It is indeed.' Just then, two students permitted to visit the gallery appeared and began to laugh. Millais flew into a rage.

'Do you know,' he almost screamed, 'that if you should live to the age of Methuselah and should improve every day by more than you will during all of your lives, you could never do anything that good. You are bloody fools!'

This outburst from a usually self-contained person is a commentary on the state of his nerves.

In 1850, for the first time, critics attended the Friday private view. On Saturday several brief notices appeared. One was in London's second most influential daily paper, the *Morning Chronicle*: 'Mr Millais is a most obtrusive sinner against all rules and laws of taste and art. [*The Carpenter's Shop*] is utterly indefensible on any pretext, either with regard to the offensiveness and repulsiveness of the subject or the childish mode of treating it . . . These absurdities have been tolerated long enough. Surely it is time that this fanatical folly came to an end. This is the most glaring offensive instance of it we have ever met with.'

The presence of reviewers at the private view was a belated acknowledgement of their importance. As the *Art Journal* said, 'For prosperity or adversity, an artist must depend upon the approval or disapprobation of the press.' With one blast a critic could destroy a career. Byron insisted that John Keats's very life was 'snuffed out by an article'. Unlike their French equivalents, nearly all British critics wrote anonymously. This gave them a license to be irresponsible, which many fully utilised. On his visit to London in 1837 American novelist James Fenimore Cooper was shocked by what he read: 'I do not remember ever to have seen in any American journal as low and as intrinsically vulgar paragraphs as frequently are seen here in journals of the first reputation.'

A low point in journalistic irresponsibility was reached in the summer of 1850, triggered by the Pre-Raphaelites. They exhibited five paintings – one by Hunt, one by Collinson, three by Millais. Each was assaulted and ridiculed, with most of the onslaught levelled against Millais. Even the Wyatt portrait was a victim. The *Examiner* called it an 'ogre-like caricature of some unfortunate grandfather'. The *Art Journal* saw 'nothing in it to justify a belief that Mr Millais ever saw a model sit'. Much more attention was paid to *Ferdinand Lured by Ariel*, characterised in various journals as 'senseless', 'unintelligible', 'bilious and dyspeptic', and by *The Times* as a 'deplorable example of perverted taste'.

Ferdinand, however, was a secondary target. The biggest guns were aimed at the untitled painting. 'This picture is revolting,' *The Times* said. 'Associating the Holy Family with the meanest details of a carpenter's shop, with no conceivable omission of misery, dirt, and even disease, all finished with loathsome minuteness, is disgusting.' Other reviews called the painting 'monstrously perverse', 'a nameless atrocity', 'an instance of studious vulgarity', 'a pictorial blasphemy', and 'a repulsive caricature'.

Critiques also appeared where they had seldom been seen before. *Blackwood's Magazine* did not commonly cover the visual arts. It had not mentioned a London exhibition since the summer of 1843. This year, 'Pictures of the Season' appeared in *Blackwood's*: 'Rejecting the experience of centuries, the Pre-Raphaelites have imitated the errors, crudities, and imperfections of artists who flourished previously to Raphael. They delight in ugliness and revel in disease. Ricketty children, emanciation, and distortion constitute their stock in trade . . . We can hardly imagine anything more ugly, graceless, and unpleasant than Mr Millais's picture of Christ in the carpenter's shop. Such a collection of splay feet, puffed joints, and misshapen limbs was assuredly never before made within so small a compass!'

Another periodical, *Tait's Edinburgh Journal*, had never taken note of a Royal Academy Exhibition. Its premier review now included this observation: 'Mr Millais gropes in lanes and alleys till he finds a whining, sickly woman with a red-haired, ricketty bantling, transfers them with disgusting fidelity to his canvas and tells us that is the representation of all that awakens our holiest, purest, and most reverential sympathies. Mr Millais's picture is conclusive against him, either on an indictment for blasphemy or a writ *de lunatico inquerando.*'

Punch had not yet formally reviewed a Trafalgar Square show, nor did it do so in 1850. It merely issued a verbal caricature, 'Pathological Exhibition at the Royal Exhibition', by 'Our Surgical Advisor', dealing only with *The Carpenter's Shop*:

The interest here is purely pathological, the figures illustrating scrofulous or strumous diathesis. Their emaciated bodies, shrunken legs, and tumid ankles characterize that morbid state . . . The boy advancing with the bowl exemplifies a splendid case of rickets, and the osteological contortions of the frame have been accurately copied from the skeleton. The child in the centre is expressively represented by red hair, light eyebrows, and mottled complexion, which betoken the extreme of struma . . . With a nice discernment, the squalid filth for which the whole group is remarkable is associated with a disorder notoriously related to dirt . . . The persons depicted, though interesting to the eye of medicine, are revolting to unprofessional beholders. The gentleman who painted this picture should draw illustrations for Cooper's Surgical Dictionary.

Finally, there was Charles Dickens. Years later, Millais expressed an opinion on the style of art reviewers: 'Their tendency is to envelop the altarpiece they would have us worship in a cloud of literary incense, often so dense that the shrine has been totally obscured, and the reader left in a vague trance, sensible only of the perfume of beautiful English, or the garlic of highfalutin gibberish.'

Whether he thought Dickens's essay was an example of 'beautiful

English' or 'highfalutin gibberish' is not on record. It was called 'Old Lamps for New Ones' and appeared in Dickens's own family magazine, *Household Words*. Here are excerpts:

> Ladies and gentlemen, walk up, walk up, and here, conspicious on a wall of the Royal Academy of Art, you shall see what a New Holy Brotherhood . . . has been 'and done!'

> You come . . . to the contemplation of a Holy Family. You will have the goodness to discharge from your minds all Post-Raphael ideas, all religious aspirations, all elevating thoughts; all tender, awful, sorrowful, ennobling, sacred, graceful, or beautiful associations; and to prepare yourselves . . . for the lowest depths of what is mean, odious, repulsive, and revolting.

> You behold the interior of a carpenter's shop. In the foreground is a hideous wry-necked, blubbering, red-haired boy in a nightgown, who appears to have received a poke playing in an adjacent gutter, and to be holding it up for the contemplation of a kneeling woman, so horrible in her ugliness that she would stand out as a monster in the vilest cabaret in France or the lowest gin-shop in England . . . Wherever it is possible to express ugliness of feature, limb, or attitude, you have it expressed. Such men as these carpenters might be undressed in any hospital where dirty drunkards in a high state of varicose veins are received . . .

> This, in the eighty-second year of the annual Exhibition of the National Academy of Art, is the Pre-Raphael representation to us, Ladies and Gentlemen, of the most solemn passage which our minds can ever approach. This, in the eighty-second year of the annual Exhibition of the National Academy of Art, is what Pre-Raphael Art can do to render reverence and homage to the faith in which we live and die!

* * *

The fifty-fifth verse of the thirteenth chapter of the Gospel of St Matthew says that when Jesus began to preach in Nazareth, sceptical neighbours asked sneeringly, 'Is not this the carpenter's son?' Taking the question as relating to a simple fact, Millais proceeded respectfully, deferentially – and realistically – to illustrate this fact. How could

[63]

something so naive and harmless have been so greatly vilified? Simply because no one had ever done anything like this. At a later date, Millais would say, 'Fashion exercises such a powerful tyranny over us that we dare not act in defiance of its voice.' In *The Carpenter's Shop* he defied the voice of fashion. He had to pay for his transgression.

We shouldn't feel smugly superior to the folks of 1850. We need only recall the response, in the United States, in Great Britain, in France, and elsewhere, to a beautifully sensitive novel, and a beautifully sensitive motion picture adaptation of that novel, Nikos Kazantzakis's *The Last Temptation of Christ*.

Because of her advanced pregnancy, Queen Victoria couldn't pay her annual visit to the Academy. But she had to see what everyone was talking about. Unprecedentedly, the picture was removed for a day and sent to Windsor Castle. When the royal inspection took place, Millais was in Oxford, working on next year's pictures. He wrote to Hunt, 'I hope that it will not have any bad effects upon the Queen's mind.'

Actually the Queen may not have been shocked. Next year at the Royal Academy banquet, preceding the opening of the show, the principal speaker for the first and only time was Prince Albert, who in the course of his speech said, 'Works of art are tender plants which thrive in an atmosphere of kindness. Unkind words of criticism pass like cold blasts over their tender shoots and shrink them, checking the flow of sap which could produce, perhaps, multitudes of flowers and fruit . . . Professional writers often strive to impress the public with a merciless manner of treating works which cost their producers the highest efforts of mind and feeling. . . . Public and private patronage is swayed by this tyrannical influence. It is, then, to an institution like this that we must look for a counterpoise to these evils.'

It is not, I think, coincidental that this was said after the assault on *The Carpenter's Shop*. And the Prince would hardly have spoken in these terms if the picture had disgusted the Queen.

As one might suppose, Millais was enjoying the notoriety. And why not? Like Byron he had awakened to find himself famous. At the age of twenty-one, still nominally a student, he was England's most widely discussed artist. Furthermore, not every review was negative.

In May there was one positive notice. The *Illustrated London News*'s reviewer found 'a thousand merits' in *The Carpenter's Shop*. The '*pre-Raphaelism*', he said, was actually 'its leading excellence'. Because of the strong points, he concluded, 'its eccentricities may be very well excused'.

June brought more good news. The *Manchester Guardian* was, as always, noted for its independence and occasional inconsistency. Earlier its critic had denounced *Ferdinand*. Now he came out with a highly favourable column on the pictures of Hunt and Millais. In *The Carpenter's Shop*, he said, 'the power of mere representation is so great that surrounding pictures look faint and conventional in comparison. This is only one manifestation of the truthfulness which pervades each countenance and figure in the picture . . . We will take Mr Millais's work as he presents it, distinguished in truth of painting and force of expression.'

Then there was this happy sentence in the important *New Monthly Review*: 'There is great character and expression in this young man's works: his conceptions are quite his own; he sets about his task fearlessly; and perhaps there is no artist from whom we have a greater right to expect great things than Mr John Millais.'

CHAPTER 7

1850–51

THE Pre-Raphaelite abuse continued through the summer, autumn, and winter. Often it was gratuitous. This, for example, appeared apropos of nothing in the *Athenaeum* on 7 December: 'The soi-distant Pre-Raphaelite ignores the principles of art and affects to dispel all fixed ideas on beauty and taste. He sits down before a model that has been selected to answer his desire to imitate the ugliness of some early master, and he searches out and imitates its disgusting details with a microscopic eye.'

The invective caused two members to resign from the Brotherhood, Gabriel Rossetti and James Collinson. And that autumn Millais wrote to Hunt, 'I cannot help thinking that we have been asses to follow the principles of nature. It is so disgustingly laborious and unremunerative.' This reflected only a momentary feeling of depression. At that very moment he was working on two paintings that were unbendingly Pre-Raphaelite. Why did he persevere? For one thing, he had a low opinion of art critics. 'I hold a painter is better able to talk of his profession than any one else,' he once wrote, 'however clumsily he may express himself. The expression "Fudge" would be a very appropriate term to apply to a man of highfalutin talk on the subject of Art, which is perpetually submitted to the public in lectures, pamphlets, and magazines.'

The main reason, however, for his steadfastness was self-confidence. He sometimes dabbled in verse, as in this stanza:

> Above all things, believe in one,
> That one yourself, as being greater

Than all the world, and you have won
Three parts of success and more.

Believe in yourself! This injunction was at the core of John Millais's philosophy of art and life.

Millais's paintings of 1850 took him in a new direction. Each had a contemporary subject, taken from a poem by a living writer. First, there was Coventry Patmore's 'The Woodman's Daughter'. Patmore, a twenty-seven-year-old assistant in the Printed Books Department of the British Museum, was the author of one slender volume, published in 1844, *Poems*, comprising four narrative pieces. A twelve-page diatribe in *Blackwood's Magazine* gave it a certain notoriety. 'Our deliberate judgment,' the reviwer wrote, 'is that the weakest inanity ever perpetrated in rhyme by the vilest poetaster of any former generation becomes masculine verse when contrasted with the nauseous pulings of Mr Patmore's muse. Indeed we question whether the strains of any poetaster can be considered vile when brought into comparison with this gentleman's verse . . . There is nothing in the writing of any former poetaster to equal his silly and conceited jargon.'

Despite, or perhaps because of, *Blackwood's*, Gabriel Rossetti loved Patmore's poetry. At the first PRB meeting he gave an eloquent reading of 'The Woodman's Daughter', which, like the other poems in the book, is weak in plot and characters, strong in description. Patmore's vision was microscopic, and his rural settings contain minute descriptions of everything. Understandably, he became the Pre-Raphaelites' favourite poet. On their List of Immortals, he was rated more highly than Spenser, Milton, Byron, and Wordsworth. He became a close friend of the Brothers and was as foolishly extravagant about them as they were about him. William Rossetti reported Patmore as maintaining 'Millais's *Isabella* far better than anything Keats ever did.' It was then hardly surprising that a Millais subject came from a Patmore poem.

'The Woodman's Daughter' deals with a common Victorian literary theme, seduction and abandonment. The title character, called Maud, is thirteen years old, daughter of the woodman on a country estate. One day the landowner's son sees her keeping her father company and is capitvated. For Millais these were the operative lines:

[67]

She fancied and he felt she help'd;
        And, whilst he hack'd and saw'd,
The rich Squire's son, a young boy then,
        Whole mornings, as if awed,
Stood silent by, and gazed in turn
        At Gerald and on Maud.

And sometimes, in a sullen tone,
        He offer'd fruits, and she
Received them always with an air
        So unreserved and free,
That shame-faced distance soon became
        Familiarity.

With the woodman in the background, the painting shows the boy offering Maud four strawberries. Never was Millais more painstakingly literal than in the landscape of this picture. Every leaf, branch, and blade of grass was seemingly reproduced.

Meanwhile in London, William Rossetti wrote in his *Journal*, 'I heard from Patmore that Tennyson on being told that Millais was doing something from "The Woodman's Daughter" observed, "I wish he'd do something from me."' This was the man who had just become poet laureate! Tennyson seems not to have been disturbed by *The Carpenter's Shop*. But then as a young man he too had suffered through a journalistic ordeal. In 1832, when he was twenty-three, his first major volume of poems was so strongly assaulted that ten years passed before he published another book. He could empathise with this twenty-one-year-old painter.

Actually Millais was doing something from Tennyson. He had left London with designs for 'The Woodman's Daughter' and Tennyson's 'Mariana'. At the end of Patmore's poem, the girl is abandoned. At the beginning of Tennyson's poem, a woman has been abandoned. For seven stanzas she laments her fate, ending with a death wish. Her surroundings reflect her mood:

With blackest moss the flower-pots
        Were thickly crusted, one and all:

The rusted nails fell from the knots
That held the pear to the gable-wall
The broken sheds look'd sad and strange:
Unlifted was the clinking latch;
Weeded and worn the ancient thatch
Upon the lonely grange.

I have discussed this poem many times with undergraduates and the response was virtually unanimous. While they admired the youthful Tennyson's technical skill, they had little sympathy for someone who bewails her predicament long enough for nails to rust. It seems as if Millais may have felt the same way. If he had followed Tennyson literally, as with Patmore, the content of his picture would have been as silly as that of the poem. But, superficially, his Mariana is nothing like Tennyson's. She wears an opulent blue dress with a richly bejewelled girdle. Her room is lavishly furnished. Beyond a window is a carefully tended garden. Abject despair has become conspicuous affluence.

If Millais was motivated as I think he was, his transformation of Tennyson's Mariana was masterful and perceptive. He presents a woman at an embroidery table. She has just risen to stretch, epitomising boredom and languor. She is probably well educated – that is, for a Victorian woman – but what good is her education? Her husband is doubtlessly out doing something constructive, but she sits at an embroidery table. If this interpretation holds up, *Mariana* makes a meaningful social comment and is another Millais picture with a message.

It should be noted that in *Mariana*, Millais was as conscientious with the indoor details as with the landscape in *The Woodman's Daughter*.

* * *

During this summer of 1850 Millais was extremely helpful to his principal Brother. Because of their notoriety, Hunt couldn't sell anything. Millais came to his rescue. Early in the summer, he stayed with Mr and Mrs Thomas Combe, a couple whose continuing kindness and generosity would have a lasting impact on him. An administrator of the Oxford University Press, Combe had begun collecting contemporary art. Unlike most picture buyers of that day (or, perhaps, of any day), he had a mind of his own. 'He does not care a bit about the papers,' Millais told Hunt, 'and so he will not be biased by opinion.' And so Millais could persuade Combe to do what no one else would do, purchase Hunt's most recent painting. 'Hurrah for PRB [underlined three times],' Millais wrote to Hunt. 'Now, old boy, work away with fresh vigour and prove the superiority of the PRB.'

After the picture had arrived and was in place, Millais wrote, 'I am delighted to think that I am the cause of your being able to go on and astonish the world. Your picture looks magnificent. Everybody is perfectly *delighted*, thoroughly appreciating it. All the university men admire. Therefore be sure ultimately you will succeed.'

Millais stayed only briefly with the Combes. During most of the summer he lived in a cottage outside Oxford, near a wood. Here he painted the background of *The Woodman's Daughter*. 'This is such a delightful place,' he told Hunt. 'I walk home through fields with cuckoos, nightingales, and rocks all singing together, and rabbits and pheasants in the coppice . . . I find it very quick, this kind of life.'

He wasn't alone. He shared his cottage, 'a most humble place', with a friend a year younger than himself, Charles Collins, son of landscape painter William Collins and younger brother of Wilkie Collins, whose first novel, *Antonina*, had just been published. Collins was a talented painter, with six pictures at the four most recent Royal Academy shows, equalling Millais's output. Personally and professionally he was so close to Hunt and Millais that everyone, including the members themselves, regarded him as a Pre-Raphaelite. In a letter to Hunt, Millais said, 'Collins is working on a painting which will be the best specimen the PRB can produce. He desires me to send brotherly affections.' In another letter, he wrote, 'Collins and I have been painting portraits and have given *great satisfaction* in the PRB style.' Perhaps Collins was not selected as a member because he was felt to be too close to the art establishment. His father, who had died in 1847, had been a Royal Academician for seventeen years. Later Collins was asked to join the Brotherhood but, feeling that he should have been chosen in the beginning, he declined the offer.

The two youths worked every day in the open air. It could be frustrating. 'We are both getting on slowly,' Millais told Hunt. 'Collins is dreadfully annoyed by flies and children, and I by the sun and children.' But neither the sun nor children could affect Millais's self-confidence. 'People better buy my pictures now when I am working for fame,' he told Thomas Combe, 'rather than a few years from now when I *am* famous.'

On 11 November, Millais returned to London, a city with which he maintained a love-hate relationship. In mid-summer he had told Hunt that he and Collins 'acknowledge to be real London cockneys and long to imbibe city atmosphere, see smoky faces, dead leaves, and green vegetation, and behold the great men in Art walking on London streets'.

But two days after coming back, he wrote to Mrs Combe, 'I had to go through the exceedingly difficult task of performing the dramatic traveller's return to his home. I say I had to "perform" because the detestation I hold London in surpasses all expression and prevents the possibility of my being pleased to return to anybody at such a place. Mind, I am not abusing the society, but the filth of the capital.' When he wrote this, he was lonely. The PRBs no longer functioned socially, and Hunt was out of town. 'I truly long for your return,' he wrote to him, 'having no friend in London except Charlie [Collins].'

It was difficult to work. 'I am ashamed to say,' he told Mrs Combe on 9 December, 'that late hours at night and ditto in the morning are creeping again on us [Collins and himself]. Now and then I make a desperate resolution to plunge out of bed when called which ends in passively lying down again. And then a late breakfast. (I won't mention the hour.)' His continuing problem was that he couldn't start a third picture for want of a subject. Then in late December he hit upon a topic. Now he thought of nothing but his painting. 'I have plenty of invitations,' he told Mrs Combe, 'all of which I have declined.' He even did evening work, which, he said, 'lasts till twelve and will continue the next few months.'

His subject, he informed Combe, 'is quite new, the dove returning to the ark with the olive branch. I shall have three figures – Noah, praying with the branch in his hand, and the dove in the breast of a young girl who is looking at Noah. The other figure will be kissing the bird's breast. The background will be very novel, as I shall paint several birds and animals one of which now forms the prey to the other.'

Despite the recent bad publicity, he sold his picture, *The Return of the Dove to the Ark*, prior to the Summer Exhibition opening. Coventry Patmore saw him after the sale: 'He was flourishing before my eyes a cheque for £150.' This may have been an instance of false bravado. Fearful that the impending season might be like the last one, he was for the first time finding it difficult to sleep.

* * *

In 1851 the Royal Academy shared the limelight with the first world's fair, the Great Exhibition, opening on Thursday, 1 May, in the Crystal Palace, Hyde Park. Promoted by Prince Albert and featuring commercial and industrial products from all over, it attracted a host of foreign visitors. In a letter to Combe, Millais said, 'Such a quantity of loathsome foreigners stroll about the principal streets that they incline one to take up a residence in Sweden, outside the fumes of their tobacco. [Millais did not yet smoke.] I expect all respectable families will leave London after the first month of the Exhibition because it will be crowded with the lower rabble of all the countries in Europe.'

On the day after the Great Exhibition opened, the Royal Academy held its private view. One of those appearing with a press pass was William Rossetti, now an art critic for the *Spectator*. He got £50 a year, supplementing his £110 salary at the Inland Revenue Office. 'I figured almost as a capitalist among the PRBs,' he said. 'Millais alone made more than I did, most of the others much less or hardly anything.' At once he searched out the five Pre-Raphaelite pictures, three by Millais, one each by Hunt and Collins. Hunt's was called *Valentine Rescuing Sylvia from Proteus*, a scene from Shakespeare's *Two Gentlemen from Verona*. Collins's was *Convent Thoughts*, a nun contemplating a flower in a garden. All but *Convent Thoughts* were well positioned, a tribute to the Academy's fairness.

The placing of the pictures made it easy for reviewers to carry on what they had started in 1850. The Pre-Raphaelite threesome were accused by the *Morning Chronicle* of 'favouring zigzagas, elbows, and angles in which the most ungraceful combinations of geometrical forms seem to have been purposely gathered together'; by the *Examiner* of having gone 'out of their way to seek deformity'; by the *Morning Post* of 'worshiping the ugly as devoutly as heretofore'; by the *Globe* of being 'retrograde freaks in painting'.

But everything was tame compared to what appeared in *The Times* on 7 May, one of the most devastating notices in the history of British art. Because it marked a major turning point for John Millais, I quote at some length:

We cannot censure as amply or as strongly as we desire that strange disorder of the mind or eyes which continues to rage with unabated absurdity among a class of juvenile artists who style themselves *Pre-Raphael-brethren*. Their faith seems to consist in absolute contempt for perspective and the known laws of light and shade, an aversion to beauty in every shape, seeking out every excess of sharpness and deformity. Mr Millais, Mr Hunt, and Mr Collins have undertaken to reform art on these principles. The Council of the Academy have allowed these extravagances to disgrace their walls for three years, and though we cannot prevent men from wasting their talents on ugliness and conceit, the public may fairly require that such offensive jests should not continue to be exposed as specimens of their profession . . . These artists have become notorious by addicting themselves to an antiquated style and an affected simplicity, which is to genuine art what the designs in *Punch* are to Giotto. With the utmost readiness to humour even the caprices of Art, when they bear the stamp of originality and genius, we can extend no toleration to a mere servile imitation of the cramped style, false perspective, and crude colour of remote antiquity. We do not want to see faces bloated into apoplexy or extenuated to skeletons, colours borrowed from the jars in a druggist's shop, and expression forced into caricature . . . The authors of these offensive, absurd productions have continued to combine the puerility of their art with the uppishness of a different period of life. That morbid infatuation which sacrifices truth, beauty, and genuine feeling to mere eccentricity deserves no quarter at the hands of the public, and these monkish follies have no claim whatsoever to figure in any decent collection of English paintings.

'The Times has sold itself to destroy us,' Millais told Combe. On the morning of Friday, 9 May, he was joined in Gower Street by Collins, Hunt, Stephens and William Rossetti. They talked about what to do in the aftershock of the explosion. Hunt said that he had heard of John Ruskin's interest in *The Return of the Dove*. Perhaps they should ask him for a letter of support, to be sent, naturally, to *The Times*. Actually it was Ruskin's father who had liked the *Dove*, but they could not have done better than to approach John Ruskin.

Since volume two of *Modern Painters*, Ruskin had brought out two more books. Now, aged thirty-two, he was Britain's most influential art critic. He was the one to confront *The Times*. And since the Pre-Raphaelites were practising what he had preached, he might agree to help.

John Ruskin, moreover, as arrogant and dogmatic as *The Times* itself, would survive a challenge of the journalistic giant, and might enjoy the experience. But how should the young men sound out the great man? They debated the question without reaching a conclusion.

As soon as his guests had left, Millais dashed over to Tottenham Court Road and hopped onto a yellow omnibus labelled 'Highgate', which took him to the northern suburb where the author of 'The Woodman's Daughter' lived. Patmore, a friend of Ruskin, rode back into town with Millais and went to the critic's current residence in Park Street, Mayfair.

The Brethren may have thought that Ruskin was a partisan of theirs, but in fact he had scarcely noticed their work. (In 1850, after glancing at *The Carpenter's Shop*, he walked away in disgust.) Patmore, however, stroked his ego by saying that the Pre-Raphaelites were being punished for following his advice. Ruskin called for his carriage and rode to Trafalgar Square and re-examined – or perhaps examined for the first time – the scandalous paintings. He was satisfied. He returned home and wrote a long letter, which appeared in *The Times* four days later. This is part of it:

Your usual liberality will, I trust, give a place in your column to an expression of regret that the tone of your critique on the works of Mr Millais and Mr Hunt was scornful and severe.

I regret it, first, because the mere labour bestowed on these works, and their fidelity to a certain order of truth, ought to have placed them above the level of contempt; and, secondly, because I believe these young artists to be at a most critical period of their career – at a turning-point from which they may either sink into nothingness or rise to very real greatness. Whether they choose the upward or downward path may in no small degree depend upon the character of the criticism which their works have to sustain . . . . I ask your permission, in justice to artists who have given much time and toil to their pictures, to institute a more serious inquiry into their merits and faults than your general notice of the Academy could possibly have admitted . . .

Let me correct an impression which your article is likely to induce, which is altogether false. These pre-Raphaelites (I cannot compliment them on common sense in choice of a *nom de guerre*) do not desire or pretend in any way to imitate antique painting as such. As far as I can judge – for I do not know the men – the pre-Raphaelites intend to surrender no advantage which the knowledge of the present time can afford to their art. They intend to return to early days in one point only – that, as far as in them lies, they will draw either what they see, or what they suppose might have been the actual facts of the scene they desire to represent, irrespective of conventional rules of picture-making; and they have chosen their unfortunate though not inaccurate name because all artists did this before Raphael's time . . .

Ruskin's letter, Hunt said, appeared like 'thunder out of a clear sky'. Because Patmore had indicated that a second letter might be forthcoming, they did not send a note of thanks so that he could continue to say that he had had no personal contact with them.

On 30 May *The Times* published the second letter. After five paragraphs of analyses of the current paintings, Ruskin said:

I heartily wish these young artists good speed, believing that if they temper the courage and energy which they have shown in the adoption of their systems with patience and discretion in framing it, and if they do not suffer themselves to be driven by harsh criticism into rejecting the ordinary means of obtaining influence over the minds of others, they may, as they gain experience, lay in our England the foundation of a school of art nobler than the world has seen for three hundred years.

Now he could be thanked. Hunt and Millais sent a joint letter from 83 Gower Street. The letter was posted on the morning of Friday, 30 May. In the afternoon Millais's guests were Mr and Mrs John Ruskin, a tribute to the Victorian postal service and a testimonial to what must have been an eloquent letter. (It has not survived.)

John Ruskin was moderately tall, slender, neat in appearance. His wife, nine years younger than he, was strikingly attractive. She had brown hair, brown eyes, a seductive gap in the middle of her upper teeth, and she spoke with a captivating Scottish burr. Her name was Euphemia, but she was known to everyone as Effie.

This was not John Everett's introduction to Effie. In the 1930s her granddaughter Lady Clara Stuart Wortley pencilled a note, now in the Pierpont Morgan Library, which says that her grandmother, aged sixteen, attended a dance at Ewell Castle, near Epsom. Fifteen-year-old John Everett Millais 'asked to be introduced to the lovely girl with auburn hair', but she 'was rather bored with him, only a boy. She preferred young men'.

Effie was not likely to be forgotten. Nor, perhaps, was John Everett. And so they probably recalled the earlier meeting. The afternoon call must have been a success because Millais received and accepted an invitation to spend the weekend at the Ruskin family home south of the river.

On the following Monday, he told Mrs Combe, 'I have dined and taken breakfast with Ruskin. We are such good friends that he wished me to accompany him and Mrs Ruskin to Switzerland.' He declined, perhaps because of potential problems of travelling as a threesome.

*　*　*

On 7 June, the *Literary Gazette* ran its fifth notice of the Summer Show, entirely devoted to the Pre-Raphaelites. 'If these pictures were badly painted,' the reviewer wrote, 'if the drawing were false, if they showed no study, or a clumsy carelessness, we might join with the Jupiter tonans of the daily press in considering them a disgrace to the Academy. But none of these faults can be brought against them.' The Pre-Raphaelites, to be sure, were guilty of 'heresy', but only 'from a desire to avoid conventionalism and to rely entirely upon nature. It is certainly better to see men following nature's teaching than painting eternally out of their own heads, repeating the same forms, colours, and expressions.'

He ended with a statement that might have come from Ruskin: 'With enthusiasm and a most devoted study of nature . . . the pre-Raffaelites employ all the modern appliances of painting in giving an exact resemblance of objects . . . It is for this devoted and faithful study we have hopes that they will become *naturalistic* just as the Caracci and Corregio did. Nature is like the conscience to a painter, a faithful monitor who, if he follow truly, will not mislead.'

This discourse in the *Literary Gazette* on the first Saturday in June of 1851 signified another turning-point for John Millais. Indeed the summer as a whole began and ended a phase in his professional life. And in his personal life.

CHAPTER 8

1851–52

Early in July 1851, Hunt and Millais boarded a London and South Western Railway train at recently completed Waterloo Station. They rode for thirty-five miles to the village of Ewell, where the Hogsmill River begins. A streamlet meandering six miles before joining the Thames at Kingston, the Hogsmill was where they would paint backgrounds and foregrounds for their next pictures. At once Hunt found a suitable locale, but, he related, Millais 'walked along beaten lanes and jumped over ditches and ruts without finding a place that would satisfy him. Almost all day we searched; nothing would satisfy him. Then toward the end of the day the "Millais luck" (a phrase which became a proverb) presented him with the exact composition of arboreal and floral richness he had dreamed of. He pointed exultantly, saying, "Look, could anything be more perfect?"'

His subject may have resulted from a particularly caustic review. Referring to Hunt's painting, the *Morning Post*'s critic remarked, 'As long as Messrs Hunt and Millais confine themselves to missal and medicinal subjects, we can bear the infliction, but we must protest against either of them meddling with Shakespeare.' Not only would Millais 'meddle', but he chose a famous passage from Shakespeare's most celebrated play, Gertrude's speech at the end of Act 4 of *Hamlet*, describing for Laertes the death of Ophelia, lines made to order for a Pre-Raphaelite:

> There is a willow grows aslant a brook,
> That shows his hoar leaves in the glassy stream.

There with fantastic garlands did she come
Of crowflowers, nettles, daisies, and long purples . . .
There on the pendent boughs, her coronet weeds
Clambering to hand an envious sliver broke,
When down her weedy trophies and herself
Fell in the weeping brook. Her clothes spread wide
And, mermaid-like, awhile they bore her up;
Which time she chanted snatches of old tunes,
As one incapable of her own distress . . .
Till that her garments, heavy with their drink,
Pull'd the poor wretch from her melodious lay
To muddy death.

After finding living accommodation, they went to work. A week or so later, Millais wrote to Mrs Combe:

Our rooms are nearly four miles from Hunt's spot and two from mine, so we arrived jaded and slightly above that temperature necessary to make cool commencement. I sit tailor-fashion under an umbrella throwing a shadow scarcely larger than a half-penny for eleven hours, with a child's mug within reach to satisfy my thirst from the running stream beside me. I am threatened with a notice to appear before a magistrate for trespassing; am also in danger of being blown by the wind into the water and becoming intimate with the feelings of Ophelia when that lady sank to muddy death, together with the (less likely) total disappearance through the voracity of the flies of Surrey, which have a great propensity for probing human flesh. The painting of a picture under these circumstances is a greater punishment than death by hanging.

Nonetheless, he persevered for more than two months before it was completed. He was pleased with his canvas, probably his most Pre-Raphaelite work. Everything – branches, reeds, foliage, flowers, moss and water – has led some viewers, mistakenly I believe, to say that his interest was less in Ophelia than her milieu. 'Perhaps the greatest compliment ever paid to "Ophelia's" truthfulness to nature,' his son John G. Millais wrote, 'is that a professor of botany, unable to

[79]

take a class into the country and lecture from objects before him, took them to the Guildhall, where "Ophelia" was being exhibited, and he discoursed upon its flowers and plants, which, he said, were as instructive as nature itself.'

This story is questionable, but it *could* have happened. Indeed the *Athenaeum*'s reviewer remarked that 'the water lily is the botanical study of Linnaeus.' If the incident did take place, the professor and his students saw something not present at the original site. A friend asked Millais about some flowers in the picture. 'Are those daffodils?'

'Yes.'

'But daffodils don't grow along the Hogsmill.'

'I know that. When I returned to London, I saw that I needed some yellow in it. So I went to Covent Garden, bought some daffodils and painted them in.'

If asked why he needed the yellow, he wouldn't have given a precise answer. 'A painter cannot tell you,' he wrote some time later, 'why he puts a bit of colour here or there. An instinct tells him it is necessary.'

* * *

When his Hogsmill setting was completed, Millais had had his fill of the river. But he didn't go back to London. He wanted to do another country picture, but without water. Hunt didn't object to leaving, and so they went to Worcester Park, then a picturesque community one mile north of Ewell, where they moved into a farm house and were joined by Charlie Collins. After about ten days, Millais wrote to Mrs Combe:

> You will see that we have changed our spot, much for the better. Nothing can exceed the comfort of the new place. There is little to write about except my mishaps.
>
> I have broken the nail on the left hand little finger at the root; the accident happened in catching a ball at cricket. I have also been bedridden three days for a bilious attack.
>
> Charlie had joined us, and we three live together as happily as ancient monastic brethren . . . I wish you could see this farm, situated on one of the highest hills in the country. In front of the house there is one of the finest avenues of elm trees I ever saw. We live

almost entirely on the produce of the farm, which supplies every necessity.

Along with cricket, he played soccer with the farm children, who called him 'Long Limbs'. He had time for sport because he wasn't painting anything. Although outwardly cheerful, he was deeply troubled about this inactivity. As early as 28 July, still amidst Ophelia's background, he had told Mrs Combe, 'I am working my brains for a subject.' Two and a half months later, he was still deliberating. His mind was not a total blank. At the foot of the hill he noted an ivy-covered brick wall that would be great for a painting. But what should he do with it? He thought of putting a pair of lovers by the wall, perhaps embracing. He asked Hunt and Collins for their opinion of this.

'Two lovers standing by themselves would be trite and hackneyed,' Hunt said. 'To be interesting they must be part of some powerful historic or dramatic story.'

Collins agreed.

Suddenly Millais sprang to his feet.

'I've got it! he shouted. 'Grisi in *The Huguenots*!'

On 10 August 1849, William Rossetti noted in his *Journal* that Giulia Grisi in Meyerbeer's *Les Huguenots* had been 'a most glorious sight'. Had Millais been in London, he might well have been sitting with Rossetti in the Covent Garden Theatre. He had loved grand opera since early childhood, when his father played arias on the flute. He went to the opera not as Degas to the ballet or Toulouse-Lautrec to the Moulin Rouge, in search of material. He enjoyed it for its own sake. A friend, William Fenn, son of Covent Garden's manager, recalled:

My father occasionally favoured acquaintances with boxes or stalls, and he said, 'I like giving Johnny Millais a seat if only to watch the intense, eager interest in his handsome, keen, intellectual young face. It is an immense pleasure to me to observe what a pleasure it is to him.'

Millais's enthusiasm for all things that attracted him found a wide field at the opera. He paid no regard as to whether it was fashionable or otherwise, to applaud vehemently. He applauded what he liked, when he liked. He would throw himself back, raise his arms and clap with the utmost vigour as Grisi, Mario, or any of the great singers brought their arias to a telling point. The overwhelming applause elicited no more enthusiastic contributor than Millais. Nor had his delight much subsided the next day. While at his easel he would give tongue to the pleasure the performance had afforded him, interspersing his talk with practical references to individual melodies. Sometimes he would criticise and say, 'Grisi was lazy tonight,' or 'Mario was not in good form. Did you see how he avoided that top C?'

His favourite opera was *Les Huguenots*. After one performance, he told Fenn, 'I should love to paint that big scene.' This was almost the only time that he ever spoke of reproducing something observed on a stage.

Les Huguenots deals with the sixteenth-century Catholic-Protestant conflict in France. The pivotal event was the St Bartholomew's Day massacre of 1572, which followed the proclamation by the Parisian Catholic Duke of Guise that 'When the clock of the Palais de Justice shall sound upon the great bell at day break, each good Catholic must bind a strip of white linen round his arm and place a fair white cross in his cap.' It would be open season on anyone without these badges.

The scene that Millais mentioned is in the last act, a great duet between the Protestant Raoul and his Catholic lover, Valentine, in her house. She begs him to let her hide him, but after hesitating he leaves by the French window.

The greatest nineteenth-century Valentine was Giulia Grisi. Her Covent Garden debut in the role was on 24 May 1849, perhaps with Millais in attendance. This is from the Manchester *Guardian* review:

'One of the most densely packed audiences we ever saw within the walls of a theatre witnessed Grisi as Valentine, and it was a decided triumph. She gave a new reading to the great scene in the third act. Instead of expressing her distress at Raoul's probable fate by frantic gestures, Grisi embodied an expression of great mental suffering and anxiety in a single look, more eloquent than the most elaborate acting. The manner in which she depicted feelings of deepest emotion brought down a perfect hurricane of applause at the conclusion of the scene. Never did Grisi declare a greater triumph.'

* * *

Millais's paintings in the summer of 1851 illustrate the diverse ways in which the creative process operates.

Some works of art are carefully mapped out and take shape as planned. Such was *Ophelia*. Everything from the moment that Millais first looked into *Hamlet* until he finally laid down his brush fell into place. Nothing was left to chance.

Then there are creative productions that come about by accident. Take, for example, James Whistler's portrait of his mother. While waiting one morning for a model to arrive, Whistler learned that an accident would incapacitate her for a few days. With time on his hands, he asked his mother to stand for a portrait. For two or three days she stood, she said, 'still as statue.' Finally she became exhausted. Somewhat reluctantly, her son let her sit down. That is the reason for her seated position. Had she remained standing, Whistler would have painted a good picture. Because she was sitting, he produced a masterpiece.

Millais's most highly acclaimed single work was just as unplanned. It exists because he happened to be stopping near an ivy-covered brick wall.

On 20 October he set up his easel by the wall and began. A few days later he told Mrs Combe of his project: 'It is a scene taking place on the eve of the massacre of St Bartholomew's Day. Two lovers are the in act of parting, the woman a Papist and the man a Protestant. The badge worn to distinguish the former from the latter was a white scarf on the left arm. Many were base enough to escape murder by wearing it. The girl is endeavouring to tie a handkerchief round the man's arm, so as to save him; but he, holding his faith above his greatest worldly love, is softly preventing her. The subject will be very quiet and but slightly suggest the horror of the massacre. I am in high spirits about this subject *as it is entirely my own*.'

This is truly disingenuous. Hunt and Collins convinced him that he needed a dramatic subject; Meyerbeer and Grisi provided almost everything else. He was particularly indebted to Grisi for his heroine's low-key performance.

Throughout the rest of October and all of November he sat alongside the wall from dawn till dusk six days a week. On Sundays, he played with the children, and with the family attended services at Kingston's Church of All Saints. On 30 November, his last Sunday in Worcester Park, he reported an occurrence in a short-lived diary:

'On our way to church, we met Mr and Mrs B——, my old flame. I wished myself anywhere but there; all seemed so horribly changed, the girl I knew so well calling me "Mr Millais" instead of "John", and I addressing "Fanny" as "Mrs B". She married a man old enough to be her father; he trying to look the young man, with a light cane in his hand . . . an apparently stupid man, plain and bald, perfectly stupefied at Mrs B asking me to make a little sketch of her ugly old husband. They left, she making a bungling expression of gladness at having met me.'

All that I know about 'Fanny' is in the above paragraph. Interestingly, it is double the length of any other entry in the diary.

*   *   *

Back in London, Millais agonised over the figure of the Huguenot. Holman Hunt was his sounding board:

6 January 1852. I am very anxious to see you as I have entirely recomposed the lower design and wish to hear your opinion on it. Manage to come tomorrow evening if possible.

26 January. I can't quite understand my state with regard to painting. I have twice rubbed out the head. [My model] comes early so that I may not lose time. I therefore keep at home and go to bed before nine . . . It will be a consolation to hear that you have a like difficulty in your first head.

20 February. I have rubbed out two days work with the legs of the Huguenot. I feel frightfully miserable and cannot make up my mind about anything.

Two or three days later he had happier news. He had had a visit from a Pre-Raphaelite three-star Immortal, William Makepeace Thackeray. *Vanity Fair* and *Pendennis*, published within the past four years, had put Thackeray almost on a level with Dickens.

'The great stunner himself called unexpectedly to make my acquaintance,' Millais told Hunt. 'He was most delighted and uttered "By Jupiter" several times. He paid me a great compliment, saying that he had not called to see my pictures but me.'

After meeting Thackeray, he gained control of his work, and finished early in March. *A Huguenot* was Millais's best painting thus far, perhaps his best ever. Its pre-eminence is due to the dramatic intensity, the quiet pathos, the extraordinarily expressive faces, and the incomparable heroine. Millais once said, 'The Dutch had no love for women. The Italians are as bad. The pictures of women by Titian, Raphael, Rembrandt, Vandyck, Velasquez, are magnificent as works of art, but who would want to kiss such women?' Has anyone ever looked at *A Huguenot* and then asked, 'Who would want to kiss that woman?'

The person who posed for this magnificent figure was a professional model, one Miss Ryan. Since Millais, unlike Raphael, could not transform an ordinary woman into an ethereal creature, we must assume that he recreated Miss Ryan approximately as she was. One might have thought that *A Huguenot* would serve as the start of an illustrious career for her, but this was not to be. She never again appeared in a noteworthy picture, and soon she disappeared entirely from the world of painters.

'Alas for Miss Ryan!' wrote John G. Millias, who on this matter may, I think, be considered trustworthy. 'Her beauty proved a fatal gift: she married an ostler, and her later history is a sad one. My father was always reluctant to speak of it, feeling perhaps that the publicity he had given to her beauty might in small measure have helped to turn her head.'

* * *

On 6 March 1852 Millais wrote to Mrs Combe, 'Today I have purchased a really splendid lady's dress – flowered over in silver embroidery – and I am going to paint it for "Ophelia". You may imagine how good it is when I tell you it cost, old and dirty as it is, four pounds.' The dress would be worn by a nineteen-year-old woman whom Walter Deverell had discovered a year earlier, working as an assistant in a Leicester Square bonnet shop. 'She is stupendously beautiful,'

Deverell had told his friends, 'magnificently tall with a lovely figure, a stately neck, and a face of the most delicate and finished modelling. She is a Phidian goddess.' Her name was Lizzie Siddal. When the others met her, they agreed with Deverell. One of them, Gabriel Rossetti, became her lover, and, some years later, her husband. A fine model, Lizzie Siddal sat for Deverell, Hunt, and, naturally, Rossetti. Millais used her for the first time as Ophelia.

She lay flat on her back in the Millais family bath tub, filled with water heated by a lamp underneath. During the final session, the lamp burned out. Lizzie spent the next several days in bed, and she didn't soon forget this incident. 'Collins,' Millais told Hunt a few months later, 'wants a model for his next picture and wrote to Miss Siddal, but was answered in a most freezing manner, stating that she had other occupations.' Millais had the good sense not to approach her again.

Lizzie hadn't suffered for nothing. Her face and hands in the finished picture are uncannily beautiful, a sufficient answer to those who contend that for Millais the setting meant more than Ophelia herself. *Ophelia* went to Trafalgar Square with *A Huguenot* and a third entry, *Mrs Coventry K. Patmore*, another portrait done as a courtesy to a friend.

*   *   *

'Come, now! Move on, please!'

This was heard repeatedly during the season of 1852 in the Royal Academy's West Room, the summer home of *Ophelia* and *A Huguenot*. Before them, Fred Stephens reported, 'Crowds stood all day. People lingered for hours, went away, and returned again and again.'

The Times, however, was unmoved. This year it had its first pre-opening notice. The reviewer, perhaps itching for another shot at his favourite target, could 'see no reason to qualify or retract the censure it was our duty to pass last year on the unfortunate productions of Mr Millais and his friends, and we now regret to find the same absence of any sense of beauty and the same mixture of the pathetic and the grotesque.' (The other exhibiting Pre-Raphaelites were Collins, with three pictures; Hunt, with one; and Stephens, making his debut, with one.)

This year *The Times* stood almost alone. The overwhelming response was a complete turnabout from 1851. The *Morning Chronicle*'s critique was typical:

Pizarro Seizing the Inca of Peru

Isabella

Christ in the House of his Parents (The Carpenter's Shop)

The Huguenot

Ophelia

The Order of Release

John Ruskin

The Blind Girl

Mr Millais's talent is budding into undoubted genius. We have no hesitation in saying that he has produced the two most imaginative and powerful pictures in the exhibition . . . *Ophelia* is startling in its originality. The beholder recoils in amazement at the extraordinary treatment, but a second glance captivates and a few moments' contemplation fascinates him . . . Still more wonderful is 'A Huguenot'. Noble and loving sentiment was never more poetically rendered . . . For strong and earnest thought, and the capability of embodying character and subjective feeling upon canvas, 'A Huguenot' is unquestionably the most significant work in the exhibition.

The most eloquent endorsement came on 15 May in *Punch*, an unsigned piece by Tom Taylor. At one time or another Taylor had been or would be an actor, an art critic, a barrister, a biographer, a dramatist, an editor, and a professor of literature at the University of London. As someone observed, he was 'an institution'. His *Punch* comments appeared in 'Our Critic Among the Pictures', which dealt with just two works, *Ophelia* and *A Huguenot.*

I have experienced a new sensation, and I hasten to record my sense of obligation to Mr Millais. I offer my hand to that Pre-Raphaelite Brother. I bow down to him and kiss the edge of his palette . . .

Before two pictures of Mr Millais I have spent the happiest hour ever at a Royal Academy Exhibition. In those pictures I find more loving observation of Nature, more mastery in reproducing her forms and colours, a deeper feeling of human emotion, a happier choice of a point of interest . . . than in all the rest of those squares of canvas put together . . .

[In *Ophelia*] I see only the face of that poor drowning girl. My eye rests on that and sees nothing else till – buffoon as I am, mocker, joker, scurril-knave, street-jester – the tears blind me, and I turn from her face to the natural loveliness that makes her dying beautiful.

In another work by the same hand . . . again what I see first is the subtle human emotion of two faces. All the rest I may find out when I have satisfied myself with that . . .

A rare quality of this picture is that it has many meanings, may be read in divers ways. The moment is chosen when nothing is decided – when two fates hang trembling in the balance, and the spectator finds himself assisting in a struggle of which he may prophesy the issue as his sympathy with the love of the woman or strength of the man happens to be stronger.

There is all that accuracy of eye and power of hand can do in these pictures, but there is still more of thought and brains. The man who painted these pictures had a meaning to express, and he has expressed it. He felt his subject, and he makes me feel it . . .

To all the RAs and ARAs . . . I say, go and do likewise. Before these pictures I commune with the painter's thoughts; before your works I criticise coloured canvas.

Three weeks after the opening a certain reviewer revised his earlier opinion. He acknowledged that he could now overlook 'puerilities' and 'singularities' because 'we have discovered genius in Mr Millais.' The man who made this discovery was the art critic of *The Times*.

As to what had caused this extraordinary transformation, I believe that, miracle of miracles, a correspondent for Victorian England's journalistic superpower had to admit to being mistaken. And this was no passing fancy. Henceforth one of John Millais's most consistent supporters was *The Times* of London.

CHAPTER 9

1852–53

'ALL the letters you have must speak of Millais,' Gabriel Rossetti wrote late in 1852 to Thomas Woolner, temporarily in Australia, 'conquering and to conquer.' Even in Australia, Woolner had heard of Millais's successes which had gained him a celebrity akin to that of his illustrious seniors, Dickens and Tennyson.

Millais enjoyed leading a full social life and hobnobbing with prominent people, as when he met the poet laureate. 'I am going tonight to Patmore's,' he told Hunt. 'Tennyson and other notables are going to be there, I have just had my hair cut, and I had a bath.' Next day he wrote, 'Tennyson was uncommonly kind to me, asking whenever I can dine with him.'

During this hyperactive summer, he went to the Lord's cricket ground for the Eton and Harrow match. Most spectators weren't there primarily for the sport. It was commonly said that four out of five didn't even understand the game. The action on the pitch was an excuse for what took place beyond the boundary. 'We all sat down to a capital dinner,' Millais told William Rossetti, 'the damask cloth, silver, wine and fruit reminding me of Boccaccio . . . I must confess that I drank pretty freely from the goblet.' By the time it was over, he had consumed half a bottle of brandy. And he didn't know who had won the match.

The biggest social event of late 1852 was, ironically, a funeral, that of the Duke of Wellington. The Duke died on 14 September, but to give dignitaries time to reach London, the services were put off until 18 November. The most sought after ticket of the year was free. It permitted the bearer to enter St Paul's for the funeral ceremonies. One lucky recipient was Effie Ruskin who obtained a ticket from the wife of the Dean of St Paul's.

Millais wasn't inside the cathedral, but he had a fine place for viewing the procession. He wrote about it to Mrs Combe: 'Altogether the sight was a most imposing one, but there is so much talk about it that I am sick of the very name of the Duke's funeral. It has taken the place of the weather in conversation. The first thing one is asked upon entering a room is, "Did you see it? Where from? What did you think of it?" Young ladies, generally dumb on the first introduction, venture upon this topic as courageously as the accustomed orator.'

He then informed Mrs Combe, 'In the "Illustrated London News" there is a drawing of the Royal carriages passing the "Punch" offices, and a likeness of me sitting in the front row between some ladies. You will see how good a position I had.'

*   *   *

Sometimes Millais's sociable activities disturbed his conscience. After the Eton and Harrow match, he confessed to William Rossetti, 'Like Macbeth at the banquet, I was troubled by a ghost, my foresaken picture, but instead of throwing away the goblet at the sight of the apparition, I solaced myself by drinking from it pretty freely . . . I trust fortune will save me from Morland's weakness, and yet it would sound natural in a new edition of Pilkington's Lives of the Painters that two of Albion's greatest artistic ornaments died from that all destructive evil, drink.'

George Morland had drunk himself to death in 1804, but Millais was picturesquely exaggerating. His drinking was generally moderate, and never interfered with his professional work, to which his correspondence repeatedly reveals his dedication, as in a letter of September 1852, from the George Inn, Hayes, Bromley, Kent, to Charles Collins's mother: 'Here I am with a sore throat . . . after working hard all day in the most cutting wind. My hand held the brush without the least feeling of life in it, paralysed by the cold. I really believe I deserve in a measure my success. Ward in two trebly wadded great coats would not have sat out in such a day.'

Ward was the popular historical painter Edward Ward. His *Charlotte Corday Going to the Execution* and Millais's *Ophelia* had contended in Birmingham for a £60 prize. Ward won, Millais told Mrs Collins, because 'his is an historical subject with many figures, and it is double the size of mine'.

When Millais wrote to Mrs Collins, she and Charles were house guests of a Mrs Otter in Southsea, a watering place near Portsmouth. Mrs Collins had invited him to join them for a weekend. He told her why he was passing up the invitation:

I leave Saturday, take ticket to Brighton, take ditto for Portsmouth. I take fly to Southsea. I arrive. I am welcomed. I enjoy myself. I go to bed. Strange room. I can't sleep. I see the morning. I *do* sleep. I am awakened. I must get up. I hear church bells. I am late. I choke with breakfast. I feel dizzy. I go to church. I take walk. I admire. I dine. I feel happy. I *must* go. General astonishment. Chorus of voices. Miss Otter: 'Oh, nonsense.' Mrs Collins: 'He's joking.' Mr Collins (feebly): 'Not tonight.' *I am firm.* Miss Otter: 'Stay till tomorrow.' Mrs Collins: 'He's mad.' Mr Collins: 'I think —.' I am weakened. Miss Otter: 'You can't go tonight.' Mrs Collins: 'You *shan't* go tonight.' Mr Collins: 'Partly —.' I am beaten. The scene acted nightly. Days spent in sightseeing. Sea, ships, tar, and pebbles. Length of visit, one week.

To neglect his work for a week was out of the question, especially when so many people wanted pictures. He had to put off potential purchasers, including the prominent patron who had wanted to buy *Pizarro*, John Miller. 'I suppose,' he wrote to Hunt, 'it is unnecessary for me to answer Mr Miller's message about painting him a picture. Therefore will you kindly (in your letter to him) let him know that at present I have so many orders I cannot promise anything.'

In Kent Millais had done the background of a picture to be shown at the next Exhibition. Back in London in October, he was unexpectedly low spirited. On the 25th he wrote to Hunt, out of town, 'I have positively no person except Charles Collins (who is so frightfully chilling) to associate with. I really don't know what to do sometimes. I run off to Hanover Terrace [where the Collinses lived], just with the old lady, say about a dozen words to her lay figure son and tumble out into the freezing night miserable . . . I am now going to bed to think upon my past life and what is probably coming, building castles in the air until I fall asleep, all very gloomy. Good night, old boy, cheer up and don't go to Egypt.' (Hunt had spoken of going to Egypt and then to the Holy Land in order to paint New Testament pictures 'on location'.)

Millais's dejection was probably brought on by the impending election of a new Associate of the Royal Academy. Forty Royal Academicians constitute the governing body of the Academy. Beneath them are twenty Associates (ARAs) from whose ranks RAs are selected. When a vacancy occurred among the ARAs, artists were invited to sign a list from which someone would be selected by the RAs. Millais was on the list; Hunt was not.

'Next Monday the election takes place,' he told Hunt. 'Ward thinks I have the best chance of getting it but seemed to think it possible [John Calcott] Horsley may manage to wedge himself in, as he has a strong lot of the Kensington friends who would vote for anybody rather than one of us. I will let you know the decision if you feel at all interested. I confess I don't care a rashlight about it, as it will not put a penny in my pocket and the honour is literally nothing. All this afternoon I have been designing but cannot get on in the least. I do long for you to get back.'

On the evening of Monday, 1 November 1852, the new Associate was elected. He was . . . Frederick Goodall. Goodall, thirty years old, had exhibited for fifteen consecutive years at Trafalgar Square. He was highly competent but not particularly inspiring. 'The picture that secured my election,' he wrote in his autobiography, 'was the Raising of the May-Pole at the Return of Charles II [exhibited in 1852]. There were hundreds of figures in it.' It is a lively scene of country people enjoying sports forbidden during the Commonwealth.

Millais at once told Hunt he had been 'so insulted' that he was 'fully prepared' never again to exhibit at the Academy. Later, given details of the voting, he calmed down. 'I have received two letters from [Charles Robert] Leslie [one of the few Academicians who had been friendly to the Pre-Raphaelites] in which he explains what occurred,' Millais wrote to Hunt. 'It appears that my name was put up, and when I had received five votes somebody stopped further voting for me on the grounds that I was not 24 years of age, which they could prove by the books. This directly put aside my name. Otherwise there is no doubt but what I should have got in. In some measure this nullifies the affair, though it is still bad enough.'

The minimum age for Associates had been twenty-four since 1796. In light of Millais's celebrity, it seems strange that the RAs were unaware of his age. Even after the matter had been clarified, he was unhappy about it. 'I openly expressed my disgust to Leslie,' he told Hunt in another letter. 'He just smiled and said that my election was only postponed.'

*   *   *

Three or four weeks later, Millais began to fill the figures onto his Kent background. This picture, *The Proscribed Royalist*, was the second instance of what was becoming a favourite leitmotif, a couple captured at a dramatic moment in their lives. An episode from the period of the rebellion preceding the Commonwealth, it shows a Cavalier hiding in a tree receiving food from a young Puritan woman. He kisses her hand as she looks and listens for any untoward sight or sound.

This is a good picture with what William Rossetti called Millais's best ever background. But it would be overshadowed at Trafalgar Square by its companion piece, a painting that Millais would regard as his supreme chef d'oeuvre, *The Order of Release*. Again, a young woman comes to a man's aid. A Highlander captured during the Jacobite Rebellion of 1745 is being freed by an order obtained by his wife. She stands barefoot at the prison gate holding their baby, the family dog alongside, as the jailer examines the paper.

When he began it, Millais faced a new challenge. 'I have to paint another kind of background,' he told Hunt, 'a prison gateway. I dread it.' After conscientious searching, he settled on part of the Tower of London, which was copied meticulously. He did the same with the accessories. He even imitated a real order of release. These details were smooth sailing compared to a couple of living models.

'I have a headache,' he wrote to Combe, 'and feel as tired as if I had walked twenty miles, from the anxiety I have undergone for a fortnight. All morning I have been drawing a dog, which in unquiet-ness is only to be surpassed by a child. Both of these animals I am trying to paint daily, and nothing can exceed the trial of patience they occasion. The child screams upon entering the room and when forcibly held in its mother's arms struggles with such obstinacy that I cannot begin my work until exhaustion comes on, generally when day-light disappears. Imagine looking forward to the day when neither of these provoking models shall come! This is my only thought at night and upon waking in the morning.'

Eventually he managed to finish them off. Then, in March 1853, he began with another model. She was also probably his only thought at night and upon waking in the morning. Her name was Effie Ruskin.

* * *

After visiting the 1852 Exhibition, John Ruskin had told Millais, 'I think Ophelia and the Huguenot are exquisite. I hailed the conversion of Punch with great delight . . . Of course you cannot expect me to tell you all I thought in a note.' And so they talked face to face. The Ruskins had moved to Herne Hill, south of the river, and settled in a small house next to the family home. A frequent guest was John Millais. Because, he said, Effie had just the face for his Highlander's wife, Millais asked her to sit. Effie, who had sat for several painters, including Watts, readily assented, and he began painting her on Monday, 14 March. Not until the rest day, Sunday, could Effie write about it to her mother:

'I have been sitting to Millais from immediately after breakfast to dinner, then through all the afternoon till dark, which gave me not a moment to myself. I am rather tired and have a stiff neck, but I was anxious to be as much help as possible as the whole importance of the picture is in the success of this head . . . He found my head immensely difficult, and he was greatly delighted last night when he said he had quite got it. The features are at once so curious and the expression he wanted so difficult to catch – half a smile . . . He says that nobody has painted me at all yet, that the others have made me look pensive [underlined twice] in order to escape the difficulties of colour and expression.'

When a handsome young man and a beautiful young woman spend a fortnight together alone, suspicion is bound to arise. On 15 April, Effie wrote to her mother, 'Mr R . . . on my wedding day [10 April, her fifth anniversary] kept hinting disagreeable things all dinner time . . . He said . . . he had never seen anything so perfect as my *attitude* as I lay on the sofa the night before and that no wonder Millais etc. etc., but it sickens me to write such nonsense.'

'The picture is talked of in a way to make every Academician frantic,' Effie told her mother when it was finished. 'It is hardly possible to approach it from the row of bonnets. Everybody is saying, "Have you seen the Millais painting?"'

She wasn't exaggerating. A less subjective viewer, the *Illustrated London News* art critic, wrote, 'Millais has more admirers than all the Academicians put together, and a good sticking crowd, who, having taken up their position do not move on, but stand gaping and staring without regard to pressure from behind of crowds seeking to occupy their places.'

On the third day a protective railing was placed in front of the picture. This had last been done in 1822, for a painting commissioned by the Duke of Wellington, David Wilkie's *Chelsea Pensioners Receiving the London Gazette . . . Announcing the Battle of Waterloo!!!* (The exclamation points are part of the title.)

The Order of Release deserved the response. A dramatic incident is presented clearly in a low key without embellishment. The characters are superb: the exhausted prisoner, the cautious jailer, and, above all, the triumphant wife, with the latest of her creator's magnificent female faces. Even the dog is outstanding. And the details, such as the jailer's keys, appear strikingly authentic. Finally, this painting, like *Pizarro*, *Elgiva*, *Isabella*, and *A Huguenot*, demonstrates John Millais's most distinctive keynote, his human compassion.

The critics gave *The Order of Release* a spirited stamp of approval. The *Morning Chronicle* called it 'the best performance of Millais that we have ever seen'. The *Daily News* saw it as 'A work of really extraordinary merit, the most perfect thing on the walls of the Academy, nearer to perfection than any modern painting we remember to have seen'. *The Times*'s critic, who confessed that he had joined 'the ranks of Mr Millais's admirers', said of *The Order of Release* that 'a more beautiful and finished work of art has seldom graced the walls of the Academy'. (*The Proscribed Royalist* was well received but was dominated by its pendant.) Several weeks into the Exhibition, *John Bull* expressed a consensus view: '*The Proscribed Royalist* and *The Order of Release* have completely established Mr Millais as our greatest living painter.'

And he was not yet old enough to become an Associate of the Royal Academy.

CHAPTER 10

1853

JOHN RUSKIN was slow in discovering the Pre-Raphaelites, but once he saw the light he was almost blinded. When he wrote his second letter to *The Times*, a new edition of volume one of *Modern Painters* was about to go to press. He appended a brief paragraph commending Hunt and Millais for 'endeavouring to paint what they see in nature without reference to what is conventional or established', in other words, for following *his* advice. Then before he and Effie left for an extended visit to Venice, he dashed off a sixty-eight page pamphlet, *Pre-Raphaelitism*. This is a curious piece of writing. He doesn't mention Rossetti or Collins or even Holman Hunt. Their prime colleague is named once: 'Turner and Millais are among the few who have defied all false teaching and have therefore in great measure done justice to the gifts with which they were intrusted.'

Millais and Turner? The champion of microscopic details alongside the master of atmospheric impressionism? Surely this is an odd couple? Not to Ruskin. In *Pre-Raphaelitism* Turner is referred to by name twenty-six times. The *Athenaeum's* incredulous reviewer said, 'The author has betaken himself, in all the pomp of his infallibility, to induce us to put trust in two opposite faiths at once, to satisfy that hot and cold are the same. One wonders if he is conscientious or comical?'

John Ruskin comical? Never! Never, that is, intentionally. He was surely conscientious – and also emphatic, arrogant, and overbearing. If he believed Turner to be a Pre-Raphaelite, then Turner *was* a Pre-Raphaelite. Like Peter in Swift's *Tale of a Tub*, he might have said, 'By God, it is so because I say it is so.'

Ruskin's mind-set comes out in his preface:

Eight years ago . . . I gave this advice to the young artists of England.

'They should go to nature in all singleness of heart and walk with her laboriously and trustingly, having no other thought but how best to penetrate her meaning; rejecting nothing, selecting nothing, and scorning nothing.' . . .

[My advice] has at last been carried out, to the very letter, by a group of men who have been assailed with the most scurrilous abuse I have ever seen in the public press. I have, therefore, thought it due to them to contradict the false statements which have been made respecting their works; and to point out the merit which these works possess beyond possibility of dispute.

Note the egocentricity of this declaration. *I* gave them advice. *My* advice was followed. Therefore *I* will come to their defence. After returning from Venice, Ruskin told his friend the essayist and poet Mary Russell Mitford that 'Millais is gifted with powers of character penetration and pictorial invention such as have not hitherto existed in my time, and capable of almost everything, if his life and strength be spared.'

He was eager to have a closer relationship with Millais. As the editor of his collected works said, 'He wanted to keep his eye on the youthful artist, to mould the ripening genius into accord with his own ideals, to instruct him in the way he should go.' His opportunity came in the spring of 1853 with a visit to London by Sir and Lady Trevelyan.

Sir Walter was the ranking member of an illustrious Northumberland family. His wife, Pauline, who dabbled in painting, enjoyed meeting people in the visual arts. Today we would call her a groupie. She had met John Ruskin and his fiancée a few weeks before their marriage. Pauline and Effie at once took a fancy to each other and for years, except for her mother, Effie had no more confidential correspondent than Lady Trevelyan. A close personal involvement of the two couples, however, did not come about until 1853.

That year the Trevelyans spent several weeks in London before and after the opening of the Exhibition, stopping at a hotel in Mayfair. The Ruskins were renting a flat nearby in Charles Street, Berkeley Square, and the four of them were often together. They attended the Royal Academy private view, and Lady Trevelyan was captivated by *The Order of Release*, returning to it again and again. Before the Trevelyans left town, the Ruskins accepted an invitation to visit Wallington Hall, their estate in Northumberland, in late June.

The trip would be part of a larger design. Ruskin had planned to take an extended working holiday in a more restful locale than London in order to compile an index to his massive just completed *Stones of Venice*, and also to prepare a series of lectures. The Trevelyans' invitation gave him an idea. From Wallington Hall, it would be convenient to go up to the Scottish Highlands for the summer.

This would not be the Ruskins' first visit to the Highlands. He and Effie had been there on their honeymoon. When it was over, Effie wrote to Pauline Trevelyan, 'John did nothing but abuse every place one after the other when he was awake. He called it the most melancholy country in the world. He slept most of the way, which I am sure you will be most shocked at, and I had the poor advantage of having the beauties all to myself.'

Why then did he intend to return for perhaps four or five months? Because he and Effie would not be alone. While in London, the Trevelyans became friendly with John Millais, who probably received an open-ended invitation to visit as well. It was only natural for Ruskin to ask Millais to join him and Effie. 'You need a rest,' Ruskin said. Millais agreed. Ruskin then told Hunt that he too needed a holiday, and Hunt signed on for the excursion.

Effie then asked her father, George Gray, a prominent lawyer in Perth, to obtain suitable accommodation for them. He recommended a picturesque inn on the River Garry. 'John thinks it will do capitally,' Effie told her father, who made a reservation. Suddenly, without citing a reason, John told Effie that he didn't want to stay there. Again Effie appealed to her father. Now he suggested a house on the River Tummel. Again Ruskin was enthusiastic. Again Mr Gray made a reservation. Again Ruskin changed his mind. Again Mr Gray had to cancel the booking. They would seem to be leaving, then, without a Scottish hotel reservation. They would also be without Holman Hunt. After he had thought it over, he bowed out because he couldn't afford to lose so much time from his work.

John Millais, who wouldn't take off in 1849 to visit the Continent with Hunt and Rossetti, and who more recently had passed up a week in Southsea, was now, when he was most in demand, going away for the entire summer. Before departing, he told Thomas Combe, 'I have worked hard for five years, and I am giving myself a well-earned holiday.'

Really? He was in excellent health and during the past year had had time for numerous relaxing activities. Moreover, he thrived on work.

* * *

'He is so extremely handsome, besides his talents, that you may fancy how he is run after.' This is how Effie described John Millais in her last letter home before leaving for Northumberland. A few weeks earlier, he had dined with Thackeray's good friend, to whom *Vanity Fair* was dedicated, Anne Procter. He 'won all hearts', she told Thackeray, 'by his unaffected manner, and his handsomeness, which he is not ashamed of'. He felt no need to apologise for his good looks. Indeed he once said, 'No painter can draw who is not well proportioned. A man always reproduces himself.'

A reproduction of himself would have revealed a man except for his attractiveness unexceptional in appearance.

He used to say [his Opera House companion Bill Fenn recollected] that he saw no reason why an artist should necessarily look like one. 'Why should a painter not dress and have his hair cut to the fashion of an ordinary gentleman?' he asked. 'Because a man happens to get his living by using a palette and brushes he need not look like a Guy Fawkes.' Thus he came to trim, 'groom', and dress himself in a becoming manner. I can't help thinking that his conduct with Opera-house society influenced him. His quick observation told him how gentlemen dressed and behaved, and he loved to linger in the crushroom at Covent Garden with members of good society. He contrasted their appearance with the careless, slovenly, unkempt aspect of the artistic world, in which many of his brethren made themselves up as what he called Guy Fawkeses, with long hair, untrimmed beards, slouch-hats, and dusty velvet jackets.

Millais didn't have to dress outlandishly to be noticed. This is how E.M. Ward's wife Henrietta reacted to their first meeting, at a ball: 'I was immediately struck with his appearance. He had a magnificently shaped head, faultless classic features, a superbly elegant figure, tall and slim, and was one of the handsomest men I have ever seen. In conversation he was charming, not the least affected . . . so frank, boyish, and breezy that he completely captivated the hearts of the fair sex.'

Including Effie Ruskin? She wrote to her mother on the eve of departing, 'So long a visit as we shall probably make in Scotland makes me extremely happy.'

* * *

John Ruskin had talked about journeying north in a carriage. Effie told her mother that 'he seems quite delighted with his idea of cutting the railroads and travelling the old way.' But on the afternoon of Tuesday, 21 June, they departed in the 'new way'. John and Effie Ruskin, John Millais, and Ruskin's valet of less than a year, Frederick Crawley, boarded a coach of a London and Birmingham Railway train. (Holman Hunt's replacement, William Millais, would join them two days later.) They left from Euston, London's most magnificent main-line terminal. With its £35,000 Doric entrance, and its resplendent Ionic-columned Grand Hall, Euston, a mid-century writer said, 'was regarded not as a railway station, but as a spectacle. Visitors used to flock to it in omnibuses and examine it with the careful scrutiny of sightseers.' It was a station without equal. What happened to this architectural masterpiece? During the heyday of 'swinging London,' in the mid-1960s, it was regarded as too expensive to maintain and, except for a statue of George Stephenson, it was totally demolished. Its successor, which opened in 1968, is visually about as exciting as a grain repository in Iowa.

The next morning, Wednesday, the Ruskin party disembarked in the ancient town of Morpeth, fourteen miles north of Newcastle-on-Tyne. Ever since 1199, when King John had granted to Roger de

Merlay the right to sell cattle in the town, Wednesday had been market day in Morpeth – the biggest cattle market in the north. They were exciting days, with the town's permanent population of 4500 enormously expanded by an influx of butchers, farmers, cattle graziers, jobbers, and dealers. One can easily visualise what William Frith might have done with this scene, but it had little or no impact on the Ruskin party. It is not mentioned in their correspondence. They just hopped into a waiting carriage and rode ten miles westward to a delightful wooded valley. In its midst stood Wallington Hall.

'This is the most beautiful place possible,' John Ruskin wrote to his father, 'a large seventeenth-century stone house in a terraced garden opening on a sloping wild park down to the brook, and woods on the other side, an undulating country with a peculiar *Northumberlandishness* about it – a faraway look which Millais enjoys immensely. We are all very happy.'

'This country is so delightful after London,' Effie wrote to a friend. 'I am so happy running into the woods and down trout streams or walking over bleak border moors. I have had such charming ripe figs and grapes out of the hot house, and fresh fish caught by the Millais brothers.'

John Millais enjoyed his fishing, but this wasn't his most pleasurable activity in Northumberland. 'Millais kept drawing all the while,' Ruskin told his father after leaving Wallington Hall. 'He could not be kept from it. First he made a sketch of me for Lady Trevelyan – like me – but not pleasing. Neither I nor Lady Trevelyan liked it except as a drawing. Then he drew Sir Walter for her, most beautifully, a lovely portrait and as like as possible – I never saw a finer thing – she was in great raptures with it. Then he drew Effie for her – and was so pleased with the drawing that he kept it for himself.'

Before leaving Wallington Hall, Millais wrote to Hunt, 'Mrs Ruskin is the sweetest creature that ever lived . . . the most pleasant companion that one could wish.' And so it isn't surprising that he wouldn't part with his drawing.

The Ruskin party left the Trevelyans on the morning of Wednesday, 29 June, travelling by post chaise to Jedburgh, across the border, where John Millais spent his first night in Scotland. From there it was by train to Edinburgh, and a day-and-a-half stop in this romantic city, which,

Ruskin told his father 'enchanted' and 'exhausted' the Millais brothers. They wanted to see and do everything. Ruskin, on the other hand, Effie wrote to her mother, was 'awfully bored and would be thankful for an express train to Callander'.

Actually a train carried them only to the ancient city of Stirling, from which they rode by carriage to Callander, arriving on the evening of Saturday, 2 July. A town with a population of 1200 in 1853, Callander was the jumping-off place for the Trossachs. As it was for the Ruskin party. On the morning of 3 July, they took the nine-mile carriage ride to their destination, the Trossachs Hotel.

The Trossachs, an enchanted labyrinth of hills and rocks, had been popularised by Sir Walter Scott's *The Lady of the Lake*.

> Here eglantine embalmed the air,
> Hawthorn and hazel mingled there.
> The primrose pale and violet flower
> Found in each cliff a narrow bower;
> Foxglove and mignonette, side by side,
> Emblem of punishment and pride.

Lured by *The Lady of the Lake*, John Ruskin had spent part of his 1838 summer vacation exploring the area. As recorded in *Praeterita*, this was his response:

The shore of Loch Katrine was exactly as Scott had described:

> Onward, amid the copse 'gan peep
> A narrow inlet, still and deep.

In literal and lovely truth that was so. By the side of the footpath (it was no more) which wound through the Trossachs, deep and calm under blackberry bushes, a dark winding clear-brown pool, not five feet wide at first, reflected the entangled moss of its margin, and arch of branches above, with scarcely a gleam of sky.

That inlet of Loch Katrine was something I have never seen the like of in lake shores. A winding recess of deep water, without any entering stream to account for it – possible only, I imagine, among rocks of the abnormal confusion of the Trossachs; and besides its natural sweetness and wonder, made sacred by the most beautiful poem that Scotland ever sang.

Several commentators have said that the Ruskin party stopped here purely by chance. As recently as 1996, a well-known art historian asserted that 'they had intended to go further into the Highlands'. I cannot possibly agree with these writers. It seems certain that before leaving London Ruskin had decided on the Trossachs, and had booked rooms at the Trossachs Hotel.

The four-storey hotel was a chateau-like building, with two large turrets, right and left, each topped by a cone. It had been built only a year earlier by Lord Willoughby D'Eresby and was the last word in luxury. This was not a place for a party of four to drop in without a reservation. In 1853, this would have been inconceivable. It just wasn't done. Clearly Ruskin had posted a written application for rooms from London, and the whole trip, including the stay in Edinburgh, proceeded as he had planned. Yet none of the others had known that this was their predetermined stopping place.

* * *

'You could go mad if you saw this scenery,' Millais wrote to Hunt on his first day in the area. 'I have never seen anything so beautiful.' But the surroundings were also disheartening. 'Although this place is so beautiful and William is with me, I feel lonely and miserable. There is something depressing about these far stretching mountains, everything looks wild and melancholy.'

He was happy, however, about his two new friends: 'The Ruskins *are the most perfect people*, always anxious and ready to sacrifice their interest in our behalf. She is the most delightful, unselfish, kind hearted creature I ever knew, it is impossible to help liking her – and he is gentle and forbearing.'

Millais was now planning to paint their portraits.

Eager to get started, he began with John Ruskin. In Millais's day-of-arrival letter to Hunt he said, 'I hope tomorrow will be fine as I long to paint. I am getting restless for work.' So much for the notion that he needed a holiday.

Although excited by the scenery, he had no artistic interest in it for its own sake. He was, however, eager to find a proper background for the portrait. He surely would find a suitable site within walking distance of the hotel. The eastern extremity of Loch Katrine, a mile to the west was a possibility. Only 150 yards eastward was Loch Achray, much smaller than Lock Katrine but no less beautiful. A half a mile farther to the east was the picturesque stone bridge of *The Lady of the Lake*, Brig o'Turk, spanning a stream in a valley called Glen Finlas.

Even though it was raining, he went early on the morning of 4 July and spent hours reconnoitering, a repeat performance of the Hogsmill River. As on that earlier occasion, he eventually found just what he wanted, directly above Brig o'Turk, along the stream of Glen Finlas.

'Millais has fixed on his place,' Ruskin told his father, 'a lovely piece of worn rock, with foaming water, and weeds, and moss, and a noble overhanging bank of dark crag – and I am to be standing looking quietly down the stream.'

Millais also wrote about it, to Charlie Collins. 'Ruskin and I have just returned from a glorious walk along a rocky river near here and we have found a splendid simple background for a portrait I am going to paint of him. I feel much too seedy to think of painting other than something quite simple so that this will be delightful. He is such a good fellow and pleasant companion . . . I will paint him looking over the edge of a steep waterfall – he looks so sweet and benign standing calmly looking into the turbulent sluice beneath.'

He still professed to be in need of rest and relaxation. He told Collins's mother that he was in the Highlands 'principally to get strong' and would 'not work too much like other years. Later, when I get back to town I begin the Deluge *for certain*, and probably I shall have more for the exhibition next year than ever.' *The Deluge* was something he had begun in London.

Continuing rain kept Millais from starting. He and his friends had time to enjoy the amenities of their hotel, which, Millais told Collins, was 'absurdly expensive'. It would have been unseemly to ask about rates beforehand, and when they learned the cost of their rooms even the Ruskins seemed shocked. The Trossachs Hotel, Millais informed

Collins, was 'ten times as expensive as the Star and Garter', near the main gate of Richmond Park and notoriously high-priced.

On 7 July, Effie wrote to Lady Trevelyan, 'They have been all day looking for another habitation, as we find this so very expensive, but I think they will find it difficult to find any place near.' In fact, they came upon a dwelling a few minutes by foot from the hotel towards Glen Finlas. The home of the local schoolmaster, Alex Stewart, who would be gone for the summer, was a one-storey whitewashed, mossy stone cottage, with a roof sloping down almost to the ground. On 9 July, the Ruskins and John Millais moved in. William Millais remained at the hotel so that they could use its facilities. (Ruskin's valet, Crawley, stayed elsewhere in a rented room.)

'Our new residence,' Millais told Mrs Collins, 'is the funniest place you ever saw. My bed room is not much larger than a snuff box. I can open the window, shut the door, and *shave* without getting out of bed.'

Writing to her mother, Effie said, 'Our parlour is nice enough, but there is *no* place to put anything in, there being no drawers. John Millais and I have two little dens where we sleep. John sleeps on a sofa in the parlour.' Despite the cramped quarters, they were 'as happy and comfortable as any people could desire. We shall be so much out of doors that we shall not be dependent on inner comforts.'

But they would spend a great deal of time in that tiny cottage, because of the weather. The rain was incessant, day after day. After two weeks, Millais hadn't even begun the portrait. 'I am restless for work,' he told Hunt. 'This rain is truly disgusting.' To Collins he wrote, 'If this wet continues I see nothing left but an immediate return *to London*.'

They didn't return to London, nor did they refrain from going out-of-doors. They were dressed for it. Before moving into the cottage, Millais wrote to Collins, 'We have purchased plaids, which we put on in the proper manner, and nothing could be more uncomfortable. They are irritating to the flesh, drag your shoulders off and lay heavily on your chest. In truth you can barely move when this beastly garment is properly worn.'

Only the men bought plaids. Effie, a Scott, after all, had come prepared for the worst. She told Lady Trevelyan, 'I have made myself a rough Linsey wolsey dress which I could not do without. With a nice jacket and large brown wide awake, I am quite independent of the weather and sit on the rocks and then wander away with the Millais when they fish up the trout stream.'

They walked, sometimes ankle-deep in water. They sat on rocks in Loch Achray. They fished in Glen Finlas and Loch Achray for trout, perch, pike, eels, and salmon, usually without success. Once they even climbed the 2800-feet-high Ben Ledi. Because of the weather, they made good use of the hotel's library as well as the teacher's personal collection of books. In letters to Hunt, Millais frequently commented on his reading:

'I have been going over Wordsworth carefully. I find him a true stunner. The peddlar story of Margaret in Excursion is perfect . . . Have you read [Samuel Richardson's] Sir Charles Grandison? . . . It is splendid . . . I am reading Jane Eyre, such a stunning novel, better almost than Thackeray . . . I have been reading In Memoriam to the Ruskins, who are stunned with admiration, particularly the lady.'

It is surprising if this well-known poem, published three years earlier, which Millais was reading for the second time, was really new to the Ruskins. John Ruskin certainly became familiar with it. The index to his Collected Works contains twenty-six references to *In Memoriam*.

Millais greatly enjoyed the poem, which he discussed in a letter to Collins, who evidently had voiced the often expressed opinion that 'In Memoriam' deals more with doubt than faith:

I think you quite misunderstood Tennyson's meaning. He does not imply that we have no light in the world, for he says:

> But what am I,
> An infant crying in the night,
> An infant crying for the light
> And with no language but a cry.

This clearly implies that it is his weakness of faith to believe the light, *which exists*, that is at fault. The poem is the expression of passing thoughts, praises of God and doubts in succession. It is very rare that great men are the *steadiest* Christians, as they are conversant with all the existing arguments against Scripture, which are very strong, as everything belonging to the Devil is . . . There is that great mistake in all believers, that they don't understand how it is that people doubt. The fact is they do, and Tennyson amongst others has had continual variations of Faith and schism. If you read *In Memoriam carefully* I think you will find it one of the most *religious works* ever written. There are many passages of weakness, but the poem is conclusive in its entire trust in Christ, which is principally required of us.'

* * *

During his early weeks in the Highlands Millais was seldom as serious as in the above letter. Mostly he and his companions were lighthearted and frolicsome. A favourite pastime was the ancient game of battle-dore and shuttlecock, the forerunner of badminton. They played at several locations. Once Effie wrote to a friend, 'The rain is really dreadful. We are obliged to have recourse to Battledore and Shuttlecock in a barn redolent of Peat rock and where a school of Gaelic bairns is held every morning.' More often they went to the hotel, which had a court, and where presumably they obtained their rackets and shuttlecocks. They also actually competed in the cottage. Millais sent Collins a report of a 'forty-round combat' played there. 'Ruskin and I have mortal combat, hitting with such rapidity that we hit each other before being able to parry like fencing.'

'He is a good fellow and pleasant companion,' Millais told Collins on day five in the Highlands.

The two men were getting along together splendidly, personally and professionally. Ruskin's upcoming lectures, to be delivered in Edinburgh, would deal with architecture, a topic in which Millais had never shown much interest. But now he wrote to Collins, 'You will hear shortly of me in another art besides painting. Ruskin has discovered that I can design architectural ornamentation more perfectly than any living or dead party . . . I have promised to design doors, arches, and windows for churches etc. etc. It is the most amusing occupation, and it comes quite easily and naturally to my hand . . . When I make a design, Ruskin slaps his hands to together in pleasure . . . The church will be designed *entirely by me* and will *for certain* be executed shortly as Ruskin is mad that it should be begun as soon as the drawings are made . . . He believes that I have almost mistaken my vocation, that I was born to restore architecture.'

He ended by telling his friend, 'Please say nothing about this, as we don't wish it to become public that we are working in consort.' Perhaps he realised that becoming an architect made about as much sense as playing racket games in that tiny cottage.

* * *

When the rain finally subsided, Millais was deliriously happy. 'I am enjoying myself so much,' he told Mrs Combe, 'that I can scarcely find time to hold a pen; it is as much as I can do to paint occasionally. We dine upon the rocks, Mrs Ruskin working [at knitting], her husband drawing, and myself painting. The midges, which bite dreadfully, are the only drawback to this almost perfect happiness.' The fountain-head of Millais's happiness was Effie, who, he told Hunt, was 'the most delightful, unselfish, kind hearted creature I ever knew, a woman whose acquaintance is a blessing.'

When confined to the cottage by rain, she had become his pupil.

'I am teaching Mrs Ruskin drawing,' he told Hunt, 'and it is wonderful how well she gets on . . . My only pleasure is teaching her. She is such a delightful creature, more delightful every day, and gets on in a manner reflecting great disgrace on me for having been so long before painting as I do now. She has drawn and painted some flowers in oil (the first time she has touched a brush) almost as well as I could do them myself. I don't understand how she does it, but I am certain she has learnt in the month I have taught her more than I did in six years. If it was not for being such a captivating person I should feel disgusted with such aptitude.'

Of course he exaggerated, but perhaps not flagrantly. Writing to Lady Trevelyan, Ruskin said, 'My saucy little wife has taken it into her head to try and paint in oil, just like a monkey, after seeing Everett do it – but the jest is she did it, and has painted some flowers and leaves nearly as well as I could do them.' (Millais had always been known as 'John' or 'Johnny' or 'Jack', but now, to avoid confusion with Ruskin, he was called 'Everett'. Effie would always refer to him as Everett.)

Effie wrote to lady Trevelyan, 'Millais's great delight in teaching me is how I am to astonish Lady Trevelyan and Mr Ruskin. When I lose confidence and say that drawing is not my forte I get such a dreadful reprimand that I go on again and make about ten dots per hour, but I like it and I can think of nothing else since I am at work which to a restless little animal like me is a blessing.'

This wasn't her first drawing instruction. Five years earlier, her husband had tried to teach her. She had also written to Lady Trevelyan about *that*: 'I confess I have been doing very badly notwithstanding Mr Ruskin's encouragements. I am afraid I am too old to learn drawing.'

She was then nineteen years old.

*   *   *

Joining the party for a week late in July was a friend of Ruskin's since their undergraduate days at Christ Church, Oxford, now Oxford's Aldrichian Professor of Clinical Medicine, Dr Henry Acland, and one of the century's most celebrated physicians. Acland had met Millais once. 'I could not read him then,' he acknowledged in a letter to his wife from the hotel. Now, after several days together, he wrote:

'I feel as though his genius should have made an impression on me for life . . .' He spelled out his current impressions:

You will be disappointed in him and wonder what I mean, for he will come to see us in Oxford. To read him you must be in the mind to value Art highly – to take it as a message from Heaven, and see the point in his work, not in his words. He is a man with powers and perception granted to very few; not more imagination, not more feeling, but a finer feeling and a more intuitive and instantaneous imagination than other men. Of this his nonsense affords the most striking proof. It was curious to see how puzzled he was by me. He found out first, that I was obstinate; second, that I was eager, third, that I was full of fun; fourth, about the third day, 'I do like the doctor. I don't know what we shall do when he is gone,' which I mention to show his dogged investigation of everything about him.

(Acland and Millais played two or three games of battledore and shuttlecock in the hotel.)

When Acland arrived, the party had been weatherbound for nearly three weeks. 'The unremitting rain,' Millais told Hunt, 'prevents our doing anything but grumble in doors.' The grumbling might have led to angry shouting, but this didn't happen. The confinement had an opposite effect. They became more intimate than they would have been outdoors. Effie and the Millais brothers laughed, joked, and held silly conversations. Acland's biographer said he was 'amazed, bewildered, and amused' by this three-handed game. Effie's husband was clearly an outsider. Millais said as much in a letter to Hunt. 'Ruskin is not of our kind. His soul is always with the clouds and out of the reach of ordinary mortals. He theorises about the vastness of space and then looks with contempt at a little stream.'

Just before Acland departed, Millais began the portrait of Ruskin. Since he had said that it would be 'small . . . something simple', he might have been expected to knock it off in no time. But in mid-August Effie referred to it in a letter to Lady Trevelyan as a 'large picture' which 'goes on very slowly as he is doing it like a miniature, about two inches a day'. He now told Hunt, 'I am getting on slowly although the weather is splendid. I feel very tired and low spirited. I don't receive gratification scarcely from anything.' A few days later, on 19 August, Ruskin wrote to his father, 'There is little chance of the picture being done till near November.'

Ruskin also noted, in passing, that William Millais had just departed for London, 'his holiday being expired'. This simple occurrence would vitally affect each of the three persons left behind.

*   *   *

When Effie received her drawing instruction, William Millais was part of it. 'I get a lesson of an hour and a half every morning,' she told Lady Trevelyan. 'John Millais watches my poor efforts to draw poor William, who sits to me and is a perfect martyr. He gets up so wearied and yawns and fidgets, upon which his brother, administering a box on the ear and a scold, gets him to sit still. Really his temper is so good and his delight in every thing so unceasing that he is invaluable to us.'

William Millais was always in a good mood, especially after a visit to the hotel bar. 'He is the happiest being I have ever known,' Effie told Lady Trevelyan. 'He is always bursting into enthusiastic fits, keeping us extremely merry, for as his brother says, if he were dying, "that boy would make us laugh."'

William didn't care if they laughed at or with him, and he could laugh at himself as he often did after abortive attempts to hook a fish in either of the nearby lakes. 'He is the most eager fisher in the world,' his brother told Collins, 'always returning home after having lost. "I brought a very large fish up to the land, but for want of a landing net," etc. etc. Occasionally these large fish are even within his grasp but curiously contrive to exhibit enough force to extricate themselves.'

On one occasion William and Ruskin together were unwittingly funny. It happened when they waded in Glen Finlas.

'They took off their shoes and stockings,' Effie wrote to her mother, 'and made about the torrent beds with great poles in their hands. They put Everett and me into fits of laughter. They were so like Tyrolese tourists or American scouts or cocknies and looked so ridiculous, their legs so tremendously white and so frightened where they put their feet.'

'They were holding their shoes,' Millais told Mrs Collins. 'Presently Will stumbles, and in trying to save a complete ducking puts out his arms and lets go his shoes, one of which the stream carries off, never to be regained. Then Ruskin, Bill, and a servant paddle about with sticks like the witches in Macbeth all in search of the missing shoe, but to no purpose.'

William was a constant source of pleasure for his companions, whether playing games in the cottage, lunching on the Glen Finlas rocks, climbing hills, rowing on Loch Achray, or singing a cappella. ('Papa will be enchanted with William's voice,' Effie told her mother.)

But he wasn't only fun and games. He had his serious side. 'William is always sketching,' Effie told Lady Trevelyan. Unlike his brother, he was inspired by the Trossachs, and his drawings of the scenery were quite good. Indeed earlier in the year, Gabriel Rossetti had told Thomas Woolner, 'William Millais has just done some landscapes worthy of almost any one except his brother.' (In 1852 and 1853 he had exhibited single landscape pictures at the R.A. Five more would appear there in later years.)

* * *

On the eve of William's departure, John Everett wrote to Collins, 'I have just returned from work a little jaded, leaving Ruskin and William building a bridge of stone across the river ... I feel too tired to paddle in water and break my back in pebble lifting. I have had a nice melancholy walk between high hills and have sung gloomy songs until my throat is dry. I have lingered by a little churchless burial ground which stands within a stone's throw from here, and my thoughts worked under each crumbling tablet to the bones there ... I feel very down in the mouth this evening.'

Surely he wasn't dejected because he was to be deprived of his brother's company. They had not lately been intimate. In recent years John Everett had been much closer to Hunt and Collins.

William did not travel alone. He left with Effie and her chaperone, a female neighbour. They spent two days in Perth with the Grays before William proceeded to London and the women returned to the Trossachs.

John Everett at once moved into his brother's hotel room. 'It is horribly dull,' he wrote to Hunt, 'having to leave the cottage at night and go up to a numbered hotel bed chamber, and being awakened by the Boots reminding the gentleman in the next room that he desires to be called at three o'clock.' But his state of mind prevented him from continuing to live alone with the Ruskins. In his next letter to Hunt he said, 'I am dreadfully unwell, scarcely a day without a headache. It is no use taking medicine as that only weakens me ... Today I have had a headache all day, and I feel intolerably depressed ... I even have a headache from writing this.'

Never had he been so dejected. During the rest of August and all of September, he had almost daily headaches. In September, with the return of bleak atmospheric conditions, he poured out his heart to Collins: 'You cannot conceive anything more dreadfully gloomy than Scotch bad weather. I feel cold, discontented, and hopeless, without the least notion of when I may get away from this place ... Everybody is marrying. All the letters I receive mention espousals. I suppose my turn will come some day. I confess I should feel considerably better for a wife ... These chilling mountains make one love little soft, warm, breathing bodies ... Last week I painted but one day out of doors ... I am seriously intending spending the winter abroad. Will you accompany me, south of France? Consider and let me know.'

Early in October, Ruskin communicated with Holman Hunt: 'I cannot help writing to you tonight, for Everett is lying upon his bed crying like a child . . . I don't know what will become of him when you are gone.' He was referring to Hunt's planned trip to the Holy Land, which, he thought, was the reason for Millais's unhappiness. One day later, Millais wrote to Hunt, 'I have discovered that last night when I felt somewhat low spirited and otherwise weak, Ruskin wrote to you and spoke of me in connection with your departure. It is true that I was thinking of that event most gloomily, but for all that I am likely to possess I would not have you influenced by any feeling of mine in regard to your leaving. Mine is purely a selfish desire to have you always within sight and not to be considered for one moment. I write fearing that you might be moved to delay going on my account. It was Mrs Ruskin who thought that I should know what her husband had written.'

Because of Middle Eastern hostilities, Hunt had said that he might have to stop in Italy until the fighting ended. This gave Millais an idea: 'If you have no objection, I will gladly join you at Florence . . . I don't think I could live in London when you are gone. I have no place to go to. You will think all of this very weak, but I don't profess to be otherwise . . . Today is filled with sunshine, but to me it is somehow very oppressive. I am so sick, all weather is miserable.'

Ruskin now spent most of his time inside the cottage working on the Edinburgh lectures, with Crawley making fair copies of the rough drafts. John Everett and Effie were left to themselves. In good weather and in not-so-good weather, they wandered through the glens and across the hills rising above Loch Katrine. They stood beneath graceful birch trees and sat on heather-covered stones. They talked and talked and talked.

At least once they were in close physical contact. Effie wrote about it to a friend: 'The other evening I was returning home with Millais, and coming to a very dark mud bank, I asked his help. It was quite dark, and he told me to walk on the edge of the grass, and I thought I was getting on nicely. He had fast hold of my arm when my foot went from under me, and of course I fell into a cold mud bath. He fell too, directly upon me.'

Rolling together in the night-time mud was an unexpected treat for both of them. By now, it seems certain, John Millais was in love with someone who probably reciprocated, but presumably was bound forever to someone else.

CHAPTER 11

1828—53

In this chapter, I interrupt the narrative to summarise the first twenty-five years of Effie Ruskin.

* * *

Euphemia Chalmers Gray was born on 5 July 1828 in Perth, the first of George and Sophie Gray's fifteen children, eight of whom survived childhood. The room in which she was born had been the site of a suicide. By an extraordinary coincidence, the victim was the grandfather of John Ruskin!

The Ruskin family had once owned the large, luxurious Gray house known as Bowerswell. George Gray was a prominent solicitor who became a Writer to the Signet, which the London *Daily News* said, 'is the highest grade and finest flower of the profession of solicitor, as practised in Scotland'. Befitting his position, he was well enough compensated for his sons to attend public schools and his daughters to enroll in ladies' seminaries.

We don't know much about all of Effie's formal education, but we have a pretty full record of the eighteenth months she spent at a school in Stratford-on-Avon, during the academic year of 1840–41 and the spring term of 1844. Founded by two sisters named Byerley in 1810 in Warwick, it moved in 1824 to an attractive three-storey white building alongside Holy Trinity Church in Stratford – Shakespeare's church – overlooking the river. In its new location it was, appropriately, named Avonbank. Everything at the school was first-class. The meals, for example, were served on the finest

china, presented to the Byerleys by their cousin Josiah
Wedgwood.

The curriculum included geography and the use of globes, ancient
and modern history, French, music, drawing, and dancing.
(Arithmetic was one of several optional extras available for an additional fee.)

This course of study, not at all innovative, was what upper strata
parents regarded as proper for their daughters. Avonbank, however,
was not just another rich girls' finishing school. The Byerleys and the
three Ainsworth sisters, who replaced them at the end of 1840,
insisted upon an intellectually demanding level of instruction. The
girls engaged in serious discussions, and they wrote challenging
papers. The school was ideal for someone as bright as Effie.

She arrived aged twelve in the beginning of September 1840 and
was assigned to a room on the second floor (American third floor),
which looked out upon the swans and boats on the Avon. In her first
letter home she wrote,

After you left me in London I enjoyed myself very much indeed.
Mr Ruskin took me to see all the sights. I was very much pleased
with the Zoological Gardens and with Westminster Abbey. . . . I am
very fond of school, and Avon Bank is a beautiful place. . . . Mr
Walker is a very amusing man. He is giving lectures on natural philosophy which are delightful, and he tells us a great many things of
which I never heard before.

Your affectionate daughter, E.C. Gray.

This letter and those that followed were grammatically impeccable
and free of spelling errors except for *receive*, which she spelled
'recieve.' ('Mr Ruskin' was John Ruskin's father. Effie had spent a few
days with the Ruskins before proceeding to Stratford.)

Avonbank emphasised competition. The highest grade was 'perfectly well'. Next came 'very well,' followed by 'well,' still a good
grade. The top girl in each subject received a prize. Additionally, a
General Attention Prize was given to whoever had the pre-eminent
over-all record. Effie loved the competition, especially in French. On
10 November she wrote to her father:

I really must tell you the delightful news. Mademoiselle [the French teacher, a Parisian] told me and Emily Sothern that we are exactly equal for the French prize, and that none of the others were near us, and today when we said our French Table we each got a *perfectly well*. If I work hard I shall either get the *Prize* or the *Card of Honour*. If we are equal, we shall draw for it, and either get the one or the other. Tell Mama that I am the best worker in the class. . . . Emily and I think of nothing else but the French Prize. When ever we meet each other she gives me a kiss to show that there is no *rivalship* [sic] between us.

On 1 December the two of them were neck and neck. They continued to earn good grades, and on 4 December and again on 7 December, Effie reported, it was impossible to tell who would win. On 16 December, the prize list was announced. The winner in French was Effie. She also captured the General Attention Prize. She was tops in her class.

One subject that did not count in the competition was music. An educated woman was expected to play an instrument, usually the piano or harp, and music lessons were compulsory in virtually all girls' schools. Effie studied the piano, and again she was number one. Because of her talent the instructor gave her additional instruction in his own time free of charge.

Although an excellent student, Effie was far from being a bookworm. She was the school's prettiest, most popular girl, with a strong outgoing personality. She spent part of the winter holiday at the home of a classmate, Louise Parker, whose mother wrote to Mrs Gray, 'I want to express our thanks for the pleasure you have afforded us in the company of our young friend, who wins all hearts by her cheerful gaiety and good humour. I assure you we shall be much pleased to secure such a friend for our daughter and trust this will not be the last time you allow her to visit us.'

This was written while Effie was still a guest. After Mr Parker had driven the two girls back to school, Mrs Parker wrote again: 'Mr Parker says that your lively little daughter was chatting the whole way. . . . Dear Mrs Gray, let me again assure you that I think you have every cause for comfort and satisfaction in the character of your dear child.

. . . She is going back with a very good resolution of trying hard for another prize in French, altho' it will be much more difficult, as Louise thinks she will be placed amongst older girls this half year.'

Her 'chatting the whole way' is not surprising. She was and always would be gregarious. Her manner of speech was part of her charm. In her letters she frequently remarked on how people enjoyed hearing her talk because of her Scottish accent, which she exploited to the fullest.

In the second term, stimulated by the competition with older girls, she again won the French prize. She also got the history prize and her second General Attention Prize.

At the end of the school year, Effie spent a few days with the Ruskin family. For her John Ruskin wrote his only fairy tale, 'The King of the Golden River'.

* * *

Despite her record, Effie did not return to Avonbank for the autumn term. During the summer, within five weeks, her three younger sisters, aged six, five, and three, all died from scarlet fever. Although Effie wanted to go back to school, and her mother too wanted her to be with girls of her age, her father said, 'No, *The house is too quiet.*' So, until the end of 1843, she was instructed by a governess from Edinburgh. Then in January of 1844 she returned to Avonbank, where she was delighted to discover that under the new head mistresses, the Ainsworth sisters, the school was academically even more exacting than before. She had studied optional German before, and was eager to get back to it. Happily now there was a new student from Germany. Only Effie spoke to her in her native language. As for her other foreign language, she wrote to her father on everyday matters a letter entirely in fluent French – idiomatic and grammatically perfect.

At Avonbank final examinations had always been important. Now, under the Ainsworth regime, the girls would be tested not only on classroom work but also on outside reading. They began preparing for the tests six week's ahead of time. 'Our class,' Effie wrote to her father, 'have the whole history of Egypt. It is extremely difficult, and having never learnt any of it before, it makes it more so. We have no time set apart to learn it in, and we are just obliged to take every two or three minutes between classes. Formerly we had a fortnight to do nothing else in.'

She did what she had to do, and she won her second history prize. She also obtained a third French prize, concerning which one of the Ainsworth sisters told Mrs Gray, 'She contended against many far superior to herself in knowledge of the language, so I conclude she has been very industrious.' Surprisingly, she lost out on the General Attention Prize, but as a final honour she was a featured piano soloist at the school's annual concert.

For whatever reason, this was her last term at Avonbank. She spent the next several years in Perth and elsewhere in Scotland and England, visiting relatives and friends, and, perhaps, breaking men's hearts. One of Avonbank's most famous former students, the novelist Elizabeth Gaskell, wrote to a friend some time later, 'Don't think me hard upon her if I tell you what I have *known* of [Effie]. She is very clever – and very vain. When she was staying in Manchester her delight was to add to the list of her offers (27 I think she was at then) but she never cared for any of them. It was her boast to add to the list in every town she visited, just like somebody in the Arabian Nights who was making up her list of 1000 lovers. *Effie Grey* [sic] *was engaged at the very time she accepted Mr Ruskin*, but he did not know it till after their marriage.'

Elizabeth Gaskell's number may be incorrect, but there were indeed numerous offers prior to Ruskin's, and Effie did break off an engagement in order to accept his proposal.

* * *

Because her family and the Ruskins had had a long-standing relationship, Effie as a girl and young woman was their frequent guest. Her most important visit came in the spring of 1847. At that time Mrs Ruskin wrote to her son, who was considering a marriage proposal,

I think very few girls at her age have equal qualifications. . . . She is very lovely, with the least vanity I have ever seen in anyone. . . . In your intercourse with the world she would indeed be a helpmeet. I think her very prudent in her expenses without the slightest meanness, her taste in dress really good, her appearance such as we may all be proud of, her family and connections equal if not superior to our own – her temper must be excellent or she would not have borne so easily your fault finding, and her natural abilities are much above the common. In conclusion I am convinced you may never meet with another so calculated to secure your happiness.'

John agreed. He proposed. Even though she was already engaged, she accepted his offer.

His frequent pre-marital letters contained lines like these:

'My own Effie – my kind Effie – my mistress – my friend – my queen – my darling – my only love.'

'I beg your pardon a thousand times, dear Effie: dress as you think best – I never saw you but well dressed.'

'I am afraid of your again thinking that I only love you "because you are pretty."'

In this last sentence, the word *again* and the quotation marks suggest that they had talked about her good looks with Effie wondering if this was why he was interested in her. She was probably right. Since he exalted all forms of beauty, why shouldn't he have been charmed by a beautiful woman, especially when she was a good conversationalist, a fluent speaker of French, a talented pianist, and an apparent devotee of the arts?

Why did Effie accept his offer? Probably because she liked the idea of marrying a well-known man of the world, after experiencing the time of her life on her visit to the Ruskins in the spring of '47. She had been entertained royally, riding in the family carriage to important exhibitions and attending numerous parties, at one of which, in the Ruskin home, she was guest of honour. She met J.M.W. Turner, Charles Robert Leslie, George Richmond, and, she told her mother, 'a number of other eminent artists who John was so kind to ask that I might meet them. . . . I am enjoying myself immensely.'

On the 10 April 1848 in Perth she became Mrs Ruskin.

* * *

'I am happier every day with John,' Effie wrote to her mother a month into the marriage. 'He is the kindest creature in the world and is so pleased with me . . . We are always so happy to do what the other wants that I do not think we shall ever quarrel.' In November she told Lady

Trevelyan, 'It is a great blessing to live with a man who is never cross but always kind and good.'

And so it went for several years, their life together apparently exciting, enjoyable, and trouble-free. They lived luxuriously in London, and took leisurely European trips finishing with wonderful winters in Venice, where Effie was courted by pillars of international society.

Because she revelled in a succession of social events, where, Ruskin said proudly, she 'was allowed by everyone to be the *reine du bal*,' Effie has been depicted as flighty, vain, and extravagant, preoccupied with superficialities, the opposite of her husband. The record does not support this characterisation.

A month after the wedding, there was a revealing incident. Jenny Lind, 'the Swedish nightingale', gave two recitals in London. 'We are going tomorrow night to hear her,' Effie wrote to her mother. 'John asked me whether I would rather go twice to the stalls or once to the boxes as the price would be the same. I at once said twice to the stalls, but Mr Ruskin thinks it infra dig to go there, so he took a box in the grand tier opposite to the Queen, in order, I suppose, that we may be properly seen.'

A couple of months later, Effie told her mother, 'We went to hear Haydn's *Creation*, which I enjoyed very much . . . John thinks all that music detestable, and so he read a book the whole time.'

Effie enjoyed reading as much as he did, at the proper time and place, and not just books in English. During her first married year, she wrote to her mother, 'I have read half of the first volume of Dumas's *Monte Cristo* [in French], but I do not think nearly so much of him as Balzac, about the same difference as between [G.P.R.] James and Sir Walter Scott, but Dumas is fertile in invention and interesting.' (If these judgments sound conventional, it should be borne in mind that Dumas and Balzac were still both alive and relatively young, and their work not yet passed into the canon.)

One person who valued Effie's opinions, literary and otherwise, was Rawdon Brown, and the intimation that she was shallow is surely controverted by their friendship. An Oxford graduate from a socially elite English family, in 1833, at the age of 30, he went on a grand tour of Europe. For him the tour ended in Venice. He fell in love with the city and lived there until his death in 1883. It was not a life of leisure;

fascinated by Venetian history, he visited the local archives almost daily. He was particularly captivated by letters from London's Venetian ambassadors to their government. The initial result of his efforts was *Four Years at the Court of Henry VIII*, a translation of and commentary upon dispatches by Sebastian Giustiniani, who served during the early part of Henry's reign. Published in 1854, it was well enough received for Lord Palmerston to give Brown a commission to calendar all Venetian state papers dealing with English history. Brown devoted the rest of his life to this commission. He examined some twelve million documents. Shortly before his death, he gave London's Public Record Office the fruits of his labours – 126 volumes of transcripts.

Rawdon Brown was the ultimate embodiment of a dedicated scholar, without wife, family, hobbies, or outside interests, and Ruskin met him on his first visit to Italy, in 1845. Later he wrote, 'I learned Venice wholly under Mr Rawdon Brown's rein.' When Brown saw Ruskin in 1849–50, he met Effie. From the start, they hit it off splendidly. Unlike almost every other man who had known her, Brown regarded Effie as more than a beautiful ornament. During the late '40s and early '50s he was working on his Henry VIII book, which he frequently talked over with the Ruskins. Subsequently Brown corresponded regularly not with John, but with Effie on what they called the Giustiniani Papers. He sent sections of the manuscript as they were completed and solicited her evaluations. This sample of her advice is from a letter sent from the Highlands in July 1853:

I think you should not only give the story, which is most interesting, but also give other details which would be equally new and interesting to the English reader. As regards your asking my opinion of its merit, I am always so interested in historical truths that I hardly know how much of what interests me would interest the public, but it appears to me that if this manuscript were carefully looked over and parts left out which do not add to the interest of the story, it would be very well received. I do not know the publications you allude to [possible publishers of all or parts of the manuscript], but I will enquire when I get back to town.... If you would give me any other hints regarding what use you would like the MS. put to, I will do everything I can to make it serve any use you intend it.

Upon returning to London, Effie found someone to edit the manuscript, a Mr Rich, whom she described in a letter to Brown: 'He seemed a sensible and agreeable person, about 35, his hair turning gray, and very black, *mesmeric* eyes – hairs once black too.' She then unearthed an interested publisher, the highly regarded Smith and Elder.

In the spring of 1854, Brown travelled to London to confer with the men whom Effie had found. After his first meeting with Rich, not yet sure if his manuscript would become a book, he wrote to her,

> My Dear Friend,
> I passed the whole morning reading over Giustianini with Rich. . . . I am gratefully mindful that it is to your exertions with Smith & Elder that I am solely indebted for a hearing. At times I anticipate nothing but failure and disappointment *in one sense*, but be that as it may I consider myself a most decided gainer of all the interest taken by you so constantly in this matter for well nigh two years, nor can any result obliterate or modify my sense of all you did in my behalf.

After the manuscript had been accepted for publication, Brown, sending Effie the good news, referred to the book as 'your God Child'.

The benefits from the Rawdon Brown-Effie Ruskin relationship were not one-sided. She gained almost as much as he did. It was exhilarating to be treated by a man of learning as an equal, with a mind of her own. Rarely, after the first few years of marriage, could she have felt like this with her husband.

'I married her,' Ruskin once said, 'thinking her so young and affectionate that I might influence her as I chose, and make of her just such a wife as I wanted, [but] she had been indulged in all her wishes from her youth and felt all restraint an insult. . . . When I had drawing or writing to do, instead of sitting with me as I drew or wrote, she went about on her own quests.' More than once he likened her to Lady Olivia, from Maria Edgeworth's epistolary novel of 1808, *Leonora*.

In the first letter of the book, Lady Olivia writes, 'What a misfortune it is to be born a woman! Condemned to incessant hypocrisy or everlasting misery, woman is the slave or outcast of society. . . . To what purpose have we understandings, which we may not use? Hearts which we may not trust? To our unhappy sex, genius and sensibility are treacherous gifts. Why should we cultivate talents merely to gratify the caprice of tyrants?'

Like Lady Olivia, Effie was fed up with being a man's prized possession. And she, too, was bored to death by her marriage. For a while it had been exciting to travel, to meet famous people, to be the 'belle of the ball'. But there was a flip side to this. 'Mr Ruskin is busy all day till dinner time, and I never see him except at dinner,' Effie wrote to Lady Trevelyan from Venice in 1850. 'He sketches and writes notes on the subject at hand . . . I cannot help teasing him about his sixty doors and hundreds of windows, staircases, balconies, and other details he is occupied with every day.'

This encapsulated Ruskin's life – hours, days, weeks, months spent in examining details, followed by hours, days, weeks, months spent in writing. Early in the marriage it was amusing. Later it became terribly frustrating.

Actually Effie and her husband had never had a real marriage, and not just because he was a workaholic. In letters to Perth, Effie sometimes referred to 'my bed room', never 'our bed room'. During virtually all of their life together, Mr and Mrs Ruskin occupied separate bedrooms. There was no need to sleep together because they didn't do anything that would require a double bed.

Effie probably revealed all of this to Millais as they meandered in the hills. And apparently nothing could be done. Four years later, the Matrimonial Causes Act would make a divorce easier to obtain, but in 1853 no relief was in sight. Effie was trapped, presumably without means of escape. John Millais could only stand by and watch. Is it any wonder that he was talking about leaving the country?

CHAPTER 12

1853–54

Wʀɪᴛɪɴɢ to his mother in September, Ruskin said:

I wish the country agreed with Millais as it does with me, but I don't know how to manage him, and he does not know how to manage himself. He paints till his limbs are numb, and his back has as many aches as joints in it. He won't exercise in the regular way, but sometimes starts and walks for seven or eight miles if he is in the humour; sometimes won't, or can't, eat any breakfast or dinner, sometimes eats enormously without seeming to enjoy anything. Sometimes he is all excitement, sometimes depressed, sick and faint as a woman, always restless and unhappy. I think I never saw such a miserable person. I don't know what to do with him. The faintness seems so excessive, sometimes appearing almost hysterical.

In a letter to Hunt, about to depart for Palestine, Millais confirmed Ruskin's appraisal:

I quite hate the thought of your leaving. I believe you will never see me again if you stay away too long. I have at night dreadful wakefulness and the most miserable forebodings . . . Here I am at 24 years of age sick of everything after winning the artistic battle and certain to realise a competence as long as I can use my eyes; and yet I don't believe there is a more wretched being alive than the much envied I. My song shall be: 'Oh, dear, what will become of me?' until you write an In Memoriam upon your departed friend.

In the midst of his despair, he learned that Walter Deverell was critically ill.

How can I assist in comforting poor Deverell? [he asked Hunt]. His sister says he would get well if he sold a picture. I will buy one tomorrow if it will give him the least relief. Let me know by return of post his circumstances, whether they require *money*, or *anything*, as I *would gladly* give all I have in *such a good* cause, and think myself lucky for having such an opportunity of doing good service. If he felt uncomfortable at receiving support from me, tell him he must paint me a picture when he gets well, or let me have something he already has in the house.

He almost welcomed the sad news which took his mind off his own misery.

* * *

In mid-October, the Ruskins left for Edinburgh. Millais had been expected to accompany them, but he stayed behind, supposedly because he had to carry on with the portrait background. Actually he probably wasn't up to travelling with the two of them. In a few days he followed along. Previously he had loved Edinburgh. Now he couldn't find anything to like in the city. His hotel, a highly rated one, was disappointing because, he told Hunt, it was 'so awfully respectable and solitary . . . with no entertainment but the Times'. The Scottish National Gallery had 'such awful things in it, patched up portraits, said to be by Van Dyck, and old Spanish pictures which have done more to knock Spain out of my head than anything. There is also a commenced picture of Wilkie's worse than the old masters.' He told Collins that he had spent five minutes in the Gallery, 'which was too long by four. I do wonder that the Edinboro people should be gulled into permitting a Fine Art Committee to purchase such awful [underlined twelve times!] old masters as they have in their Gallery. Oh, my stars, what things!'

In the letter to Hunt, he spoke again of his personal turmoil: 'I feel under the lash of some demon. I can understand so well your desire to get away into new scenes. It is the only thing left for us.' He stayed in Edinburgh for two of Ruskin's four lectures, leaving on 4 November for London. Three days later the Royal Academicians would elect their newest Associate.

* * *

Millais was heavily favoured to win, but he took nothing for granted. On the 7th, a Monday, he was too nervous to stay home, or even in town. He and his brother, along with Charles and Wilkie Collins, spent a day in the country. Upon returning in the evening, they called at the Academy and were greeted by Charles Landseer, RA, who said, 'Well, Millais, you are now in *in earnest*.' He was alluding to the election earlier in the day and to the form in which the newest Associate's name had initially been registered, 'John Ernest Millais'. Until then the youngest ARA had been Turner. Now, at the age of twenty-four years and five months, Millais edged Turner by six weeks. No one younger has since been chosen.

* * *

About six weeks after his election, Millais wrote for the first time to Effie's mother, answering a letter from her. They had met in Edinburgh at a Ruskin lecture. He learned then that she shared his growing distaste for her son-in-law. Now he referred to Ruskin as 'an undeniable giant of an author but a poor, weak creature in everything else'. A couple of days later he again wrote to her. After calling Ruskin 'a plotting, scheming fellow, a quiet scoundrel [who] ought to be ducked in a mill', he spoke of the time when he and Effie had roamed about while Ruskin stayed indoors: 'His absence from us seemed purposed to give me an opportunity of being in his wife's society. His wickedness must be without parallel if he stayed away to that end, as I am inclined to think.'

Especially in light of the indisputable professional debt of gratitude Millais owed to Ruskin, this language must come as a shock. Nothing hitherto can prepare us for it. I can think of no rational explanation for such obvious hatred. The real explanation might be found in the most famous work of Millais's favourite novelist, Thackeray's *Vanity Fair*. John Everett's position resembled that of Mr Osborne, whose unreasonable animosity toward Mr Sedley was thus accounted for by the author: 'When one man has been under very remarkable obligations to another, with whom he subsequently quarrels, a common sense of decency, as it were, makes of the former a much severer enemy than a mere stranger would be. To justify your own hardheartedness and ingratitude in such a case, you are bound to prove the other party's crime.'

And so to rationalise his own feelings, Millais had to demonstrate that Ruskin was a scoundrel. Even so, might not there be some merit to the accusation that Ruskin actually had planned for John Everett and Effie to have an affair? Perhaps Ruskin's character might be said to rule it out. But then his behaviour throughout this summer should raise some questions. Could he not have known, especially after the prolonged sittings for *The Order of Release*, that something was going on between Effie and John Everett? If he did realise that they were more than just friends, why did he extend the summer-long invitation to Millais? Why did he decide upon the Trossachs? Because it was the most romantic spot in Scotland? Why was he so willing to move from the hotel? Was a wealthy man who always went first-class really concerned about the cost, when twice he and Effie had stayed for an extended period at Venice's famous Hotel Danieli? Could he have desired more confining quarters than those of a luxury hotel? Finally, when day after day Effie and Everett – a beautiful young woman and a handsome young man obviously attracted to each other – were exploring the hills, could he really have thought that nothing would happen?

All in all, the implications of these questions lead me to conclude that John Ruskin did indeed predesign this affair in the Highlands.

* * *

On Christmas Day the unhappy couple returned home. Soon thereafter, John Ruskin turned up in Gower Street to resume his sittings for a portrait which, it must have seemed, would go on forever. Never had Millais spent so much time on a picture, which, he told Hunt, he was 'heartily sick of'. To Mrs Gray he wrote, 'If I had only myself to consult, I should refuse to go further with the most hateful task I ever had to perform, but I am anxious that Effie should not suffer for any act of mine, and I will put up with anything rather than increase her suffering.'

After one sitting, he wrote to Ruskin:

Don't come on Wednesday as I shall not be able to see you. Dr Acland called last Friday, and I had breakfast with him the next morning at Sir Benjamin Brodie's hotel, where he was staying for a day on business. I went so that the great doctor might give his opinion upon the mark on the underlid of my left eye. [Brodie was a famous surgeon, but he was not an eye specialist.] He considers that it should be removed at once as it might ultimately interfere with my sight. I thought he would recommend an oculist, but when he saw me he determined to remove it himself and commenced by nearly burning my eye out. He is rather old, and I think in pouring the acid into the lid he gave much greater pain than is necessary. The agony is almost insufferable.

At no other time did Millais suffer from a visual impairment. The psychological basis of experiencing the one disability that would prevent a painter from working seems too clear-cut to require comment.

After resting his eyes for a few days, his sight was restored, and he returned to his loathsome task.

* * *

Within a period of thirty days early in 1854, Millais endured two painful events. In January, Hunt left for Palestine. After finishing a picture one afternoon, he dashed off to Waterloo Station without taking time to have dinner. Millais saw him off, and Hunt recalled how his friend had 'rushed into the buffet and seized any likely food he could find, and, running alongside the moving train, tossed it into my compartment'.

Three weeks later Walter Deverell died. In December his health had completely given way, and he was confined terminally to bed. During his final weeks the person most attentive to him was Millais, reading to him by the hour and helping out in various ways. Deverell faced death with equanimity; he was concerned only with the financial state of his brothers and sisters, of whom he had been the sole support. And so Millais bought, for a good price, his major unsold painting and had an acquaintance pretend to be the purchaser. (A fine picture of a woman standing with a caged bird, it is now in the Tate Gallery.) There was one thing that he could not do. Gabriel Rossetti told Woolner about it: 'Millais did not come to the funeral; you know his excitable nature, and I fancy he would not trust himself not to break down.'

* * *

In February he informed Mrs Gray that when her son-in-law's portrait was finished he would join Hunt in Cairo and 'begin a new life or rather try to end this one'. A month later he delayed his departure date. He told Hunt, 'I shall certainly join you next autumn.' In April his plans were more modest: 'If you will let me know when you come home I will meet you half way and travel home with you.' He never seriously intended to join Hunt. He disliked travelling and detested foreigners. He was just restless.

He did, however, move from London. But only across the river. Late in April, his parents left Gower Street and settled in a cottage overlooking the Thames at Surbiton. John Everett joined them and converted a stable into a studio. He didn't seem to be sad to leave the place where he had done the work that made him famous. He told the philologist Frederick Furnivall that his new home would be 'out of the way of callers in town. You will understand how much better I shall be able to get on away from the excitement of society. I believe it to be a great mistake to go out too much. I mean to alter my way of living.'

Actually he hadn't been having much of a social life, or any other kind of life. Before going to Surbiton, he wrote to Hunt, 'I have been out very little into society this winter, deriving no pleasure from anything. The desire for work gets less every day. I shall die a pauper if I do not alter soon. I try hard to think of subjects, but nothing ever seems worth painting. London is dreadfully miserable, and you were wise to get away. I assure you I feel very wretched here.'

* * *

Several years earlier, in Surrey, Millais had seen his first fox hunt, which he called 'savage and uncivilised'. Never thereafter would he have anything to do with this pastime. Until now. The popular *Punch* cartoonist John Leech asked him to join a Saturday chase, just for the ride. Willing to do almost anything to alleviate his misery, he accepted the invitation.

> I have been in the country with Leech [he wrote to Hunt]. We went to the Puckeridge hunt, I only attending to watch, but when I saw them off, I could not resist joining them, so away I went to the fright and astonishment of Leech over the first ditch, after which I quickly gained confidence and rode surprisingly to myself. I made five leaps without feeling the least insecure. So much for my first attempt at fox hunting. The exercise is better than any other. I rode between 10 and 40 miles, riding until the break-up. What pleased me that we had all the excitement without killing the little red *verming* [who escaped from the hounds] . . . I never felt so jolly in my life. All troublesome thoughts were shaken out of my head, and I felt as though I could have jumped with the best of sportsmen. . . . By George, there is nothing like the sensation of riding 'over the hills and far away'.

He became a lifelong enthusiast, once telling a friend, 'I enjoy the chase above all other recreation.' For Leech, hunting inspired hundreds of drawings. But except for a few drawings done in this – for him – artistically dead year of 1854, nothing related to the sport ever came from Millais's brush or pencil.

*   *   *

Effie Ruskin didn't have anything to relieve *her* despondency. During the early months of 1854 she was even more miserable than Millais. 'Effie is never happy,' Ruskin wrote to lady Trevelyan in January, 'which makes her ill.'

Every day she lamented that she was sick, but her husband and her in-laws were not sympathetic. 'Since she returned,' Mr Ruskin wrote to Mr Gray, 'she complains of ill health and the place not agreeing with her – but I see no look of ill health, nor is she ever unable to go to parties or theatres.'

The Ruskins could never have understood her ailment, which was something from which her counterpart, Maria Edgeworth's Lady Olivia, had suffered. 'My love for my husband was extinguished,' Lady Olivia confessed. 'Alas! we were not born for each other. The attractive moment of illusion was past. The repulsive reality remained. The living was chained to the dead and, by the inexorable tyranny of English laws, that chain can be severed only by the desperation of vice. Divorce, according to our barbarous institutions, cannot be obtained without guilt.'

This 'guilt' was the only grounds at that time for a British divorce. To be freed from her husband, Effie would have had to apply to Parliament and, in proceedings that were expensive and humiliating, prove to the complete satisfaction of the Ecclesiastical Court, and also the House of Lords, that her husband had been guilty of adultery as well as desertion. The procedure was indeed 'barbarous'.

*   *   *

On 3 March Millais wrote to Mrs Gray: '*It is my belief that steps should be speedily taken* to protect Effie from the harassing behaviour of the Rs . . . I am not sufficiently acquainted with the law to know whether something more than a separation could be obtained, but I think you should enquire into the matter.'

It seems strange that George Gray, a distinguished lawyer, apparently hadn't thought of this. In point of fact, a marriage that had never been consummated physically, could be annulled. Since Effie was childless after six years of matrimony – highly unusual then – the Grays had their suspicions. But they hadn't queried her on it. Now, after hearing from Millais, they asked the crucial question. On 7 March she sent her answer:

I have to tell you that I do not think I am John Ruskin's wife at all – and I entreat you to assist me to get released from my unnatural position. To go back to the day of my marriage . . . I had never been told the duties of married persons to each other and knew little or nothing about their relations in the closest union on earth. For days John talked about it but avowed no intention of making me his wife. He alleged various reasons – hatred of children, religious motives, a desire to preserve my beauty, and finally last year (and this is as villainous as all the rest), that he had imagined that women were quite different to what he saw I was, and that the reason he did not make me his wife was because he was disgusted with my person the first evening. [His knowledge of naked women had come from paintings and statues. It has been suggested that he was 'disgusted' by the sight of his wife's pubic hair.] I argued with him and quoted the Bible, but he silenced me and said that after six years, when I was 25, he would marry me. This last year I spoke to him about it. [Her twenty-fifth birthday was 7 May 1853, six weeks before the departure for Scotland with Millais.] He then said that as I professed quite a dislike to him it would be *sinful* to enter into such a connexion.

The letter was signed, for the first time since her marriage, 'Yr. affectionate Daughter, Effie Gray.'

* * *

How did Ruskin explain or justify matrimony without sex?

Immediately after our marriage [he told his solicitor], we agreed not to consummate it for some time, so that my wife's state of health might not interfere with a proposed journey to the Continent. For my part I married in order to have a companion – not for passion's sake; and I was particularly anxious that my wife should be able to climb Swiss hills. I was delighted that she seemed quite relieved at the suggestion.

Soon afterward we agreed that the marriage should not be consummated until my wife was five and twenty.

Before that period had arrived, I had become aware of points in her character which caused me to regard with excessive pain any idea of having children by her, and therefore neither pressed nor forced consummation, but I offered it again and again; always it was refused.

Probably neither was eager for sex. For Ruskin it was unimportant. The same, I think, was true of Effie. A disdain for sex was common to the Victorian 'modern woman' who is often encountered in novels. (A prime example is Sue Bridehead, in Thomas Hardy's *Jude the Obscure*, an exact contemporary of Effie.) In any event, Effie didn't complain until after she had become friendly with Millais.

In concluding his statement, Ruskin said:

My wife's feelings of affection towards me gradually became extinguished and were at last replaced by a hatred so great that she told me, at the end of September or the beginning of October in 1853, we being in Scotland, that if she should suffer the pains of eternal torment, they could not be worse than going home to live with me.

I took her home nevertheless. She has remained in resolute anger, venting itself in unexplained insults, and rejecting every attempt of mine to caress her as if I had been a wild beast.

* * *

'When I think of his double dealing,' Effie wrote to her mother early in April 1854, 'I wonder how I can speak to him. He is quite loathsome to me . . . I am quite decided that to live on any terms with him is to continue in sin.'

This last sentence clearly echoes a declaration by the woman whom Ruskin called his wife's precursor. In one of her letters, Maria Edgeworth's Lady Olivia had said, 'To live with a man I cannot love is, to a mind like mine, legal prostitution.'

Rawdon Brown, the Venetian history scholar, was in London to confer on his book. Effie told him, 'I have no more dependence on JR than on a piece of slippery ice. Delay is no longer possible.' She was alluding to a planned escape. Four days later, on 14 April, her parents arrived clandestinely and moved into lodgings in Bury Street, St James's. Effie told Brown, 'I am off to Scotland on Wednesday [the 19th]. The R's have not a suspicion as to what is about to happen. What a state of astonishment they will be in on Wednesday night!'

Actually she left on the morning of the 25th, ostensibly for a brief visit to Perth. I doubt that the Ruskins were oblivious of what was happening. For ten days Effie had been going regularly from her home to St James's, and then, just prior to departing, she sent off her luggage. The Ruskins would have had to be quite dense if they had 'not a suspicion' of what she was doing. I think they pretended to be in the dark because they were as glad to be rid of her as she was to leave. Anyhow, John Ruskin accompanied Effie to King's Cross, along with Crawley, who was to ride with her to Perth. He was in fact dismissed at the next station, when Mr and Mrs Gray, who had left London an hour earlier, boarded the train. The threesome proceeded to Perth.

* * *

The Grays had conferred at length with lawyers in London. The first fruits of these meetings were realised on the afternoon of their departure. John Ruskin received a citation to answer the allegation that, because of an inability to fulfill his basic responsibility, the marriage should be annulled. On the same day, the senior Ruskins got a parcel containing Effie's wedding ring, the household keys, and a letter to John's mother. After delineating her real or imagined grievances, Effie said, 'The Law will let you know what I have demanded, and I put it to you and Mr Ruskin to consider what a very great temporal loss, in every point of view, your son's conduct has entailed upon me for these best six years of my life.'

On the next morning Mr Ruskin saw his solicitor. He wanted everything to be done quietly. In order to expedite the proceedings, his son would offer no defence.

The Ruskins were naive if they thought that this affair could be swept under the carpet. The cast of characters ensured a groundswell of publicity. Additionally, Lady Elizabeth Eastlake, wife of Sir Charles Eastlake, President of the Royal Academy since Martin Shee's death in August 1850, despised Ruskin because he had written critically, and honestly, about her husband's work. She spread the news of the separation, augmented by a personal interpretation. To a friend she wrote, 'I tell the tale whenever and wherever I think the *truth* can do good.'

On 29 April, the Royal Academy held its private view. *The Times* observed that 'the Pre-Raphaelites are only represented by Messrs. Hunt and Collins.' Millais, for obvious reasons, was an absentee, even though his name would have been followed by 'ARA'. He put in a brief appearance and then wrote to Mrs Gray, '*Everybody glories in the step*

Effie has taken and only wonders at her delaying so long . . . I did not hear what most people said as I would escape when the subject was mentioned.' A few days later, he told Hunt, 'I never go to the Cosmopolitan [which, along with the Garrick, was one of his two clubs] as I should only hear nasty jokes. Everybody is full of the Ruskin business.' Again to Mrs Gray: 'Some of the most barbarous stories are in circulation regarding my absence from the RA wall. I have avoided as much as possible going out where there was a chance of *that* being the conversation.' Therefore he didn't go *anywhere*.

Fortunately for the involved parties, the newspaper gossip column did not exist. Even so, the news travelled rapidly. Gabriel Rossetti, who had been staying in Hastings, knew all about it. 'That Ruskin row seems to have grown into a roar,' he wrote to Ford Madox Brown. 'Mrs R will get a divorce it seems – her husband is – or *is not* – I know not what . . . It seems Mrs R's seven years of marriage have been passed like Rachel's seven marriageable years – in hope. I suppose it is not the right time to be in favour with Ruskin. He seems to take it very cool as he wrote to me a good deal about Art etc.'

Ruskin indeed kept his cool. He carried on as if nothing unusual had happened. Except for a letter to his solicitor, which he insisted be kept out of the proceedings, he apparently wrote about the affair only to Acland. 'Effie found my society not enough for her happiness,' he told the doctor, 'and was angry with me for not being entertaining. Gradually the worst part of her character gained ground, more especially a self-will quite as dominant as my own and less rational . . . Have you read Miss Edgeworth's *Leonora*? Effie is "Lady Olivia" (with less refinement) mingled with Goneril in *King Lear*.'

*   *   *

'I am so disgusted with London society,' Millais told Mrs Gray in mid-May, 'that I shall be right glad when I am out breathing the pure air of the country.'

He was about to return to Glen Finlas for the final details of the portrait. Just before leaving, he heard from Furnivall, his friend as well as Ruskin's, that the folks in Mayfair assumed that he was leaving town to meet secretly with Effie.

'You will, I know,' he at once replied, 'have the kindness to contradict any absurd conjecture about myself and Mrs R. I am *disgusted* with the way in which Society has mixed up my name in the affair. I am going to the Highlands truly to finish the background of Ruskin's portrait. I should indeed be sorry to hear that any friend of mine imagined that I had the *bad taste* to see Mrs R whilst the matter is in lawyers' hands. I beg you will positively state that I shall make a point of avoiding *all persons connected with the business*.'

The letter originally ended thus: 'Don't joke about this matter any.' Apparently realising the impropriety of saying this to a distinguished philologist, Millais had the good sense to scratch it out. (It wasn't totally obliterated.)

On 25 May, Millais left for the Highlands. Three days later, Effie and her father went to London. On the 30th she was examined by two court-appointed physicians. They deposed, 'We found that the usual signs of virginity are perfect and that she is naturally and properly formed, and there are no impediments on her part to a proper consummation of marriage.'

A few days after returning to Perth, Effie told Rawdon Brown that she was 'eating heartily, sleeping well, and walking long distances'. She had to wait five weeks for the good news. On 15 July, the Commissary Court of Surrey held a brief hearing in which the only evidence was Effie's deposition. When it was over, the presiding judge signed a decree nullifying her marriage because 'the said John Ruskin was incapable of consummating the same by reason of incurable impotency'.

Ruskin told his lawyer, 'I can prove my virility at once, but I do not wish to receive back into my house the woman who has made such a charge against me.'

Perhaps William Gladstone summed it up most charitably when he said to his daughter, 'Should you ever hear any one blame Millais, or his wife, or Mr Ruskin, remember there was no fault: there was misfortune, even tragedy, but all three were blameless.'

CHAPTER 13

1854–55

In mid-June, at the place where he had begun almost a year earlier, Millais could finally say that he had finished the portrait. No viewer without prior knowledge would guess that its creator had hated this picture with a passion. The rocks, the foliage, and the water are superb. The full-length portrait – completed earlier in London – is probably the best likeness of Ruskin. This hardly supports the premise that to do well, one must love one's work.

As soon as the painting had been shipped off, Millais, joined by Charlie Collins and Mike Halliday, began a Highlands walking tour. In his present frame of mind he had to do something physical. 'The only books I can read at this time,' he told Furnivall, 'are Thackeray's. His last number of "Newcomes" is as fine as it can be. I know no praise too great for it.' (In October 1853, *The Newcomes* had begun publication in monthly parts.)

After about four weeks of walking, he informed Hunt that 'Mrs Ruskin is now Miss Effie again and is entirely free.' He himself was 'much stronger, stouter, and happier than ever'. Never before had the world been so beautiful: 'The scenery of Scotland beats everything I have seen in England or abroad. [Except briefly as a child in Brittany, he had never been abroad.] The grandeur of the moutains, the vast glens, the inaccessible heights, the clouds rolling about in their deep purple tops, while the middle distances and foregrounds from the quantity of heather present every thing from the brightest maize to the richest crimson and purple. We have been sketching but alas it is sickening to think how faint an idea one can give of the sublime scene before us.'

This was perhaps a first for Millais, an expression of interest in doing landscape art.

On 21 July, he wrote his initial letter to 'Effie Gray':

I have been painting out of doors all day, or rather pretending to paint – so that I might be away from my friends and have some quiet to think upon this wonderful change.

I must see you before returning to London, *if you will invite me.* Oh, Countess, how glad I shall be to see you again. This is all I can say now, and you must imagine the rest. I can never be sufficiently thankful for God's goodness to me – I really believe that I should have grown a selfish, callous fellow if this altercation had not come about.

'Countess' was Effie's nickname, acquired in the Trossachs, which Millais explained to Collins: 'We give ourselves titles here as there are no people to dispute them. I am a Duke.' Effie did not send his invitation. 'The world will watch your every move,' her past head mistress, Mary Ainsworth, had warned. Her parents agreed. A visit from Millais at this time was out of the question.

Writing to Effie on 26 August 1854, Mary Ainsworth said, 'People gossip about when you will marry, usually giving you to Millais. I deny it positively, and I do not scruple to say that I hope and trust no such thing will *ever* take place.' So spoke the Stratford spinster. The Venice bachelor, on the other hand, Rawdon Brown, asked her directly, in September, when she would remarry. This was her response:

I am at present gaining health and strength and very happy teaching my sisters [ten-year-old Sophia Margaret and nine-year-old Alice Elizabeth]. I am not fit to marry anybody, believe me, and after what I have suffered could not do so without very much time for thought and deliberation, and you know it would never do to be wretched twice. If I marry it must be to somebody who wouldn't require me to live in London. I am very unfit for living in town although I should like to go occasionally. I could not be shut up in a street without pining, and I cannot have a man again be unkind to my parents . . . Now all this surely will take a long time to get and will leave me peace to teach music and lessons to my heart's content.

Attached to this letter in the archives of the Pierpont Morgan Library is a handwritten note by an eminent Ruskin scholar, the late Helen Viljoen: 'In its combination of piety and patent lies, this letter conspicuously shows Effie as a *perfect* replica of Becky Sharp . . . the dear little woman protecting her dear parents against the unkindness of another J.R. and *so* happy simply to teach her little sisters. This is fantastic!' Reflecting a lifelong devotion to John Ruskin, Ms Viljoen may have been a trifle unfair, but she had a point. Effie was not just writing a private communication. Rawdon Brown could be counted on to reveal its contents to British residents and visitors in Venice. With the speed of an express train the news would travel to Mayfair. If there are no 'patent lies' in the letter, there is the misleading implication that Effie had not thought about remarrying. Their subsequent conduct makes clear that she and John Everett had agreed to marry after 'a decent interval'. Naturally nothing in writing on this matter could have survived.

*   *   *

In mid-October, Millais returned to the metropolis, but not to Surbiton. He found rooms with an adjoining studio in Langham Chambers, lately built especially for artists across from the conical-spired All Soul's Church in Langham Place, the short stretch joining Portland Place to Regent Street. Gabriel Rossetti told his friend the minor poet William Allingham that Millais's lodgings were 'handsome'. But Rossetti, who lived alongside Blackfriars Bridge, added, 'I had rather have my bridge river view than his indoor magnificence.' This says something about both of them.

While still in the Highlands, Millais had told Hunt, 'I have been playing cricket, fishing, and grouse hunting on the moor, but now I intend working in the old way until sending-in day. I mean to do much better things than I have hitherto done.' 'Working in the old way' meant that John Millais, ARA, was still a dedicated PRB. He added emphasis by saying, 'I am more than ever convinced that it is our duty to reform.'

Now settled in Langham Chambers, and raring to go, he faced a familiar problem: want of a subject. Despite his ravings about beautiful Scotland, he had not seriously thought about doing a landscape. Before he could give much consideration to this matter, he heard from Alfred Tennyson. The poet laureate would be pleased to receive a visit from Mr Millais. For about a year Tennyson had lived on the western end of the Isle of Wight. So secluded was his house that to reach it visitors had to walk two and a half miles. Millais didn't mind. This invitation couldn't be declined and, besides, he enjoyed walking.

Tennyson's publisher, Edward Moxon, had decided to issue a luxurious anthology of his best previously printed poems. A novelty in 1854, it would be illustrated. Tennyson, who liked Millais's *Mariana*, asked him to be the principal artist. The response was unhesitatingly affirmative. Millais would do eighteen illustrations, his first major work in black and white. This was a commission of some significance. Millais had been concerned about being reproached for his perceived role in the Ruskin affair. An invitation from the laureate, known for a stringent moral code, would have a restraining effect on anyone who might wish to cast stones.

*　　*　　*

Early in December, soon after returning from the Isle of Wight, Millais received a letter from, of all people, John Ruskin:

> We have just got the picture placed – in, I think, the very light it wants – or rather – for it cannot be said to want any light – in that which suits it best. I am more delighted than ever with it . . . My father and mother say the likeness is perfect, but that I looked bored. Certainly after standing looking at chimneys in Gower Street for three hours, on one leg, it was no wonder I looked rather disinterested in the world in general. But the more they look at it the more they come to it. Please send me your proper address, as I may often want to write to you. Faithfully and gratefully yours . . .

Millais responded:

My address is Langham Chambers, Langham Place, but I can
scarcely see how you conceive it possible that I can desire to continue on terms of intimacy with you. Indeed I concluded after finishing your portrait that you yourself would have seen the necessity
of abstaining from further intercourse.

Ruskin answered with a formal note, beginning 'Sir' and ending 'Yr.
Obedt. Servt.' It was the last communication to pass between them.

* * *

On 23 January 1855, Gabriel Rossetti informed Allingham that
'Millais is painting his picture of a fireman rescuing some children.'
This would be his current subject, but it wasn't something he had hit
upon lately. Six months earlier, in the Highlands, he had written to
Collins, 'For the life of me I cannot get an outdoor subject this year
that I like and must return soon and go on with the fireman.' When
the new year arrived and he hadn't come up with anything fresh, he
turned back to his fire fighter.

This painting would be a ground-breaker. All of his earlier pictures
had been historical or literary. He had never done anything that could
stand by itself, apart from a written source. Now for the first time his
source was an event that he had personally witnessed. It had happened early in 1854, a spectacular evening fire at the Meux Brewery in
Tottenham Court Road at the corner of Great Russell Street, in which
two fire fighters lost their lives. He saw possibilities for a picture here
but didn't follow through until he was desperate for a topic.

Once he had made up his mind, he was exhilarated about his work.
After spending more than a year on the most loathsome picture of his
career, he was now doing something that he *wanted* to do. Arthur
Hughes, a follower and friend of the Pre-Raphaelites, recalled meeting
him on the street: 'The moment I saw him he began to describe his
subject, "to honour a set of men quietly doing a noble work, firemen",
and he poured out, in words of vividness and reality, the scene he
would put on canvas. I never see the picture without seeing also the
picture of himself glorified with enthusiasm as he was describing it.'

A few days after conversing with Hughes, on 29 January, Millais dined at the Hanover Place home of Harriet Collins. Five people were there: Mrs Collins, her sons Charles and Wilkie, John Millais, and Charles Dickens. The event had been initiated by Wilkie, in hopes of a friendly meeting between two of his close friends.

Millais had seen Dickens at large gatherings, but they had never spoken to each other. Thanks largely to amiable, tactful Harriet Collins, everything proceeded smoothly. Millais mentioned his new picture, whereupon Dickens offered to send him a copy of an article on the London fire brigade. It had appeared in *Household Words*, the journal which, four and one-half years earlier, had carried Dickens's denunciation of *The Carpenter's Shop*.

On the next day, the article arrived, along with a letter:

My dear sir, I send you the account of the fire brigade.

If you have in mind any previous association with the pages in which it appears, it may be a rather disagreeable one. In that case I hope a word frankly said may make it pleasanter.

Objecting very strongly to what I believed to be an unworthy use of your great powers, I once expressed objections in the same journal. My opinion on that point has not in the least changed, but it has never dashed my admiration of your progress in which I suppose are higher and better things. In short, you have given me such great reasons (in your works) to separate you from uncongenial associations that I wish to give you in return little reason for doing the like by me. Hence this note.

Millais's research for his present picture was as thorough as for any of the others. He interviewed officials of the brigade and accompanied a unit on several missions to watch the men in action. At least once he wore a fire fighter's coat, helmet, and boots and helped out at the scene. He was not much concerned about technical effects in the scene that he would depict. He was interested mainly in human beings. A fire fighter would be descending a staircase in a burning residence, carrying a child under each arm, with a third clinging to his neck. Their mother would be at the bottom of the stairs, kneeling with outstretched arms.

He began his picture, *The Rescue*, late in January and worked steadily until sending-in day, with one brief interruption. At last permitted to see Effie, in mid-February he spent two days in Perth. The wedding day was set for July.

This painting, with a new type of subject, was not easy. In late March, only three weeks before the deadline, William Rossetti reported in the *Pre-Raphaelite Journal*, which he still maintained sporadically, that 'more than half of his canvas is still uncovered'. Yet on sending-in day it was carted away. 'How he does it, I can't tell,' Rossetti wrote, adding that Millais 'told me he had terribly scamped his picture, but he thought he *must* send it in this year'.

After *The Rescue* had gone off, he had his first night out in three months. He, his brother William, Charlie Collins, and William Rossetti had dinner at a favourite restaurant of the Pre-Raphaelite circle, Campbell's Steak House in Beak Street, just off Regent Street. Rossetti reported on the occasion:

Millais summoned the waiters and with utmost voice ordered everything in the place that was good. He kept up such a noise that very soon everything was brought, and Millais ate as only he can. A modest man in the next box had asked for a chop and continued asking, till Millais, well stuffed and ready to leave, suddenly takes to pitying the ill-used man.

'Sir,' says he, 'these waiters behave very badly to you. Were I in your place, I would bully them frightfully. Why, sir, we've actually got our dinner and eaten while you've been waiting for your chop. Were I you, sir, when it came I would send it back – leave it on their hands.'

The man, incensed, did so, which, having witnessed, out stalked Millais *triumphans*. William suggested that he would have to go elsewhere and begin waiting again for his chop.

*　*　*

Several weeks later, at the private view, Millais was less amused than at the steak house. *The Rescue* was three feet above the line. In 1846, when *Pizarro* hung under the ceiling, and in 1847, when *Elvira* was in the Octagon Room, he had accepted his fate without a whimper. He was a teenager happy to be in the show. Now conditions had changed. He was an Associate of the Royal Academy.

He was hardly the first artist to protest the hanging of his pictures at the Academy. The most celebrated instance, in 1783, involved Thomas Gainsborough, a founding member of the Royal Academy. His submissions included fourteen interrelated *Portraits of the Royal Family*. When he found that the hanging committee had not gone along with his request for their positioning, he delivered a letter to the committee:

> Mr Gainsborough presents his compliments to the gentlemen appointed to hang the pictures and begs leave to hint to them that if the 'Royal Family' are hung above the line, alone with the full lengths, he never more, whilst he breathes, will send another picture to the Exhibition. This he swears by God.

The hangers rearranged the pictures. In 1784 Gainsborough, again unhappy, wrote to the committee:

> Mr Gainsborough's compliments to the Gentlemen of the Committee and begs pardon for giving them so much trouble; but as he has painted his Picture of the Princess in so tender a light, he cannot possibly consent to have it placed higher than five feet and a half, because the likeness and Work of the Picture will not be seen any higher; he will not trouble the Gentlemen against their Inclination but will beg his pictures back again.

This time the committee did not capitulate, and the pictures were returned. Never again did he exhibit at the Academy.

Millais was less literary and more physical than Gainsborough. 'I almost dropped down in a fit from rage in a row I had with the three hangers,' he told Hunt. 'I forgot all restraint and shook my fist in their faces, calling them every conceivable name of abuse.' He threatened to remove his picture and even to resign his Associateship. At once the painting was lowered by three feet.

The poet William Bell Scott recalled that for days thereafter 'Millais's amusement was to go about and rehearse the scene at the Academy betwen him and the ancient magnates.' Some two weeks after the incident, Ford Madox Brown also wrote in his diary, 'Millais described for us with gestures his battle with the Academicians; he shook his first in their faces, etc., etc., and talked to them for one hour.'

* * *

It is 'the most wonderful thing Millais has done, except perhaps the Huguenot', Gabriel Rossetti said of *The Rescue*. One of the most popular pictures in the show, it elicited a highly emotional response from viewers, one of whom, Thomas Spence Baines, wrote to Charlotte Brontë, 'Those children! Ah me. I can hardly bear to think of it, as yet the agony is too near, too intense, too awful, for present rejoicing even at the deliverance. And that smile on the young mother's face expresses such a sudden ecstasy of gratitude and joy that it quite unmans me to look at it. It is the most intense and pathetic utterance of pure human love I have ever met.'

As is often true, many critics did not see the same picture that was viewed by those who had paid the entrance fee. *The Times* called it 'a curiosity'; the *Daily News* proclaimed it Millais's 'latest escapade'; and the *Athenaeum* said it 'would be cheap for any public office wishing to save coals in bad weather'.

This year the corps of reviewers included an illustrious newcomer. His name was John Ruskin.

For years Ruskin had been asked for his views on various pictures at the Royal Academy. Now, in 1855, his opinions became available for a shilling. He issued the first of a series of annual pamphlets on some of the exhibited works, his *Academy Notes*.

In the 1855 preface, he stated, 'The following remarks have at least the virtue of *entire* impartiality . . . Some of the painters are my friends, and some quite other than friends. But the reader would be strangely deceived who, from the tone of the criticism, should endeavour to guess to which class a painter belonged.'

Ruskin was asserting the principle of critical 'disinterestedness' which Matthew Arnold would enunciate. Not much mid-century English criticism was disinterested. Even less was signed. But every issue of *Academy Notes* bore the author's name. As for disinterestedness, consider Ruskin's treatment of *The Rescue*: 'It is the only *great* picture this year, and it is *very* great. The immortal element is in it to the full . . . I have heard it was hastily finished, but except in the face of the child kissing the mother, it could not be much bettered. For there is a true sympathy between the impetuousness of the execution and the haste of the action.'

George Du Maurier, soon to become noted for cartoons in *Punch*, wrote amusingly to his brother, 'Happy Millais! fortunatus nimium sua si bona nôrit – who ran away with Ruskin's wife and became the ideal theme of Ruskin's pen. Some people say however that Ruskin has a sneaking gratitude – ayant l'honneur de connaître la dame en question, je m'abstiens de commentaires, but by jove *I'd* run away with her to be praised by Ruskin.'

Not long after the critique appeared, Millais wrote to Hunt, 'I can scarcely trust myself to speak of Ruskin, who certainly appears to me . . . to be the most wicked man I have known in my life. This I say *without hesitation and methodically.*'

* * *

One reason for Millais's uncharacteristic behaviour at the private view was the state of his nerves because of a coming event. 'Next month,' he wrote to Hunt, 'I shall be a *married* man. What think you of that? . . . Good gracious!; fancy me married, my old boy . . . All London knows of my marriage and comments upon it, as the best thing I *could* do, the *noblest*, the *vilest*, the most impudent, etc. etc.'

On 18 June, Wilkie Collins presided over a bachelor party for Millais. The next morning he left for Perth. During the period leading up to the wedding he wrote three letters to Charles Collins. In the first one he said, 'I feel quite a different person.' A habitual late riser, he was now up at seven every morning with 'nothing to do but walk with Effie and play bowls and take long rides through every kind of scenery conducive to a romantic effect'. In his second letter, he insisted that 'painting sounds like some vocation I remember to have followed three hundred years ago, so long has it been since I gave it a thought.' Then just before the event, he wrote, 'Fancy, my dear friend, what I am come to. I am able more clearly to understand it. We are both resigned to my fate . . . On Tuesday drink my health and wish me well.'

* * *

[148]

Under the heading 'Marriages' *The Times* of 6 July 1855 announced 'On the third instant, at Bowerswell, by the Rev. John Anderson, of Kinnoull, John Everett Millais, Esq., A.R.A., to Euphemia Chalmers Gray, eldest daughter of George Gray, Esq., writer, Perth.' The ceremony took place in the Bowerswell living room with William Millais and Gray family members as witnesses. Afterwards the couple left on a month-long Scottish wedding trip. I quote from their honeymoon correspondence:

11 July. [John Everett to George Gray, Jr., from Brodick, Isle of Arran] Effie has been combing her hair like a mermaid before her looking glass all afternoon.

27 July. [Effie to George, from Oban] After a long drive Everett had a bad nervous headache from exhaustion and excitement, but he recovered after tea and rest . . . He diverts me beyond everything. I don't think I have laughed so much since I was Alice's age [her ten-year-old sister]. His perception of character is wonderful, and we see very few people who are not perfect oddities.

As a painter, Millais's greatest interest was people and his best pictures uniformly demonstrate a wonderful perception of character.

29 July [John Everett to Harriet Collins, from Inverness] The Countess sings every morning and is very cheerful. We are the happiest couple in the world. I was wise . . . to venture. All my friends should follow my example. It doesn't matter now what people may think about the propriety of our marriage. If they only knew what a blessed change has come upon two bodies in this world, they would hold their tongues . . . Effie looks well again and is a strong woman. I am so proud of such a wife. Everybody looks at her and pays attention. I believe that she had forgotten everything connected with the Past and doesn't care to do anything but please me. No wife could be better and kinder . . . *Poor bachelors —* pity them.

29 July. [John Everett to Charles Collins, from Inverness] Effie is dressing for dinner, which she will do wherever she may be. The Countess is certainly the sharpest woman alive, without being objectionably knowing. She is really beautiful and improved by her marriage beyond all expression . . . I feel as if I possessed all the world and a great deal more. To be a married man is *very* great. I wonder at my earlier misgivings. I *was* and *you are quite mistaken* in your estimate of women. The creatures we artists meet go far to destroy the just estimation of a *lady's character*. Now I have a wife who I believe is more happy than any woman living. By George, Charlie, I am a truly favoured man. The delight of feeling a woman always about one part of oneself is indescribable. . . . I am convinced that as a married man I will show the public what I am capable of doing . . . Just think how few men in this world at my time of life are so blessed. It is really *astounding* [underlined three times] to me. I am convinced that with the *exception of imperfect creatures* all men should marry. It is one of God's laws.

1 August. [Effie to her mother, from Aberdeen] We had a lovely drive yesterday. . . . Everett had another headache. Seeing many things and new places just finishes him. I am rather the strongest of the two.'

1 August. [John Everett to George Gray, Jr., from Braemar] Effie is always entertaining unless she's in pershoot of historical knowledge, when she's relentless. I watched her harass a coachman cruelly about details of Scottish history *a propos* of some heap of stones, and then the coachman reveals his distress by driving wildly . . . Effie talks to everybody, and a French waiter will remember her as one of his conquests.

2 August. [John Everett to Mr Gray, from Braemar] I look forward to bringing back your altered girl with rosy cheeks, a good appetite and never a complaint. Now I am your man for backgammon, golf, or bowls.

4 August. [Effie to her mother, from Fortingall] For castles in the air, I think Everett is quite up to Papa, and he has begun to puff cigarettes.

On 6 August, the newlyweds moved into their new home, Annat Lodge, next door to the Grays' home, which they leased for a year. 'It was very strong and delightful,' Millais told Collins, 'going over the house with the servants peering at us to see their future master and mistress.' Probably feeling guilty for neglecting his art, he assured Collins that he would 'absolutely' begin work 'tomorrow'. Then he spent the entire next day fishing for salmon. Clearly Millais looked forward to the perquisites of his new life – hunting, shooting, fishing, and golfing. He wrote to Mr Gray, temporarily absent from Bowerswell, 'I have got so strong . . . that I shall be for ever striking golf balls into the town of St Andrew's [the golfing shrine was twenty-five miles away] and be compelled to desist from the game from the expenses incurred in the destruction of windows and other property.' He wasn't really an avid golfer and rarely mentioned the sport to anyone but Mr Gray, who, like most men living near St Andrew's, was a golfing enthusiast.

After a day revelling in his new sporting ventures during this month of August 1855, he wrote, perhaps defensively, to Collins, 'I am not at all sorry to be away from Art . . . The news of it quite maddens me. Write me news, *but not of Art*. Carefully avoid mention of everything connected with it.'

CHAPTER 14

1856

CONTRARY to what might have been inferred from his correspondence, Millais did not actually neglect his art. He had never before had more than three paintings at a Summer Exhibition. Only once, in 1851, did he send three major pictures. Now in his first show as a married man, he would have five entries, four of them major.

Early in the year Hunt had returned from the Holy Land. In February, Millais wrote to him about his current creativity: 'I could never have done in London what I have painted here in four months. Marriage is the best cure for that wretched *lingering* over one's work which racks the brains and makes one miserable . . . I cannot help touting for matrimony. It is such a healthy, manly, and right kind of life. I feel I am fulfilling at least one duty, with less fear of becoming selfish and a disappointed groaner, with a responsibility of a household on my shoulders . . . After all, a man by himself plays but half of his part in this world and is ignorant of much which he should know. A man does not live this life over again, and he should not shun one of its chief responsibilities. *Man was not intended to live alone.*'

Effie was also writing about married life, in slightly different tones, to Rawdon Brown: 'I had so fatiguing a day today. Everett has been poorly with a bilious attack, and he complains so much and requires so much attention that I am beginning to feel the want of sleep. Otherwise I cannot be thankful enough that I have been so strong . . . When Everett is working, I read aloud and play the piano as much as he wishes.'

Effie probably did more for her husband than read aloud and play the piano. She was, I believe, the creative force behind the most innovative picture he had yet painted, a substantive and stylistic breakthrough.

'He wished to paint a picture full of beauty without a subject,' Effie wrote in a briefly kept diary. What emerged was *Autumn Leaves*, four girls piling leaves, apparently for burning, with a background of blue hills and a sunset sky. It's a self-contained work independent of dramatic, literary, historical, or legendary associations, completed nine years before Albert Moore's first 'non-story' painting, eleven years before James Whistler's first 'symphony'.

Never had Millais even thought of a subject picture without a clearly defined story. Rarely since the formation of the PRB had he begun a painting until completing days or even weeks of research. And except for *The Rescue*, done hastily for want of an alternative, he had not had a contemporary subject. This abrupt change, in my opinion, could not have been self-generating. Intuitively, I am convinced that Effie was responsible for *Autumn Leaves*. She thought it was counter-productive to agonise over a subject. 'Take an ordinary incident and get on with it.' This, in a nutshell, was her attitude.

Effie's influence wasn't confined to subject matter. She had strong feelings about frittering away time over a picture. Not coincidentally, *Autumn Leaves* was completed more quickly than any of the earlier major works. Instead of trying to reproduce every single leaf, he painted the whole scene freely, semi-impressionistically, and rapidly. Seemingly in no time at all it was done. He then moved on to another picture.

This altered methodology was necessary, and not just because he was pressured by his wife. When he began *Autumn Leaves*, in October 1855, Effie was in her second month of pregnancy. Before the next Exhibition was a month old, he would be a father. Punctilious Pre-Raphaelitism was out of the question. He hadn't abandoned his ideals. He still regarded himself as a Pre-Raphaelite painter, faithful to nature, but he was no longer an exact copyist. Instead of imitative truth, *Autumn Leaves* represented a truthful impression of nature. This was a more sophisticated type of Pre-Raphaelitism. But it was still Pre-Raphaelitism. Actually, if his art did not stagnate, it would inevitably change. No innovating style can remain unaltered without becoming as immutable as that which it had opposed. Even though his motives may have been questionable, he was doing the right thing.

* * *

Millais's best picture of 1856 was *The Blind Girl*. Like *Autumn Leaves*, its subject was simple, a poor blind woman, about nineteen years old, holding a concertina as she sits with a younger girl by the side of a road. Farm animals and village houses punctuate the background beneath a brilliant rainbow. Another manifestation of his compassion for simple human beings, it is a touching scene, of sentiment, not sentimentality.

His two remaining major works tell conventional 'stories'. *L'Enfant du Regiment* (sometimes called *The Random Shot*), a scene from the French Revolution, shows a little girl hit by a stray bullet. Covered by a soldier's coat, she is lying asleep against a statue at the entrance of a church. *Peace Concluded*, his largest current painting, was crassly commercial. It shows 'a wounded officer, returned from the Crimea, and his wife reclining on a sofa, their two children playing beside them. The officer holds a copy of *The Times* announcing the end of the war; the children are playing with a Noah's Ark.'

Millais's major offerings of 1856 were thus two potboilers and two works of sincerity and integrity, not a bad ratio. (His fifth entry showed a three-year-old boy inspecting a book of John Leech's woodcuts.)

* * *

'Here I am, safe with my pictures,' Millais wrote from London on sending-in day. 'I am in high spirits and jolly . . . Now, my darling, take "awful" good care of yourself and particularly be careful about crossing that run of water between Bowerswell and home. That place haunts me.'

The letter was signed, 'Your affectionate *husband* [underlined six times].'

After his paintings had been hung, he said:

Nothing could be better. The largest [*Peace Concluded*] is next to Edwin Landseer's in the large room. 'Autumn Leaves' is in the middle room, beautifully seen. The 'Blind Girl' is in the third room on the line, of course. The child on the tomb is also there, beautifully hung. The little portrait is in the middle room on the line. Altogether I have never been treated so kindly.

This was only what he deserved:

The success of my pictures is far beyond my most sanguine expectations. Now that they are in their frames, they certainly astonish me. They *must* without doubt put me as much above all other painters as any one man can get. I wish, my darling, you were with me, but perhaps the excitement of this truly surprising success would do you harm . . . My brother artists are all in a fix and imagine that my pictures are the result of years instead of a few months. They look nearly perfect.

A couple of days later he wrote:

I know every picture in the place, and I get greater comfort every day I see my own in comparison with the others . . . This great mercy from God is very awful, and I cannot help feeling a little frightened. It is so alarmingly conspicuous to me in everything I undertake that I fear for a turn in my fortune. I cannot help seeing how differently he deals with the many about us.

Everyone, he added, was wild about his work:

Indeed, it is *startling* [underlined twice] the admiration my pictures occasion. Really, no words can tell you the impression they make upon people. All other years pass into absolute insignificance after this . . . The report [of his pictures] is already all over London . . . Rossetti visited the Academy and was *aghast* [underlined twice] with admiration.

Rossetti told Allingham, '*Autumn Leaves* is very lovely and *The Blind Girl* is one of the most touching and perfect things I know, but *Peace Concluded* is a very stupid affair to suit the day.'

[155]

After the opening, Millais wrote, 'I never expected such complete success as the pictures are making. People cannot *get near* them, but *every other picture* can be seen immediately ... *Everybody* are [sic] *enthusiastic*. The only people who are silent are the Academicians.'

Autumn Leaves was as popular as any of the others, but it perplexed some reviewers, who tried to find 'deep meaning' in it. This, for example, is from the *Art Journal*: 'Shall these withered leaves be read as a natural consummation, a type of death – that the human forms in their youth signify life, or shall the twilight of the day describe the twilight of the year? The figures represent, perhaps, priestesses of the seasons offering on the great altar of the earth a burnt sacrifice in propitiation of winter. In what vein of mystic poetry will the picture be read?'

Millais initially was amused by nonsense like this. But after a while he began somehow to agree that his painting was indeed more than just four young women and a pile of leaves. Late in the year, two or three months after the show had closed, Fred Stephens wrote this for an American journal:

Of all Millais's pictures, unquestionably the most impressive is *Autumn Leaves*. By the margin of a valley-wood stand four fate-like children burning leaves . . . The sun has sunk and dark night cometh, the whole valley is full of a luminous mist, out of which stark, denuded poplars rise at intervals, standing sharp against the sky, which has been golden, but now fadeth to a dun brassiness, while in the zenith is the black-purple of night: 'For the night cometh in which no man can work.' [John, 9:4] The children's faces are turned from the glowing west, and are in the shadow; there is a strange impassivity upon them, as if they knew not what they did, senseless instruments of fate; they gather the leaves and cast them upon the pile, half unconscious of the awful threat:

'For wickedness burneth as the fire; it shall devour the briers and thorns, and shall kindle in the thickets of the forest; and they shall mount up like the lifting up of smoke.

'Through the wrath of the Lord of hosts is the land darkened, and the people shall be as the fuel of the fire; no man shall spare his brother.' [Isaiah, 9:18–19]

[156]

Nothing more awful than this picture can be conceived, or out of fewer materials have we ever seen so much expressed.

This is a splendid example of critical humbug. But instead of smiling, Millais sent Stephens this response:

You certainly understand what I intended. I nearly put in the catalogue an extract from the Psalms of the same character as you have quoted, but was prevented by a fear it would be considered an affectation. I am always insulted when people regard the picture as a simple little domestic episode, as I intended it to arouse by its solemnity the deepest religious reflection. I chose the subject of burning leaves as most calculated to produce this feeling, and the picture was thought of and begun with that object *only* in view. These kinds of pictures are more difficult to paint than any other as they are not to be achieved by faithful attention to Nature. Such effects are so transient and occur so rarely that the rendering becomes a matter of feeling and recollection . . . I know I am not accused of very deep religious reflections. However as you have certainly read my thoughts in this matter, I do not hesitate to acknowledge so much. *Tear this up* as I rather feel ashamed of having written this.

Perhaps at the end he realised that what he had written was ludicrous. He had also, without doubt, been affected by comments on Holman Hunt's principal entry. Hunt had returned from Palestine with a number of drawings and one major painting, of a solitary goat standing in an exactingly particularised spot of wilderness. It was called *The Scapegoat*.

This picture exemplified the ultimate in Pre-Raphaelitism. Most of his friends and colleagues loved it. Ford Madox Brown, for example, wrote in his diary that it 'requires to be seen to believe. Only then can it be understood how, by the might of genius, out of an old goat, and some saline incrustations, can be made one of the most tragic and impressive works in the annals of art.' Partly because of the dangers and hardships Hunt had endured, this picture easily drew the most attention at the private view. At the show itself, the *Art Journal* reported, it 'constantly attracts scores of gazers'. The critical response was mixed. Everyone took note of the effort that had gone into *The Scapegoat*. Several writers, however, suggested that it wasn't really worth the trouble. The *Athenaeum*'s reviewer could see only 'a dying goat which has no more interest for us than the sheep that furnished yesterday's dinner'.

Hunt's answer was that he had not spent two years in Palestine just to paint a goat. The animal was symbolically significant, and he underlined this by attaching to his picture frame two Biblical verses: 'And the goat shall bear upon him all their iniquities into a land not inhabited.' (Leviticus, 16:22) 'Barely he hath borne our griefs and carried our sorrows, yet we did esteem him stricken, smitten of God and afflicted.' (Isaiah, 53:4) For months Hunt continued to emphasise this point. On 10 November, he wrote to Millais, 'I am sanguine that [*The Scapegoat*] may be a means of leading any reflecting Jew to see a reference to the Messiah as he was, and not as they understand, a temporal King.'

Hunt's letter reached Millais at almost the exact time that he received a copy of Stephens's over-imaginative reading of *Autumn Leaves*. In advancing his own fanciful interpretation of his picture, including the surprising news that he had intended to include Biblical passages with it, he had to have been influenced by Hunt.

Since the opening of the Exhibition, Millais had been preoccupied with Hunt. He resented the attention accorded *The Scapegoat*, and he was especially irritated by comments on Hunt's position in the Pre-Raphaelite movement. After contrasting the skimping of details in *Autumn Leaves* with the careful attention to everything in *The Scapegoat*, the *Daily News* called Millais 'the *quondam* leader of the brotherhood, who had lost that distinction to Mr Hunt'; the *Morning Advertiser* said that 'the reigning brother of the school is certainly Mr W.H. Hunt, and the acme of the school is displayed in "The Scapegoat"'; the *Illustrated London News* referred to Hunt as 'the Agamemnon of the Pre-Raphaelites'.

Millais was incensed, but he could do nothing but belittle Hunt in letters to Effie. 'Poor Hunt,' he wrote, 'returned with not so much work as I have done in a few months and, not of the excellence his friends expected. His work disappoints all, most of all me, for I expected as good or better than his work of five years back . . . The comparison which has often been made of our relative merits ceases forever with this year's [Exhibition]. There can be no more mentioning us in the same breath.' A day or two later he gloated, 'Poor Hunt has not found a purchaser for his "Scapegoat" in spite of the absurd lowness of his price, £400, for a highly finished picture, *twice* my largest size. This speaks volumes as to whether his work is more deserving of praise than mine.'

Eventually he obtained his £400, Millais meanwhile realising for his pictures more than seven times that amount. Additionally, he told Mr Gray, 'I sold a little sketch for 35gn., the *only* unsold one. People are as greedy for my things as a pike for a minnow . . . I might have got more for the "Blind Girl" [sold for £400] as it is a great favourite.' This last piece of information did not please Effie. Nor was she happy about the sale of *Peace Concluded*.

Effie's letters to her husband in London during the fifties have mostly disappeared, doubtlessly destroyed by one or more descendants (for reasons best known to them). Like readers of Browning's 'Andrea del Sarto', who must infer Lucrezia's comments from Andrea's words, gestures, and movements, so we must conjecture from John Everett's letters what Effie had written.

In the matter at hand, they had decided on £1000 for *Peace Concluded*, from his Liverpool patron John Miller. When John Everett accepted £900, Effie was piqued. Millais explained, or rationalised, his action:

I made up my mind to get *2000* for the three, and I have got it. [*Autumn Leaves*, *The Blind Girl*, and *Peace Concluded*. The others had already been sold.] I must not be greedy. If I put by three thousand this year, I will be doing uncommonly well, and I see every reason to expect it, seeing I have every hope of getting a thousand for copyrights. [Only the copyright owners, usually the artist, could have a painting engraved. A picture buyer often paid additionally for the copyright.] I must repeat, my darling, that *nine* hundred is a very large price, particularly as the 'Order of Release' was only *four* hundred. Raising prices is always done gradually. You may rest assured that I will not be taken in by any man. [Miller] is delighted, and I shall lose nothing by having taken off a hundred . . . I did not like to appear *grasping*.

Some years later, lecturing at the Academy, he made his position clear on this point: 'An artist should be careful not to ask too much . . . He should always err on the right side if he is in any doubt, and under-selling will invariably tell *in his favour* in disposing later productions.'

* * *

In the summer of 1856 John Millais for the first time was hyper-sensitive to criticism. 'On the whole,' he told Effie, after about ten days in London, 'the critics are worse than ever, but it really doesn't matter much beyond making ignorant people say very foolish things . . . Leech made me look at some to see how absurd they were.'

This was a strange remark. The reviews were predominantly favour-able. Ruskin was again generous. He called *Autumn Leaves* 'by far the most poetical work the painter has yet conceived, and also the first instance, as far as I know, of a perfectly painted twilight'. On *Peace Concluded* he was embarrassingly extravagant: 'This picture is as brilliant in invention as it is consummate in executive power [and] will rank in the future among the world's best masterpieces. I see no limit to what the painter may hope in the future to achieve; Titian himself could hardly head him now.'

Millais had said that he would never read anything that Ruskin wrote, but he did see *The Times*. Its reviewer said *Autumn Leaves* marked an 'advance in his style' of treating objects in nature, and he compared the picture to *The Return of the Dove to the Ark* of 1851: 'There every straw was painted with a minuteness which it was painful to follow; here the leaves are given with great truth and force.' The writer also called *The Blind Girl* 'full of feeling', *L'Enfant du Regiment* 'sweet', the *Portrait of a Gentleman* 'capital', and *Peace Concluded* 'both very good and very bad'.

Only hours after the appearance of this notice, Millais wrote to his wife:

I hope this will come to hand before you see the 'Times', which is more wickedly against me than ever. However I will discover who writes these articles and make some effort to stop his further writing. It is *well understood* that the criticism is not '*above board*', and that there is more than ignorance in the man. I was not much distressed, as it has been my fate from the first and will probably be to the last to meet with injurious treatment from newspapers. A young man doesn't get £*900* for a picture without an attempt at detraction . . . There is more *underhand* villainy which must sooner or later come to light. I am not at all sure it doesn't spring from the *Academy itself*. Indeed I think there is every reason *to suppose that it does* . . . The feeling is generally expressed *in my presence* that the influence is so great against me that I need not look for any good criticism from the Times for many years to come.

This is extraordinary not just because of his reaction to a mostly friendly critique. How could he complain of consistently bad press treatment? Except for the years of notoriety, 1850 and 1851, he had regularly had good notices. How could he have charged the Academy with plotting against him? He was the youngest ever ARA, and his current pictures were all on the line.

His belief in an Academic conspiracy became obsessive. In his next letter he wrote:

The envy, and this determined cabal against me, make me long to return. In one word, I have the whole of the R. Acad. against me . . . The only people who are silent [about his pictures] are the Academicians. Not a kind word was said of 'Peace' by any of them. They all insulted me by admiring the child's portrait, not three inches square. This is always the way with them. They avoid mentioning the larger, important works. I never saw anything so well arranged as the treatment by the RA of my works. Every year it is the same . . . Certainly there *never* was such cunningly divined *machinations against any character*.

Effie, surely astonished by these fulminations, apparently asked why the RA's were conspiring against him. 'I believe *sincerely* [underlined twice],' he told her, 'that the chief reason why my pictures are so picked to pieces is from their being out of the scale of received conventionalities.'

She probably reminded him that only *Autumn Leaves* was unconventional. He then produced another explanation:

I think one *great reason* for their opposition is the sudden great *increase in my prices* because there is such an extraordinary demand for my work. Such a tribute to my pictures, when others have only one or two men desirous of purchasing theirs, for a quarter of the sum, makes the profession generally mad with jealousy.

'I have great faith in the mass of the public, who are the only *really* disinterested critics,' Millais had said after the opening when crowds gathered around his work. But then he changed his mind about the voice of the people. He heard 'such frightful remarks' from 'hopeless ignoramuses' that he believed public opinion to be worthless, and 'not just at the RA'. 'It is *just the same* with music and literature. Last night I saw a man make a complete *buffoon* of himself with wretched comic songs, and the audience were *screaming* with *enjoyment*. And at the Haymarket Theatre the old worn out jokes and bad acting were received with enthusiasm, and parts meant for pathos mistaken for fun and laughed at accordingly.' Maybe only future generations would appreciate his work: 'It's a matter of time, perhaps beyond our lives, but ultimately truth must prevail.'

Clearly Millais was suffering from pananoia, brought on, I think, by loneliness.

As soon as he was in London, he wrote, 'I am already anxious to get back with you. I cannot bear being away from you.'

A couple of days later he poured out his feelings:

I am really sick all day for want of you near me. What I used to feel for you when I wrote from here before my marriage is trebled now, and all day I tingle with love for you, my [illegible word] Effie. My darling, I love you so dearly you ought to be the happiest woman living. This absence tells me how much I love you, for it is really suffering to be away from you, and I am sure you will never get me away again without you . . . What a treat it will be coming back. From that moment you will feel how much I depend upon you. All last night I was longing for the moment of seeing you again. If possible, after this parting, we shall be happier than before, for this tells us both how much we love each other. Do for my comfort write me *every day* [underlined twice]. As soon as I can get away, I will, for life is too short for us to be away from each other when it may be otherwise. I feel sickish *all day* [underlined twice] without you . . . My darling, I think of you all hours in the day and night and shall not be comfortable until I return . . . I am miserable without you.

* * *

But he wasn't always wallowing in self-pity. Every evening he went out. One morning he wrote to Effie, 'I had a little dinner party of eight at the Garrick. We *all drank to your health*, my darling, and I need not tell you how I felt. Everybody, *all ladies* [underlined twice] ask so kindly after you. When I meet anybody who forgets to ask after you they immediately fall in my estimation, but on the whole people are very thoughtful and kind.'

The Garrick was one of London's newer clubs, founded in 1831 in King Street, Covent Garden. Its charter announced it as a club 'in which actors and men of education and refinement might meet on equal terms'. (Does this imply that an actor was probably not educated or refined?) Also, according to the charter, 'Patrons of drama and its professors are to be brought together and a rendevous offered to literary men.' Most of London's leading actors were members, along with prominent writers, including Dickens, Thackeray, Trollope, and Charles Reade. Familiarly called 'the G', it was less formal and more sociable than most of the other clubs. Its casualness was captivating. Thackeray called it 'the dearest little place in the world'. He was a club fixture, as was Millais, who regularly used the library, the writing room, the dining room, and the card and billiard room. It was his second home.

Even apart from the Garrick, he led an active night life. He attended concerts and 'heard delightful music, quartets, and good singing'. He watched a troupe of Spanish dancers at the Haymarket. He had an uproarious time at the Victoria, the Waterloo Bridge Road theatre which became the Old Vic: 'We went for the fun of the thing, to see a regular out and out melodrama, and we were not disappointed. We got a box for five shillings and laughed so immoderately that we were nearly turned out.'

Toward the end of his stay, he felt guilty for enjoying himself while Effie was home alone awaiting childbirth: 'I am quite tired of this kind of excitement, but I should be miserable without it away from you.'

* * *

On 30 May 1856, Millais posted a two-sentence note to Holman Hunt: 'Just a line to say another PRB has come into the world. My wife was taken ill last night and is now the mother of a fine little boy who will be called Everett.'

CHAPTER 15

1856–57

'MY baby robs me of a great deal of my time,' Millais wrote to Hunt. 'I am continually in the nursery watching its progress and its ever-changing expression.' The man who had often objected to children was a tenderhearted father. 'I find myself approaching the confines of imbecility,' he told Hunt. 'I find the greatest pleasure in watching my boy in his shoutings or comical ways. When I was called upon as a bachelor to enter into the feelings of fond parents who delightedly watched the movements of their children, I used to think how far gone they were in obliviousness of the outside world. Now I understand this and pay visits on tiptoes to his nursery to kiss my baby before I got to bed.'

He ended with a sentence that could not have pleased Hunt: 'If my work next year is less careful, you will know the reason.'

Millais's work for 1857 was not less careful than in 1856, but there was less of it. His output was reduced to three pictures. To his credit, they were major works. One of them was blatantly commercial, following upon the success of *Peace Concluded*. Called *News from Home*, it showed an officer in the Crimea reading a letter from his wife. One reviewer properly called it as 'an innocent little bit of very common claptrap'.

The other two paintings deserve more attention. The impulse for one of them came from William Prescott's recently published *History of the Reign of Philip II of Spain*. Prescott emphasises Philip's avariciousness and describes in detail the intrigue, corruption, and violence of his regime, carried out under the aegis of the Catholic

Church. 'How can any one talk about the *good* old times?' Millais asked Hunt. 'The cruelties committed in the middle ages are so *extravagantly fearful* that they make a hell hereafter absolutely inevitable with justice. The unscrupulous murderings of defenceless creatures, the gloating over torture, and the indifference to the most stirring entreaties of starving widows and children, were committed in the name of sanctity. I have felt all afternoon desirous of pulling Philip II's royal nose.'

The upshot was *The Escape of a Heretic*, designed as a typical incident in Philip's reign. A beautiful young woman, Millais's first since 1853, is in prison wearing *auto-da-fe* clothing. She is a convicted heretic. Her lover, in the uniform of a jailer, whom he has bound and gagged, has come just in time to bring about her escape.

The idea was superior to its realisation. This was no *Huguenot*. The scene is energetic, but instead of drama we have melodrama. The rescuer is laughable. His gestures are theatrical and his expression is grotesquely ludicrous. This is something that might have been performed at the Victoria Theatre.

Millais's major work of the year measured forty-nine by sixty-seven inches and was the largest easel picture of his career. Entitled *A Dream of the Past. Sir Isumbras at the Ford*, it shows an elderly knight carrying two small children across a stream. Beyond, there is a fully detailed background.

The catalogue entry would contain a passage of what appears to be Middle English verse:

> . . . and als he wente by a woode schawe,
> Thare mette he with a lytille knave
> Came rynnande him agayne
> Gramercy, faire syr Isumbras,
> Have pitie on us in this case,
> And lifte us uppe for Marie's grace!
> N'as never childe so fayre
> Theretoe of a mayden he was ware
> That over floude ne mighte not fare,
> Sir Ysumbras stoopede him thare,
> And uppe ahent hem twayne.

There is a metrical romance called *Sir Isumbras*, but these lines are not part of it. They were written a few weeks before sending-in day by the versatile Tom Taylor.

As the Exhibition approached, Millais was upbeat. He was enjoying the joke of passing off Tom Taylor's verse as the real thing. He was certain that *Sir Isumbras* would be a big success. And this year he wouldn't be in London alone. Even though pregnant again, Effie was his travelling companion. Early in April, they moved into rooms in Savile Row. This was to be a trial run to see if she could reside in London without feeling uncomfortable. Then, too, she probably wanted to be sure that the picture fetched the best possible prices. Effie remained until just before the opening. While she was there, two paintings were sold, each for an excellent figure. Indeed, *News from Home* was Millais's best sale thus far, £1000 without the copyright. The big one, however, *Sir Isumbras*, had not been claimed. Its unconventional subject and mammoth dimensions led potential purchasers to hesitate. They would await the reviews.

*   *   *

When he sent off his pictures, Millais was convinced that *Sir Isumbras* would be the hit of the show. A painting of this size could not go unnoticed, and before the Exhibition had begun it attracted much attention. But it was not the sort of attention he had in mind. In its Saturday pre-opening remarks, the *Illustrated London News* predicted that *Sir Isumbras* 'will probably excite more than customary controversy'. The controversy began on that day. The *Morning Chronicle*'s reviewer asked, 'What can we say to Mr Millais? If he had wished to show the inherent error of his school he could not have shown it more glaringly. The Knight is not a man – he is gilt ornament. The horse is not a horse – it is an illustration to a mediaeval book.'

During the first week of the show, *Sir Isumbras* was sweepingly assailed. The *Daily News* called it 'grotesque in the extreme'. The *Saturday Review* saw 'a rocking-horse, and an ugly rocking-horse, too'. The *Athenaeum* said that a 'pudgy and dwarfish' knight was riding 'such an animal as Noah would have shut the door against'. The *Illustrated Times* spoke of 'a monstrosity' that 'makes you doubt whether to charge the artist with imbecility or impertinence'.

Millais was not disheartened. He had faith enough in *Sir Isumbras* to turn down a dealer's offer of £800.

'All those whose opinions I care about,' he told Effie, 'think the picture *far* beyond what I have hitherto done. I find the public so *tremendously* admire it that I must get at least *1200*. Leech and Rossetti think it far the best thing I have done and advise me not to sell it for less than *1500*. How stupid these dealers are.'

He was particularly emboldened by a report he had received concerning the journalistic powerhouse: 'I hear all the Times men are enchanted with my picture. One of them only yesterday said that the Knight was the finest thing in the show. I scarcely think they will avoid following out their promises.'

Three days later, *The Times* published an extended commentary on *Sir Isumbras*. This picture, the reviewer declared, 'sins so conspicuously and unmistakably against positive laws of proportion and light that we can scarcely believe Mr Millais is blind to the worst of his mistakes'. Point by point, paragraph by paragraph, the writer ticked off flaws which 'rob the work of any redeeming merit'. He ended by saying, 'We are fearful for the future of this rarely gifted young painter.'

The next day saw the appearance of John Ruskin's third *Academy Notes*.

One sentence in the preface was a forewarning: 'The Pre-Raphaelite cause has been doubly betrayed, by the mistimed deliberation of one of its leaders and the inefficient haste of another; we regret that the pictures of Holman Hunt were too late for the Exhibition and that those of Everett Millais were in time for it.'

In the body of his pamphlet, Ruskin derided *News from Home* with a question: 'Does Mr Millais imagine that Highlanders at the Crimea always put on new uniforms when reading letters?' He referred to *The Escape of a Heretic* as 'at once coarse and ghastly, exaggerated and obscure'.

Ruskin reached a crowning point with an analysis of *Sir Isumbras*, consuming five and a half pages of a thirty-three-page booklet, the longest discourse on a single picture in any edition of *Academy Notes*. It didn't contain one friendly syllable. Ruskin even mocked the poetry in the catalogue: 'I am not sure whether the bitterest enemies of Pre-Raphaelitism have yet accused it of expecting to cover its errors by

[168]

describing them in bad English.' The painting itself illustrated a 'change in manner from the years of "Ophelia" and "Mariana"' which 'is not merely Fall – it is Catastrophe, not merely a loss of power but a reversal of principle'. After detailing at length its deficiencies, Ruskin concluded, 'The time has come when this painter must choose whether his eminence will make him conspicuous in honour or in ruin.'

Millais told Effie, 'JR's pamphlet is out and I hear blows me up awfully, but he has lost such cast in London among *all* circles that it doesn't matter one bit. [Actually, his standing as a critic was higher than ever.] . . . I have been to the Cosmopolitan once or twice, and all the members appear unusually civil, which is always a good sign as to one's success.'

No one from the Cosmopolitan, however, nor apparently anyone else, thought about owning *Sir Isumbras*. It remained unsold until late 1858, when it was bought by Millais's friend from the Garrick, novelist Charles Reade. Holman Hunt said he paid £400. John Guille Millais said the price was £300.

* * *

In his last letter to Effie from London, Millais rationalised his failure to sell *Sir Isumbras*: 'There is no encouragement for large pictures. I find all men dislike the great size of the Knight picture . . . Next year I will do only small pictures. It will pay us *double*.'

During the rest of 1857 and most of 1858 his pictures were so small that he exhibited nothing at Trafalgar Square in 1858. His work consisted mainly of illustrations for magazines and books.

It is not surprising that he turned to illustrating, and not just because of *Sir Isumbras*. The so-called golden age of black-and-white drawings had begun, and nearly all artists were accepting commissions from publishers. There were good reasons for doing so. Illustrators didn't have to look for a subject, nor were they concerned about sales. And the artists were well paid.

John Millais's first illustration had been done in 1851, the frontispiece to Wilkie Collins's novelette *Mr Wray's Cash-Box*. This was only a favour to a friend. His illustrating career really began with the publication of Edward Moxon's edition of Tennyson's poems, in May

1857, the month of his Trafalgar Square failure. While his painting was being slashed, his illustrations were getting a good reception. And so, for the time being, he would be an illustrator.

He easily adapted to his new role. Joseph Pennell, an American best known for his relationship with Whistler, himself a fine creator of black-and-white drawings, accounted for Millais's success as an illustrator: 'He possessed a remarkable fitness to become the eye and hand of another man's brain. He did not have persistent visions of his own to come between himself and the page and lead him, as they led Rossetti, into fantastic embroideries upon the text. Millais saw in the reading what the average Englishman saw, and he put it down.'

The Moxon volume was a case in point. A recent biographer of Tennyson noted that he 'disliked having artists distort his words and took them seriously to task if any illustrations contained a single detail that could not be plainly justified by the words of the poems'. He loved Millais's work, but, Rossetti told Allingham, 'Tennyson loathes mine.' William Rossetti explained this reaction: 'It must be said that himself only [Grabriel Rossetti], and not Tennyson, was his guide. He drew what he chose, taking from his author's text nothing more than a hint and an opportunity.' Millais, however, was closely in touch with, and a faithful interpreter of, the poet's work.

Actually as an illustrator Millais was only duplicating what he had done in his early years as a painter. *Pizarro, Elgiva, Isabella, Ferdinand Lured by Ariel, The Woodman's Daughter, A Huguenot,* and *Ophelia* might properly be called top-grade 'illustrations'.

* * *

Millais was a first-rate illustrator, and he was conscientious about his work. He would never, however, regard black-and-white drawings as more than a lucrative sideline. A superb colourist, he could not have felt otherwise. Then there was the matter of prestige. Even the best illustrators were regarded as hacks. Good painters were West End celebrities.

Millais's true life's work was painting and, while fulfilling publishers' commissions, he found time for his real calling. Thus in the autumn of 1857, while loaded down with black-and-white work, he attempted the most demanding painting he had ever undertaken. He told Hunt about it:

'I have been groaning over a night, candlelight subject . . . I now have misgivings of everything I begin. I think the public require and ask for very simple treatment, everything so *evident* that a design which wants a moon to show it is night will be taken for the representation of a London fog, and when the moon is introduced the chances are it will be taken for the sun. I hate candlelight effects, but I find myself in the middle of one before I know where I am, a regular Dutch painter's lodge, only it hasn't an old woman selling a fish under a tent, as those masters invariably favour us with . . . I am going to get some artificial good spirits by drinking some whiskey and water.'

One of Millais's current illustrations was, in fact, a night scene, which might have caused him to 'groan', but it would certainly not have led him to 'have misgivings of everything I begin'. And he hardly would have erected 'a regular Dutch painter's lodge' to do an illustration. It is extremely unlikely that by himself Millais would have thought of doing this. And so it was probably at the urging of Effie who, as Ruskin's wife, had heard all too much about Turner's evening scenes, that he had been led from his illustration to attempt this moonlight painting some fifteen years before the appearance of the first of James Whistler's nocturnes.

* * *

Late in the autumn of 1857 Mr and Mrs Charles Dickens announced the engagement of their daughter Kate to the man who had courted her for some time, Charles Collins. A little earlier, writing to Millais from the Dickens' country house, Collins had expressed envy of his future father-in-law because of his fame. Millais responded straight from the heart:

I agree with you as to the enviable *worldly* position of your host, but when he gets so much wordly comfort and adulation, you may depend upon it that if his mind is prone to uneasiness he will find quite enough to destroy his peace in the inconstancy of public favour. *Present* [underlined twice] success is, *all in all*, the only thing to make such a man happy, and his last book [*Little Dorrit*] I hear from all sides is '*a falling off*' – *that horrible* [last two words underlined twice] expression which the kind hearted public always make when they have not received so much pleasure as they have before from the same man. The knowledge of this is enough to upset his equanimity. . . . The real happiness he seems to get is out of his family, and, I suspect, very little from his profession. His reputation will be made a scourge against all his future efforts, and a man gets to hate his own successful works when they are continually brought up against him as reflections on present shortcomings, as though he could go on writing every year fresh 'Oliver Twists' when the chief element of its excellence is in its novelty. . . . One great advantage he has over painters is that he can turn his critics into ridicule, where the unfortunate artist is compelled to sit and bear it.

*   *   *

The four trial weeks in Savile Row had been without unpleasantness, and so Effie and John Everett would move to London. They were both frightfully bored in Annat Lodge. In a letter to Hunt, explaining why he hadn't written recently, Millais said, 'The fact is I have really nothing to say. Nothing ever happens and I never go near the town of Perth.' London was where the action was.

On 27 October, Millais went down, and his wife wrote to Rawdon Brown, 'Whenever Everett finds a house I shall follow . . . I hope we get a nice house for six months and during that time look for a permanent residence. At Kensington there are many nice villas, but too many artists. The Little Holland House society is too much for my practical turn. [A small mansion near the junction of Kensington High Street and Holland Road, Little Holland House was a popular gathering place for writers and painters.] Poets and artists have their own place in the world like other people, but Tennyson and Wattsworship is very disgusting. Everett gets it also and he dislikes it as I do. It is such nonsense.'

Far from Kensington, they leased for six months a three-storey dwelling at 16 York Terrace, Regent's Park.

From the start of their residence, they had a busy social life. The high point occurred on the evening of 23 December at a party in the Onslow Square home of the sculptor Baron Carlo Marochetti. The guests included Sir Walter and Lady Trevelyan, whom Effie had not seen since the summer of 1853. Lady Trevelyan walked over to Effie and extended her hand. Effie turned her back and began to converse with another guest.

On the next day, Millais wrote to Mr Gray, 'Effie must have told you of yesterday's recontre with the Trevelyans, when if she has the slightest feeling of *retaliation* must have been gratifying to her feelings. She is but mortal if she felt a naughty pleasure in refusing to accept the hand of Lady T.'

What had Lady Trevelyan done to deserve this? She and her husband had not abandoned John Ruskin nor joined in the condemnation of him. They hadn't said or done anything contrary to John Everett or Effie. They just remained loyal to an old friend.

That was enough for Effie.

CHAPTER 16

1858–59

SINCE they could not afford to live luxuriously in London, the Millais did not renew their lease when it expired. They returned to Scotland a few days before the opening of the 1858 Exhibition.

A few weeks later, John Everett demonstrated that he was still a loyal PRB. Someone suggested that the expanded Pre-Raphaelite circle of artists should boycott the Academy and hold a competing show. Asked by Hunt for his opinion, he replied: 'I think withdrawing ourselves a *great mistake* because they gain by *avoiding the comparison*, and we would lose by battling against each other. We should *court* comparison and exhibit with the rest, which is the only way we can show our superiority. I believe nothing would please the general body of painters better than our separating ourselves.'

The letter ended thus: 'Do you plan to go to Egypt again? I wish you would go at the head of an army and destroy all Mahomedans. The brutes, they are massacring all Christians they can get hold of.'

When Hunt wrote again, he was bemoaning the fact that he painted so slowly. For four years he had worked on one picture, *The Finding of Christ in the Temple*. He wondered if it would ever be finished.

My poor dear old boy [Millais replied], what is the matter with you? I know *too well* your sensations. I have them, and perhaps they are true. What of it? Let us be thankful that we are as well to do as we are. Certainly I have no reason to complain of my position with all its anxieties and difficulties and I think I may say the same for you. After the Temple picture is done, 'put money in thy purse,' and then a wife in thy house . . . Don't you think you would greatly ease your mind if you would begin another kind of picture altogether with the determination of *doing it right off*. Rapidity is not incompatible with *perfectness* if the objects chosen are simple . . . My wife, who is reading your letter, told me *peremptorily* to cheer you up and command you *instantly* to finish the 'Temple'. Why you had nothing to do to it when I saw it last, all drawn and colour complete with nothing wrong. As a matter of course you will see defects, but where is the work without them? No amount of care will shield you from error . . . You are a hopeless fellow as long as you work so hard. Why can't you take a holiday like other folk and feel independent for a week. *Kick art and pictures to the wind* and enjoy yourself in this very short life . . . For a week *go somewhere*.

After signing the letter and sealing the envelope, he went out and spent the rest of the day shooting at partridges. ('Shooting partridges,' Effie told Rawdon Brown, 'is a sport which refreshes Everett at once when he gets tired.')

* * *

The Millais's second child, George, was born on 18 September 1857. One year later, on 8 September 1858, Effie informed Rawdon Brown that their third child was due later in the month. 'This time,' she said, 'I hope for a little girl and then *'basta'*!' She did in fact give birth to a girl, named Effie.

Young Effie provided John Everett with an added stimulus. Later in the year he told Hunt that he was 'working very hard', hoping to earn enough for a permanent return to London. 'My pictures,' he said, 'are out of door subjects. I am painting *figures* and *entirely* [underlined twice] in the open air, which adds to the difficulty, but the result is so much more satisfactory that I don't hesitate, although it is sometimes great pain from the intense cold.'

He would have two out-of-door pictures to exhibit, neither of which told much of a story. One, reminiscent of *Autumn Leaves*, was called *Spring*, later changed to *Apple Blossoms*. Eight gaudily dressed young women are standing, sitting, squatting, or lying in an orchard of apple trees. Less simple and more suggestive was *The Vale of Rest*. At this time, Effie kept a notebook in which she documented the origin and commencement of this painting:

> It had long been Everett's intention to paint a picture with nuns in it, the idea occurring to him on our wedding tour. On descending the hill by Loch Awe he was extremely struck with its beauty, and the coach-man told us that on one of the islands there were the ruins of a monastery. We imagined the beauty of the picturesque features of the Roman Catholic religion, and transported ourselves, in idea, back to the times before the Restoration had torn down, with bigoted zeal, all that was beautiful from antiquity . . . The vesper bell pealed forth the 'Ave Maria' at sundown, and the organ notes of the Virgin's hymn were carried by the water and transformed into a sweeter melody, caught up on the hillside and dying away in the blue air. We pictured white-robed nuns in boats, singing on the water in summer evenings, chanting holy songs, inspired by the loveliness of the world around them.
>
> Everett said he was determined to paint nuns some day, and one night this autumn, being inspired by the beauty of the sunset, he rushed for a large canvas and began at once upon it, taking for the background the wall of our garden at Bowerswell, with the tall oaks and poplar trees behind it.

The painting shows two nuns in a convent garden. One is digging a grave while the other rests on a stone, silently meditating. In the background, poplar trees stand out against a sunset sky with a large coffin-shaped cloud. The scene is starkly realistic, and the two women seem admirably suited to their calling. The digging nun might have been created by Millais's homophonic namesake, Jean-François Millet. Her colleague stares at the sky, apparently thinking of the Scottish super-stition that a coffin-shaped cloud at sunset forebodes death.

The Vale of Rest and *Spring*, Millais's major works of 1859, were accompanied by a third painting, *The Love of James I of Scotland*. Another of Millais's beautiful young women is outside a dungeon window handing a flower to her imprisoned royal lover, represented by an outstretched hand.

* * *

In April, John Everett went to London with his pictures. Effie remained behind, visiting relatives in Edinburgh. She wrote to him, 'I see clearly that you will find your works so appreciated that you will sell them immediately.'

Actually she didn't see very clearly.

'I came to get some money,' he wrote on the day after arriving. 'Now I feel in rather low spirits . . . The *nastiest* things are afloat about my pictures . . . There has been no decided wish expressed for them, and I am half alarmed at the state of things. Your father wants me to ask *3000* for the two, but if I get 2000 I shall consider myself lucky. At present I have had no offer beyond Gambart saying that he would take them although he didn't like them.'

Gambart was Ernest Gambart, the most successful Victorian art dealer. He was one of a small group of men bringing about a big change in the relationship of painters to the buying public. This was the frequent subject of contemporary commentaries, as in this passage from an article in the *Saturday Review*. 'A class of middlemen has arisen who intervene between artists and buyers, and they have acquired great power and influence. The picture dealer is a merchant who buys what he knows is likely to sell. As a general rule, he will not buy pictures on aesthetic grounds, but simply with a view to the state of the market. Dealers will ascertain the direction of public opinion and then push actively in that direction . . . The advice of dealers to artists is to cultivate qualities which sell and neglect aims which the public can't understand – to be diligently commercial.'

Eventually Millais would be grateful to dealers. Some years later he wrote: 'I am inclined to think we are chiefly indebted to the much abused dealer for the great advance in prices paid for modern art. It is he who awakened the spirit of competition. When the artist knows of only one purchaser, the dealer knows many. He has on the whole been the artist's best friend and scores of times has bought on the easel what the connoisseur has from timidity refused.'

He didn't feel like this in 1859.

'Oh, this isn't a nice profession,' he wrote to Effie. 'I have no faith in anything connected with art and will sell my pictures for anything.' He was distressed because of the 'total want of confidence in my pictures amongst the dealers'. They were mildly interested in the 'commercially safe' one, *The Love of James I.* As for the other two, '*None of the dealers even spoke to me about them*,' he told Effie. 'They are not anxious to *look into my eyes just now.*'

A painter didn't *have* to sell to dealers, and Effie thought John Everett was too beholden to them. She told her sister Sophia that he was 'foolish in ignoring prospective orders from private gentlemen'.

Actually he didn't entirely overlook them. Upon hearing that Thomas Combe had shown interest in *The Vale of Rest*, Millais wrote to him, offering the picture for 1000 guineas. Combe's reply was non-committal. He said that he also liked Hunt's still incomplete *The Finding of Christ in the Temple*, and he couldn't afford both paintings.

'If Combe buys Hunt's "Temple",' Millais told Effie, 'it will be like sinking money in a gutter, for I never saw such a *sad, sad* failure. The proportions and drawing are absolutely *execrable*. However it has been so much the fashion lately to praise this work that no one seems to dream that it can be bad *after four years labour* [underlined twice].'

Combe's response revived his persecution complex: 'The enmity against me is overwhelming. The clique has been most successful. Everywhere I hear of infamous attempts to destroy me.' The conspiracy included everybody, even his club companions: 'At the G, [Charles] Reade and Shirley Brooks [a minor poet-essayist] were curiously silent about my works. There is something puzzling in all this, and it requires all the confidence in myself I profess to keep my heart from falling into my boots.'

The one thing he did not lack was self-confidence. After leaving the private view, he told Effie, 'I am *most completely* [underlined twice] convinced of the superiority of my pictures to all living work.' He went even further on the day of the opening: 'Conscientiously, I believe my pictures are as clear from fault as the very best work that ever has been achieved.' This was an exaggeration which he could not have believed. He was just trying to make a point. Regardless of what anyone might say, he knew that his major works were good. He was right. *Spring* excellently presents its simple subject. And *The Vale of Rest* is strikingly provocative. But Millais recognised that the critics wouldn't agree with his own evaluation. 'I am prepared for disappointment,' he told Effie. 'It always happens.'

On the Saturday before the opening *The Times* started the ball rolling. It referred to the nuns as 'coarse and ugly' women who, if 'they attract the eye it is simply to repel it'. And *Spring* was a display of 'the most sordid coarseness and slovenliness' and 'almost hottentot repulsiveness'.

This was only the beginning. The Exhibition opened at noon on Monday, 2 May. A few hours earlier two daily papers had appeared with the most vitriolic reviews of his work since *The Times*'s assault of 1851.

The *Morning Post* thus characterised *The Vale of Rest*:

The incidents in this miserable Golgotha are the most dispiriting that can easily be imagined; the characters are ghastly, and the scene is dreary in the extreme . . . A more unprepossessing pair of women than these we don't remember to have seen. The figure of the lady digging is gaunt and ungainly, and her face is neither of the colour or substance of human flesh; yet she is an angel in comparison with the lady sitting, whose hollow cheeks, saucer eyes, shaggy eyebrows, ponderous jawbones, crooked mouth, and horrible expression combine to create a pre-eminence of ugliness akin to that enjoyed by the female of whom Charles Lamb said to have seen her once was an event in one's life never to be forgotten. It is just conceivable that there may be in real life a woman as ingeniously ugly as Millais's 'Gorgon' but a high work of art should exhibit only the most beautiful in nature. As an eminent critic said, 'An ugly picture ought to be burned.'

The reviewer said of *Spring* only that it was 'better than "The Vale of Rest".'

The other pre-opening onslaught appeared in the *Daily Telegraph*:

John Everett Millais . . . is fast becoming a warning and 'frightful example' to artists. Two of his three pictures the Hanging Committee should at once have rejected as examples of dangerous pictorial *rabies* . . . The faces of both nuns in *The Vale of Rest* are intolerably ugly. The cheek bones are as high as those of Scotch midwives. Their eyes, lobster-like in their protrusion, are smeared with apparently the *khol* with which Turkish women heighten the dusky attractions of their eyelids and lashes . . . [The reviwer checked off other details, all of which he detested.]

[179]

Spring is even more open to animadversion. The figures are abominable, a parcel of girls inconceivably ill-favoured. One girl sprawls on the turf and leers at the spectator, with her head upside down, as if to say, 'Here we are! All alive! What do you think of us? Isn't it funny? Isn't Mr Millais a great painter, and isn't this picture worth a thousand?' . . . All the lips are smeared with red lead, all the eyes swollen and darkened, all the cheek bones high . . . When we remember what the painter of this abortion has done, what poetic insight and appreciation of beauty he manifested years ago, and survey now his lamentable decadence and miserable inefficiency, we turn away in sorrow and disgust, believing that the most charitable hypothesis respecting the picture is that Mr Millais, when he sat down to paint it was not in his right mind.

On the evening of opening day, Millais wrote to his wife:

Leech and others are of the opinion that my work is *far* beyond anything I have as yet done. I have not read the papers, but I hear the abuse is *very great* . . . I am in very good spirits as I see everybody acknowledge my *superiority* and place me with Landseer. It is most strange that there shd be a kind of panic amongst the purchasers with regard to these pictures – they are so undecided they cannot make up their minds. I am bullied *right* and *left* with regard to ugliness, which surprises me as I see nothing ugly in either picture . . . I *am* [underlined five times] so certain *of the goodness* of my pictures and their absurd superiority over all other Exhibition work. At the same time I want confidence in the wretched commissions. The universal ignorance of Art *is lamentable*. The people individually appear to know nothing . . . If I could sell one it would keep me from feeling embarrassed, but if not I shall have to work at small things like mad. All this certainly sets my stomach more determinedly against the profession.

*   *   *

The two morning papers set the tone for the critical evaluation of Millais in '59: the *Illustrated London News* asked, 'Where does he get such positively ugly female models?' The *Saturday Review* said that 'the painter of "Ophelia" has sunk to the manipulation of a sign-painter.' The *Standard* judged the pictures to be 'utterly unworthy of an Associate of the Royal Academy'. The *Art Journal* concluded that 'Mr Millais must now be practising on the toleration of his friends.' A brand-new periodical, *Bentley's Quarterly Review*, in its first review of an art show kept up with its elders: 'There are not many men with the heart to paint eight young girls as so many clothed skeletons, every one ugly and ungraceful, with hard features, stained skins, and in broad day with cheeks and lips painted as if for the footlights . . . In his other painting, the unnecessary ugliness of the women is positively provoking. It is truly lamentable to see Mr Millais willfully taking the wrong road.'

At this time Millais wrote his most comprehensive response to appraisals of his work, in an eight-page letter to his father. This is part of it:

I am convinced that nothing earthly from me will meet with an entirely fair criticism . . . There is *nothing* [underlined three times] absolutely ugly in the pictures, and the drawing is nearly irreproachable, but where there is an inequality (*as there must always be*) [parenthesis underlined twice] it is seized upon to destroy all the beauties. However, my position is *established* [underlined three times] beyond all doubt . . . I understand from a man at the exhibition yesterday that my pictures were mobbed so that it was quite impossible to get near them. [Several reviewers acknowledged the crowds surrounding his paintings, hardly surprising in light of what had been written.] I have no doubt of ultimately selling them in spite of all that has been said. The purchasers seem quite *staggered* and uncertain and so dependent on the judgment of the dealers that they hang back. Directly some enlightened man possesses one of the pictures the others will follow . . . Mind you, the uproar is immensely favourable to me, for it creates an excitement which renders all the other work as nothing. Really, London is ringing with the subject of my pictures, and this is no small proof of their excellence . . . There is no doubt that whatever I do will be *torn to pieces*. JR will not be backward. I expect him to say I have gone to the dogs.

Actually Ruskin was one of the few critics who liked Millais's paintings. He called *The Vale of Rest* 'a great work'.

* * *

'There is no doubt,' John Everett told Effie a week after the opening, 'the critics have ruined the sale of my pictures.'

His situation reinforced his opinion of art critics. A little later, in a calmer mood, he spoke about reviewers passing judgment on artists, foreshadowing what Whistler would say in his libel suit against Ruskin. Millais proclaimed: 'Why should a man of very, very superficial knowledge, on the strength of having travelled abroad and studied foreign or English schools put himself on the same level on the subject of art with a professional artist? . . . A man may be always reading law reports but he would be bold indeed to tackle a Lord Chancellor on that subject.'

He then fantasised on how a Victorian critic would treat a 'great picture' from the past, Raphael's *Sistine Madonna*:

Mr Raphael sends one of his many Madonnas, a substantial matron, evidently of the peasant class, holding a fleshly child in her arms . . . with a figure on either side, showing no novelty of composition, and two rude Cupidian monsters (for where are such limbs to be found?) resting their elbows on what appears to be the front of an opera box minus the lorgnettes. The illusion moreover is increased by the disposition of a curtain on each side of the group, over which we must suppose is an unending Heavenly roof devoid of any mundane arrangement of brass rod and rings for suspension. There is some dignity of expression in the principal heads, but when will Mr Raphael give over that hard manner of execution which was the besetting sin of his late master, Mr Perugino?

In May of 1859 Millais didn't joke about critics or anything else. Unprecedentedly, it was possible that he would sell nothing.

'If this happens, God help us,' he told Effie. 'If I don't sell them here, I must go to New York and see what I can do there.'

He had an overseas connection. His sister had married a well-known American actor, Lester Walleck, and lived on West 30th Street,

New York City. But because of his distaste for travel he would cross the Atlantic only as a last resort. In any event, one thing seemed certain. He and Effie would have to control their spending.

'My darling,' he wrote, 'I am so sorry for your sake that there does not appear to be a promise of comfort for us this year . . . I never had such a trying time in my life. I would not care a farthing if I were a bachelor, but for your sake I cannot take such injustice calmly. I only hope it will not affect you overmuch. But we must *economise as much as possible* [underlined twice].'

Even more troubling than Effie's apparent extravagance was something that her husband mentioned in another current letter: 'How I long for us to be together as other healthy married people are. Our life together for some time has been most unsatisfactory, but I will not speak more of this.'

* * *

When Millais was in the depths of despair, fortune's wheel took a favourable turn. 'Yesterday,' he wrote to Effie on 16 May, 'I was offered by [D.T.] White [a Maddox Street dealer] £700, and I have sold the Nun. It is much lower than we hoped, but the *original* [underlined twice] price I *always intended to ask*. Now we shall be comfortable again . . . I am *sure I have done right* . . . I certainly begin to feel *very happy*, as I see all is coming right, no thanks to the press.'

A few days later, Ernest Gambart bought *The Love of James I* for the asking price, £300. 'So we are not badly off,' Millais told his mother-in-law. But nobody wanted a picture of eight young women in an orchard. *Spring* would remain unsold until mid-1861.

In his last letter before returning to Scotland, he wrote, 'These pictures have been such torments to me that I want to wipe their memory from my mind for ever.'

CHAPTER 17

1859—62

THE Exhibition of 1859 would seem to have ended what might be called the first phase in the career of John Everett Millais. After the critical demolition of *Spring* and *The Vale of Rest*, he said that he couldn't carry on. No longer did he consider himself to be a practising PRB. Never again, he said, would he attempt anything truly original or innovative. It was all over. Finished! That's what he said.

From time to time, for his own amusement, he wrote poems. One of them, written a few years later, might fittingly be quoted here:

'A Way to Get On'

Firstcultivate a gift of gab,
For John Bull fears the man who bellows.
Play through life the game of grab
And have contempt for all your fellows.

Push, cringe, and grovel to men in power.
Make friends of editors.
They are helpful in an evil hour
If you are b—d by creditors.

A safe role with a certain class,
Professional excellence despise.
Some few will write you down an ass,
But most of all will think you wise.

After the painful summer of 1859, Millais was determined just to 'get on'. He knew what people wanted, and he would give them what they wanted.

* * *

'I have had a great many commissions,' Millais told Mrs Gray on 25 May 1859. 'Next year I shall paint only these. The press has not quite ruined me yet.'

As in 1857, he planned to bypass the next Exhibition in favour of commercial work with assured income. This was 'getting on'.

One early commission is worth noting. It came from the publishers of a new journal, *Once a Week*, subtitled 'An Illustrated Weekly of General Literature'. This was not the nation's first illustrated periodical. The *Illustrated London News* had been founded in 1842, but it was a news weekly, with pictures of current events. *Once a Week* was different. Its illustrations accompanied stories, poems, and brief articles. This publication was the first of its kind in Britain. During its initial year, *Once a Week* ran drawings by twenty-eight different persons. Two, John Leech and Charles Keene, were staff artists for *Punch*. The others were mostly nonentities, people like G.H. Bennett and W. Harry Rogers, and some identified only as 'Wolf' or 'Miss Lane'.

The only well-known painter among the twenty-eight was John Millais, probably engaged to provide *Once a Week* with instant credibility. And so the first illustration of the first number, appearing on 2 July 1859, was a drawing by Millais, appended to a poem by Tom Taylor, 'Magenta', inspired by an armed conflict in the Italian town of that name. Taylor wrote about the grieving family members of men killed in action. Millais's drawing showed an attractive young woman burying her head in a sofa cushion alongside an open newspaper, presumably containing a list of casualties.

Millais was not a prolific *Once a Week* illustrator. In the first year he did thirteen, compared with fifty-four by Leech and seventy-three by Keene. But, Effie told her mother, he received 'capital pay'. There was also an attractive fringe benefit, an expense-free week in Paris for himself and his wife.

On their way over, they stopped briefly in Surbiton, Effie's first sojourn with her in-laws. She hoped it would be the last one. 'If I was not going to Paris,' she told her mother, 'I would go straight home as they are so irregular and noisy. They dine at all hours, have no proper meals. I have not had a proper, well-cooked meal since I came.'

One would think that Millais was sent to Paris to illustrate a Parisian story. But not one of his total of sixty-nine *Once a Week* drawings has anything to do with Paris. Perhaps this was a gesture of good will from the new publication to its most prestigious illustrator.

What did he do during his first visit to a foreign city? What did he think of the Louvre? the Luxembourg gallery? the Latin Quarter? Montmartre? Notre Dame? Versailles? Who knows? If he wrote anything from Paris, it hasn't survived, and Effie's one letter doesn't help. She told her mother that they were staying at the luxurious Hotel du Louvre in the Rue de Rivoli. About Paris, she said only this: 'The shops are full of lovely things for presents, and if I had any money I would invest it in presents, but I have none. I feel it would be delightful to spend money and go all out. The children's things here are so neatly made. But I have nothing to spend.'

* * *

In July, Millais spent a couple of weeks in London conferring with dealers, engravers, and publishers. It was uncommonly hot. His letters kept pace with the weather.

'I have been thinking of the raptures at meeting you,' he told Effie after only a couple of days in London. 'I am very much afraid I shall not be able to keep my hands away from you long enough to do any work as I shall be terribly amorous. I will *gobble* [underlined twice] you up.'

In his next letter he wrote, '*I never was so anxious in my life* [underlined twice] as I am to get beside you. I so long for a renewal of that delight that I lose my sleep and toss about. All pleasures are literally nought to compare with the private *ecstasy* of a married couple.'

When his return trip drew near, he wrote, 'I think I shall go to bed with you whatever hour I arrive and not get up for 24 hours . . . Nothing compensates for the ecstasy of being with you.'

Never was it more regrettable that their surviving correspondence is one-sided.

* * *

In November, Millais was again in London. He was house-hunting. He and Effie would move to the big city once and for all.

He found satisfactory rented accommodation to occupy while looking for a permanent home, at 1 Bryanston Place, off Bryanston Square, about a hundred yards from Marble Arch. It was spacious, with a large drawing room, a dining room, a library, a well-lighted studio and seven bedrooms. The rent was ten guineas ($52) a week.

While in London, he attended a dinner party at the home of the John Leeches. One of the guests was William Russell, the world's first full-time war correspondent, who gained fame while covering the Crimean conflict for *The Times*. It was he who reported that the heroic but foolhardy charge of the Light Brigade had been a 'hideous blunder'. Millais received expert advice from Russell on his painting for 1860.

He would return to the big Summer Show, after all. Primarily a painter, not an illustrator, he found it difficult to stay away. He would have one entry, his first post-Pre-Raphaelite painting.

Repeatedly since 1852 he had been asked, 'Why don't you give us the Huguenot again?' For seven years he had resisted the temptation to replicate his number one triumph. (Today we would probably have *Huguenot, II, III,* etc.) As a dedicated Pre-Raphaelite, he constantly sought fresh, original subjects. He could not in good conscience repeat something simply because dealers promised to sell it for a good price. Then came the response to *Spring* and *The Vale of Rest*. He capitulated. He would do it.

In October he tentatively decided on a subject but didn't mention it to anyone. Then after speaking to Russell, he confided in Effie:

Yesterday I dined with Leech, who had a small dinner party . . . Billy Russell (the Times corespondent) was there. Oddly enough he touched upon the subject of *the picture I am going to paint*, and I asked him to clear up one or two things. I told him my project (as it was absolutely necessary) but he promised to keep it secret, knowing how things are pirated. It was very fortunate my meeting him, as he is the very best man for military information. My subject appears to me, too, most fortunate, and Russell thinks it first-rate. It is connected with the Brunswicker Cavalry at Waterloo.

'Brunswickers' they were called, the best gentlemen in Germany. [At Waterloo they joined the anti-French coalition.] They wore black uniforms with death's head and cross-bones, and gave and received no quarter. They were nearly annihilated but performed prodigies of valour. I intend having the sweetheart of a young soldier sewing crape round his arm and vainly supplicating him to keep from the bugle-call to arms. It will be a perfect *pendant* to 'The Huguenot'. *I have it all in my mind's eye, and feel confident that it will be a prodigious success.*

This conversation with Russell demonstrated that John Millais would not and could not throw off the principles of the body to which he had devoted ten years. He would never work haphazardly. He would plan his subjects with great care. He would be truthful in depicting details. But for the time being he would *not* take chances.

He began his picture soon after moving to London. His female model was Kate Dickens, soon to be Mrs Charles Collins. The scene is a room in the woman's house. As in *A Huguenot*, she and her lover stand face to face as she makes her appeal. (Thankfully, Millais didn't go through with his intention of having her attach something to his arm.)

When the painting was done, at least one thing could be said for it. The man's uniform, the woman's dress, and the room itself measure up to the standard of Millais's earlier works. Otherwise, it is, like most sequels, a pale imitation of the original. There can be no comparison between the earlier superb expressions and these almost passionless faces. Also, the man's duty is to depart. This might have made it difficult for some viewers to be empathetic.

Apparently realising that his couple needed help, Millais included a couple of things not present in *A Huguenot*. The man and woman aren't alone. As in *The Order of Release*, a dog is standing on its hind legs, leaning against its mistress. One reviewer thought that she cared more for her dog than her lover.

This last opinion was not really farfetched. Millais's second appendage to the new painting was a picture on a wall of the room, a copy of David's *Napoleon Crossing the Alps*. What does this mean? That the woman was an admirer of Napoleon, which was really why she was trying to hold back her companion? In his earlier works, Millais had been straightforward. Now he seems deliberately ambiguous, suggesting perhaps that he may have had some doubts about the painting. The picture was called *The Black Brunswickers*, the plural title taking it beyond the immediate scene and honouring a group of men.

* * *

The *Athenaeum* congratulated Millais for 'abandoning the bizarrerie of his recent productions'. Since the figures were attractive, and the picture easy to understand, the critics liked it. (Suffering from exhaustion and nervous depression, Ruskin did not bring out his *Academy Notes*. It would reappear once, in 1875.) Millais expected to fetch his best price yet. He was confident because of good reviews and because of the payment to Hunt for *his* most recent painting.

Early in the spring, after nearly six years of work in Palestine and England, Hunt had completed his magnum opus, *The Finding of Christ in the Temple*. Super-dealer Gambart bought it with copyright for £5500, the highest sum ever paid in Britain for a modern picture. In late April it was exhibited by itself in Bond Street's German Gallery with an admission fee of one shilling, the same as at the Royal Academy. The gallery was packed every day throughout the summer.

Millais was envious. He was also pleased to report to Effie, visiting her family in Perth, that despite his good fortune, Hunt was 'in low spirits. He feels no pleasure in the success of his picture. He says it has cost him 2000, that he has nothing in the world after six years work laid by, and he will have to pay very heavy bills.'

If the *Temple* could be sold for £5500, Millais thought, his own picture surely would bring in £2000. Yet early in June it was still unsold. 'I will get more than 2000 if only we wait,' he told Effie. A few days later he was less confident: 'To sell my picture is not so easy. I feel certain I shall . . . get 2000 . . . but it may not be as shortly as you seem to imagine.'

Before the end of June, Gambart bought it for £1000. He earned a fair profit by re-selling it for £1150.

* * *

On 17 July 1860 at St Mary's Church, in Higham, Kent, wedding bells rang out. Kate Dickens became Mrs Charles Collins. The bride was twenty, the groom thirty-two. There was great excitement in Higham. The church was festooned with flowers. A special train brought dozens of wedding guests from London, including, naturally, Holman Hunt, who devoted three pages of his autobiography to the affair. There was one conspicuous absentee. Even though Charlie Collins had been one of his two closest friends, and Kate Dickens had sat for his current painting, John Millais was not there.

Although he did not explain it in any piece of writing known to me, I think I know why Millais failed to put in an appearance. It was for the same reason that he did not attend Walter Deverell's funeral. If would have been too painful. Charles Collins was incurably impotent. After what he was convinced Effie had experienced with John Ruskin, how could he have stood by and watched this marriage of a woman for whom he had a genuine affection? Since he could not have concealed his feelings, it was probably better for him to stay away. As Millais might have predicted, the marriage was a failure. Collins died when his wife was relatively young. She remarried and presumably lived satisfactorily with her second husband.

* * *

After seeing what Hunt had received for his large picture of a dramatic incident from the distant past involving a child separated from his parents, Millais in the summer of 1860 began a large painting of a dramatic event from the past focusing on two children who had been separated from their parents. They were kidnapped girls being returned to their father, a medieval knight. He called it *The Ransom*. It would take many months to complete. During this period he also worked on numerous commissioned drawings, including those for two of Anthony Trollope's novels, *Framley Parsonage* and *Orley Farm*, serialised in *Cornhill Magazine*.

'Altogether Millais drew from my tales 87 drawings,' Trollope recounted, 'and I do not think that more conscientious work was ever done. It was open to him simply to make a pretty picture, or to study the author's work. The former method was certainly easier. An artist will frequently dislike subordinating his own ideas to those of the author, and sometimes he is too lazy to find out what these ideas are. But Millais was neither proud nor idle. In every figure he drew his object was to promote the views of the writer, and he never spared himself any pains in studying that work.'

These drawings did not come easily. These are excerpts from letters to Effie, in Perth: 'I haven't done the second "Orley" yet. It has given me more trouble than all my former drawings put together.' 'Yesterday I finished the "Orley" illustration, which is a *great thing* off my mind.' 'I wish I cd. get the "Orley F" illustrations done. They are like a millstone round my neck right now.' He also told Effie, 'I cannot let illustrations interfere with my painting.'

But they did interfere. He couldn't complete *The Ransom* for the 1861 Exhibition, from which he was absent for the second time in four years. He couldn't help it. He needed the guaranteed income from illustrations, now more than ever. On 22 April 1861, he and Effie signed a lease for their first relatively permanent residence, at 7 Cromwell Road, in newly developing South Kensington. They didn't move immediately and, after the signing, Effie left for a prolonged visit with her parents. Before going, she had a strange encounter with her first husband.

* * *

The Royal Institution of Great Britain, in Albemarle Street, Piccadilly, was founded in 1800 'for the promotion, diffusion, and extension of useful knowledge'. Its facilities include a lecture hall, where in the spring of 1861 Professor Frankland spoke on 'Some Phenomena of Combustion in Rarefied Air', and Professor Helmholtz discoursed on 'The Application of the Law of Conservation of Force in Organic Nature'. The lecture following those of Professors Frankland and Helmholtz, on 17 April, was entitled 'Tree Twigs'. This doesn't sound exciting but, as a magazine reported, 'the eminence of the speaker secured a most brilliant audience.' The speaker was John Ruskin.

Because of his health, this was his first public appearance in many months. It was therefore a fashionable West End event. Elizabeth Gaskell told a friend that 'great interest was made to obtain tickets, and the place was very crowded'.

Ruskin was even more fidgety than usual. Gaskell said that 'he begged to have a door either open or shut – I forget which – and asked for it publicly, alleging some good reason, but one of the directors refused to allow it to be done.' He in fact wanted the entrance door closed, but because some members of the smart audience were stylishly late, it remained open.

'The lecturers that usually appear here,' Ruskin began as latecomers were arriving, 'have been the greatest philosophers of the age, and the deepest truths and latest discoveries of science have been the engrossing topics on which they have dwelt. No such high interest will attach to what I have to say. I will only endeavour to point out the connection between the laws of nature and those of art.'

At this point he looked up and staggered. Two well-dressed women had just entered. One of them was Lady Eastlake. Her companion was Effie Millais. As he stood in shocked silence, they took their seats, in the first row, dead centre.

'When he saw *Lady Eastlake* and *Mrs Millais* sitting right opposite him and staring at him,' Elizabeth Gaskell gleefully related, 'he entirely *broke down*. This finished him. All his friends are indignant and sorry.'

Gaskell, who was not present, apparently believed that Ruskin couldn't continue. This wasn't quite true. The venerable sage of Chelsea, Thomas Carlyle, was in the audience – sitting in the gallery, no less. He told his brother, 'The lecture was thought to "break down", and indeed it did *as a lecture*.' Ruskin put aside his prepared notes and for about an hour spoke extemporaneously. 'I do not recollect,' Carlyle said, 'to have heard in that place any lecture I liked so well as this chaotic one.' When Carlyle learned of why Ruskin had come apart, he blamed 'that termagant of a woman called Lady Eastlake,' who he said, did it 'on purpose to disconcert him'.

* * *

On 1 May 1861, in Perth, Effie had a miscarriage. Some may have seen this as punishment for what she had done to Ruskin. I don't think that she felt that way. Recall how in 1858 with the birth of her third child she had said, '*Basta!*' Then in 1860 she had a second daughter, Mary. And so she probably didn't grieve over the loss of what would have been her fifth child. Actually the miscarriage, occurring just after her arrival home, perhaps resulted from the co-operation of a friendly physician.

While Effie was in Scotland, her husband was involved in an embarrassingly amusing episode in London.

Two well-known engravers, George and Edward Dalziell, who had worked with Millais on his illustrations, were producing a book of thirty water-colour drawings by Myles Birket Foster, eventually a prominent water colourist, now starting his career. The Dalziells wanted a page of verse with each picture. Late in May, they spoke about it to Millais. He volunteered to ascertain if Tennyson would take on the job. One of the two or three most meticulous craftsmen in the history of English poetry, Tennyson had been poet laureate for eleven years, but Millais did not think it inappropriate to ask him to dash off some verses for an artistic novice.

Because her husband was probably too embarrassed to respond, Millais's letter was answered by Mrs Tennyson. She wrote, 'I am sorry to have to say the thing is impossible. Poems do not come to him so, and if they did not *come*, you are, I flatter myself, too much his friend to wish them there or anywhere.'

Millais told one of the Dalziell brothers, 'I should have thought it easy to write a few lines to each picture as I should find it easy enough to illustrate anything.'

When the strangely naive appeal was made to Tennyson, Effie had been away for a month with no sign of returning soon. Fashionable London was basking in the height of the season, the period from Easter until the first week of July. Nowadays, seasons aren't like those of the Victorians. A popular writer, Hawley Smart, in his novel of 1870, *Bitter Is the Rind*, alluded to a West End season:

'The heart of Piccadilly throngs strong; the fitful pulse of Bond Street knows no rest. Carriage after carriage rolls home with its freight from the Park. The tide of pedestrians ebbs, flows, and eddies between Apsley House and the Regent Circus [Piccadilly Circus], anon whirling fiercely up Park Lane, then sweeping more tranquilly down decorous St James's Street towards Marlborough House and the Palace.'

John Everett's letters of May and June reflect his seasonal activities: 'I feel rather seedy this morning. So late at night drinking and smoking.' 'I dine out so much and keep such late hours that I cannot naturally progress much.' 'This dining out is not conducive to working steadily. This last week I have done nothing.' 'I was up very late last night, two o'clock in the morning playing whist at the G.' 'I have wasted the whole morning playing billiards with Campbell, who I met by chance.' 'Today I have got myself in my best to loaf about. I am going to watch the cricket match between Oxford and Cambridge at Lord's.'

With all this socialising, Effie thought it only proper to inquire about the big painting begun more than a year earlier, *The Ransom*. When she had left for Scotland, it was nearly completed, and now she asked again and again when it would be done and sold.

In one of several letters on the subject, John Everett said, 'I don't agree on the necessity of [illegible word] a sale. I shall sell it all in good time and for more than I can get just now . . . I *must keep the picture* until I can get my price, which I see no likelihood of getting just now. I am not in the least anxious, so don't you be.'

A few days later he wrote, 'I have your two letters and will do my best to carry out your suggestions. To finish and sell my picture isn't so easy, especially the latter part of the recommendation, but *I feel quite certain* [underlined twice] that with patience I *must* ultimately sell it and get my *2000*.'

Effie's eagerness for an early sale, he believed, was due to her desire for ready cash. This led him, on 12 June, to write an obviously painful letter on what must have been an often discussed topic:

I am sorry to have to speak to you about expenses, as you can never hear a word on that subject quietly. My only reason is simply from looking at the check [sic] book. I find from the *17 April* to the present moment *160* [underlined twice] within two months, this chiefly for living expenses, not including my professional expenses. Surely that is a large sum, and I do hope the next two months will not come to half of this amount. You see it approaches a rate of 1200 a year. I know *perfectly* well you can account for every farthing most satisfactorily, but that does not take away from the fact that we have spent the 160 within *one month and a half*. I think that is a great deal too much. Fortunately working *every* [underlined three times] day here has *nearly* kept us as we were when we came, but directly I get to my big picture I shall cease having an *immediate* return. I myself *spend less than £5* a week over lodging. I *hate* [under-lined three times] talking on this subject, but it does seem we are living at a rate that is quite unnecessary.

In defense of his night life, Millais wrote, 'I am obliged to dissipate a little to feel your absence less. I *am not enjoying* it by any means.' A little scepticism is proper here, but the statement contains some truth. John Millais did acutely miss his wife.

When she left, late in April, he expected her to be gone for a couple of weeks. Supposedly because of her mother's illness, she remained in Perth throughout May and June and into July. The painfulness of their separation is shown in his letters:

25 May. I am *half crazy* away from you.
2 June. I was awake early and longed to be beside you. It is perfectly dreadful. It is impossible to destroy nature.
15 June. I confess that being with you is *so far* [underlined twice] above every other consideration that I wd do anything to shorten the time . . . I am growing so outrageously anxious and feel so con-stantly giddy, it is quite past endurance.

Obviously, he missed more than her companionship. In one letter he wrote, 'I think *continually* of having the most ecstatic enjoyment with you.' Again: 'Oh, I so long to be with you, you can't think how much. I feel I shall eat you up when I see you . . . *Art, Money*, everything disappears before the prospect of meeting you.'

It was unnatural, he repeatedly emphasised, to be so long separ-ated. 'It is *truly impossible*,' he said, 'for a young man to stay away from his wife.' And 'remember', he told her, 'I am not an old fogey yet.'

Some attractive residents of Mayfair knew that he was far from being an old fogey. 'I find many ladies *overwhelmingly* complimentary to me,' he wrote. 'I don't think I shall run away with any of them, but don't keep from me too long. They certainly are dreadfully tempting and suggestive in their sweet summer dresses.'

And they were ready and willing to be accommodating: 'The things some ladies say are *disgraceful* [underlined twice]. Many things said to me have been immodest . . . There certainly is an *immense* deal of immodesty here. I am not prudish, but there is a license in society amongst some members that is tremendous. A lady told a friend of mine that she wondered that *you left me* ten days by myself here.'

If he was trying to arouse Effie's anxiety and hasten her return home, he didn't succeed. After it became clear that this course of action wasn't accomplishing anything, he used another approach:

8 June. I have been trying to work, but the heat and the interruptions are so great and I *cannot* [underlined three times] get you out of my head . . . I wd work splendidly if I was beside you. I am *perfectly certain* [underlined twice] I could finish both pictures [*The Ransom* and a large portrait] in less than half the time if I were with you.
12 June. I have tried to work but unsuccessfully. It is so warm it is difficult to do anything . . . I don't know whether I shall ever be able to stick sufficiently at the picture to finish it before seeing you.
18 June. You do not know how irksome every moment is to me. I cannot possibly work . . . I am quite in a tremble all day. I will try and work tomorrow. I *must* try and do something.
23 June. It is too hot to do much, and so I just sit in my shirt sleeves all day. I am so sick of looking forward to joining you that I am quite dull and indifferent about anything. The most I can do is a drawing for *Once a Week*. I haven't the energy to paint.

His complaints about the heat were valid. In a novel of 1864, *Thornycroft Hall*, Emma Jane Guyton looked back upon this summer of 1861: 'Ah! those close dreary squares and those dull hot streets – oh, the glaring dusty parks, and the roar and bustle of that wearisome Oxford Street! And the weather grew almost unbearable. Old Nabov chuckled and said it was like Calcutta. People were reported as dying of sun-strokes, stray dogs suggested hydrophobia, and penny ices were greatly in demand.'

Heat or no heat, Effie was not coming. John Everett then came up with a new idea: 'If the mountain won't go to Mahomet, the prophet must go to the mountain. *Write and say come* and I will leave at once.'

After an unenthusiastic response, he became more insistent: 'I really think it wd be best to finish my picture at Bowerswell. *I am quite sure of selling it* [underlined three times], and if I come by sea I could bring it and Mrs Atlkins [his portrait] and finish both there *better* than here. Certainly I shd be less disturbed . . . I shd be so quiet at Perth. Do let me do this and make me happy.'

Then he asked, 'Surely you must want me?'

Her answer may be surmised from his next letter, dated 3 July: 'You say that another week is not much longer to stay, but for me it is *dreadful to contemplate.*'

Actually he stayed for two and a half more weeks. Just before leaving, he wrote, 'I can't help thinking that a quarter of a year, three months, have gone by and I have *scarcely* seen you and not the children at all. That can't be called drawing much pleasure out of a family. I suppose I will see you for a week or two, and then you will go off somewhere else.'

After Effie and John Everett were reunited, they were together for only a week or two. But it was *he* who went 'off somewhere else'. He spent more than four weeks fishing and shooting.

While gone, he was a punctilious correspondent, providing Effie with almost daily reports of his doings. In one letter he told her, 'I fished all day . . . I caught salmon, grilse, and sea trout.' Then there was this exultant message: 'I sent off four brace of grouse, also a beautiful pike of seven pounds which I caught this morning . . . The one I sent afforded me splendid play, having just come up from the salt water. It was most difficult to land. I have quite got into the way of playing them and have confidence in myself.' Not once during this sporting holiday did he appear to be lonely. Indeed after being away for four full weeks, he wrote, 'Yesterday I held for a moment a *fifteen* pounder, but he was badly hooked. I suppose I shall stay until Saty. as I am always thinking to catch another . . . I long to get back to you, but I think it best to give every day to fishing.'

* * *

Late in November 1861, the Millais family – Effie; John Everett; Everett, aged five; George, four; Effie, three; and Mary, one – moved into their home at 7 Cromwell Place. South Kensington was beginning a growth which would transform it from an almost vacant district into a domain of broad roads, stately houses, and lofty institutions. Peter Cunningham, author of the most popular

Victorian guidebook to London, would soon call it 'the most residentiary quarter in the metropolis'. The recently built Millais house, across the road from where the Natural History Museum would stand, was quite large enough to accommodate the present family. According to William Allingham, it was furnished at a cost of more than £2000 ($10,000).

The first Summer Show following the move introduced the 'new' Millais. He had four entries, two of which were major works. All four, however, were important.

At last the medieval *Ransom* was finished. The costumes and household effects show that, as usual, Millais had done his homework. But otherwise it was a disappointment. Except for the deliberate ambiguity in *The Black Brunswickers*, his earlier historical pictures had been without obscurity. This isn't true here. The ransom apparently paid, the two girls have been returned home and cling to their father, dressed in full armour. Surprisingly, the three abductors are also present, seemingly demanding more from the knight, painstakingly handing over jewellery. Why in his own house should he be so solicitous and the captors so bold? And why, unlike Millais's other historical scenes, is there no real feeling in what should be an emotional moment? It looks like a routine transaction.

This long-awaited picture had to be a letdown. Millais didn't seem to resolve the story clearly in his own mind. He was probably diverted by commercial assignments. But more than that, he had lost his enthusiasm for historical work. He was finding it to be boring. (As I implied, the principal stimulation for the work was perhaps the enormous sum Hunt got for *his* historical painting.) It is thus not surprising that his other main entry, *Trust Me*, was much more successful.

If *The Ransom* is bewilderingly vague, *Trust Me* is disarmingly simple. The scene is the breakfast room of an upper-middle-class country house soon after the morning meal has been consumed. The silver breakfast service, the table and chairs, and a folding door are done with Pre-Raphaelite fidelity. Further rearward, however, it is less distinct. Millais is now concentrating on the main event. Two figures are standing, a middle-aged man and a nineteen- or twenty-year-old woman, obviously his daughter. Wearing a hunting outfit and holding a whip, he is about to go out on a chase. Before leaving, he asks something of his daughter and holds out an open hand. The morning post has arrived, and she clutches behind her back an unopened letter. We can see a portion of the envelope, which bears a cancelled red stamp and is addressed to a 'Miss' in the county of Norfolk.

Here is a simple, easy-to-understand incident, with an element of uncertainty, exemplified by the title. *The Times* commented, 'The "trust me" may be put into either mouth. Is it a love letter? Is the man recalling the absolute confidence in which they have lived till now and asking the girl to continue it? Or is she reminding him that he has never had cause to doubt her, and must not begin now if she decline to show him the letter? It may be breaking to her some painful news which she feels it better he should not know. In short, the picture gives us the pleasant duty of cracking the nut.'

The daughter, Millais's latest great beautiful woman, doesn't help us in this matter. 'The young lady,' the *Saturday Review* observed, 'is totally devoid of expression. We can read in her face neither timidity, wavering, guilt, merriment, defiance, nor yielding.' The creator of *A Huguenot* and *The Order of Release* was a master of feminine expression. If this woman is 'devoid of expression', it was intentional, as in *The Black Brunswickers*, a deliberate ambiguity.

Unlike *The Ransom*, which got a muted response, *Trust Me* was the most popular picture in the show. It deserved the acclamation. The slight but not trivial incident shows how eminently paintable ordinary life can be in the hands of a master. To paint a meaningful picture, one doesn't have to travel thousands of miles, as Hunt had done, or delve deeply into the past, as Millais had done repeatedly. *Trust Me* began a trend.

It wasn't the only current manifestation of the 'new' Millais. Also worth noting are the so-called minor entries.

One entitled, *Parable of the Woman Seeking for a Piece of Money* shows a house-maid at night, broom in one hand and a candle in the other, looking for a lost coin. The *Saturday Review* called it a 'Rembrandt-like sketch'. This demonstrates what can be achieved with comparatively slight elements.

Millais's fourth picture was a small head-and-shoulders portrait of a Mrs Charles Freeman. It was mostly overlooked, but the few reviewers who mentioned it liked it. As one said, it 'possesses wonderful truth and individuality of character'. This picture's importance cannot be measured by its size or the attention it received. Like *Trust Me*, it was the start of something new. Although Millais had painstakingly portrayed faces in his subject paintings, he had never shown much interest in straight portraits. The few that he had painted were favours to friends – portraits of James Wyatt, Mrs Coventry Patmore, and Mrs John Leech. Mrs Freeman was different. Her picture was his first straight portrait commission to hang in an exhibition gallery.

Just as 1859 had ended one stage in John Millais's career, 1862 began a new one.

Ten or twelve years later, he jotted down some notes, which are germane here:

Historical art is most surely fulfilled in the record of passing events. Hogarth, Copley, Sir Joshua, Gainsborough, and most other men of that day painted what they saw. From Hogarth we have life, character, and manners; Copley the death of Chatham and Major Passion in the Square of St Heliers, Jersey; while Sir Joshua and Gainsborough gave us the charming ladies, warriors, statesmen, and wits of their day – all of which work is essentially historical – and the very Highest Art also.

The splendour of the nose and dignity of expression in the picture of Mrs Siddons [by Gainsborough] is not surpassed by any work in the whole world of art; in this and in Sir Joshua's portrait of Hunter I see the same intellectual inspiration which enabled Raphael to paint the San Sisto [Madonna]. Many of these men attempted Biblical and classical subjects but are remembered almost entirely by contemporaneous subject matter . . .

Historical art, is most surely fulfilled by a record of the subjects of an artist's own time, for if art should be faithful, it gives the world a fact as it is, surrounded by the veritable actors of the scene. In this sense all portrait art is, so to speak, historical . . . A man can hardly paint other than his own nationality.

*   *   *

Soon after he had seen *Trust Me* and called it 'the finest thing at the Academy', George Du Maurier met the artist and his wife.

'The other day,' he told his mother, 'I dined at Little Holland House with Millais and Mrs Millais, and the sight of the fellow gave me the blues for a week. Such liveliness and vitality, such a spoilt child of nature and society and everything – and much of it owing no doubt to his astonishing beauty and naif impudence – he is not more than 30. [He was in fact thirty-three.] I was much disappointed in Mrs Millais. She is quite passée – wasn't she fascinated by my singing though.'

This objective response to Effie by someone who saw her for the first time is perhaps a commentary on what a succession of children had done to an excitingly effervescent young woman. She was probably right when some years earlier she said 'Basta!'

Du Maurier wrote to his brother, 'I was fascinated by the young god; the beauty, loudness, immense animal spirits did envelop me, although his sayings were not awfully wise.'

Maybe Millais had his mind on his annual fishing holiday. Late in the summer of almost every year of his married life, he went to Scotland to fish and shoot. Here he could smoke a pipe and grow a beard (to Effie's dismay) and, while enjoying himself thoroughly, bombard Effie with letters telling her how much he missed her:

7 September, Inveran Inn. Yesterday we caught a very good basket of trout. Tomorrow we begin three days of shooting [for grouse and deer] . . . The only two things which hinder my happiness is being away from you, which is really dreadfully sickening, and the midges, which don't trouble me nearly so much now since my skin has hardened in their nourishment. The first named drawback I won't suffer again if I can help it as I will take you with me another time. Being away from you affects my health, and I always feel feverish. The other morning in bed my nose began to bleed . . . I have come to the conclusion that no sport is worth separating from you. The one thing I have gained is to feel more acutely how delicious being with you is. It appears the longer we live together the less able is one to bear a separation. I certainly feel it more this time than ever before.

The letters in which Millais spoke of his loneliness and pains of separation were written on successive Sundays, when he had time on his hands because for sportsmen Sunday was a mandatory day of rest. Always on Monday morning he would regain his spirits and be eager to get started. He began one Monday letter by declaring, 'I work like a labourer at the rod, and if anyone can get the salmon I will.'

Never at any time did Effie accompany her husband on a shooting and fishing holiday.

CHAPTER 18

1863

Late in 1862, probably pushed again by Effie, Millais returned to what he had attempted in 1857, a moonlight painting. It was not a plain, unadorned moonscape. He needed a subject. He found it in John Keats's 'Eve of St Agnes', Madeline undressing for bed beneath rays of 'the wintry moon' shining through the 'casement'.

The place he chose for painting the picture was Lord Sackville's fifteenth-century mansion in Knole Park, Sevenoaks, Kent. Since this was presumably her venture, Effie agreed at once to sit for Madeline. With the arrival of November's full moon, they rode from Victoria Station on the newly constructed line to Sevenoaks. John Everett got permission to enter an unoccupied room, unlighted and unheated. He used a bull lantern to shine on his canvas. For three frigid nights he painted while Effie stood in a thin nightgown. Not once did she complain. Can one doubt that this picture was done at her behest? It was finished after two more days of work in London, five days in all.

Unlike *Isabella*, the picture only hints at its origin. Millais paid little heed to the poem's precise details. Keats's bed is behind Madeline; Millais's is in front. The poem has a medieval milieu; the painting's room has Jacobean furnishings. A 'triple-arched' window became square-mullioned.

Ten years earlier Millais would never have been so cavalier. But this was 1862, not 1852. Instead of transcribing Keats, he was showing a young woman retiring on a moonlit night. The resultant product was a nocturne, appearing nine years before the first of Whistler's nocturnes. Calling it *The Eve of St Agnes*, and including seven lines from the poem in the catalogue, stimulated interest in it.

He was pleased with the critical response. Typically, the *Illustrated London News* said of the moonlight that it had been 'painted with more literal truth perhaps than moonlight has ever been painted by anyone'. Critics raved about the moonlight and denounced Madeline. The *Athenaeum* saw a 'commonplace girl of our own day loosening her bodice after a ball'. The *Art Journal* called her 'little short of ugly, unpardonable in illustrating a poem of Keats'. But Millais *wasn't* illustrating a poem by Keats. His Madeline might very well have been returning from a ball.

Through the years *The Eve of St Agnes* has been one of his most highly acclaimed works. The historical painter Philip Calderon, RA, for example, wrote to Millais regarding his retrospective exhibition of 1886: 'If you ask me *which* of all the glorious pictures in the show is the most *perfect* I would say at once "The Eve of St Agnes". It has the poetry of the earlier works, allied to the mastery of materials of the later ones. It is pure in conception – simple and grand in arrangement – magnificent in its subdued splendour of colour – altogether, to me, more like a lovely dream than a thing of this earth.'

Millais surely was proud of it. But he would never attempt a second moonlight, another reason for believing that he had responded to urging, perhaps nagging, of his wife.

*   *   *

The Eve of St Agnes was Millais's gem of 1863. His other two Exhibition entries, however, were of more lasting significance. They could hardly have been more unlike the *Eve*.

He was now the father of five. (His fifth child, Alice, was born in mid-1862.) None had sat for a picture. Nor had Millais ever painted any child alone. Then came *My First Sermon*. *My First Sermon* shows a pretty little girl in a high-backed pew (in Kingston's All Saints' Church, where Millais's parents were parishioners), wearing a red cloak, purple dress, scarlet stockings, and black Garibaldi hat, listening attentively. Her model was the artist's eldest daughter, four-year-old Effie. After finishing this portrait, Millais immediately painted a picture of several of his youngsters playing under the family's grand piano. It was called *The Wolf's Den*.

Before the show started, *My First Sermon* received some praise that was unexpected. On Saturday night prior to the opening, one of the most select events of every season took place, the annual Royal Academy banquet. This year's principal speaker was the Archbishop of Canterbury. During his address, *The Times*, which alone was permitted to cover the affair, reported that he had said, 'I cannot forget that in its early days painting was the constant handmaid to religion, and that those great early masterpieces were powerful aids to reverence and devotion. (Cheers) Altered circumstances, in later days, somewhat changed the direction in which the current of genius flowed. But still art has, and ever will have, a noble mission to fulfill. That man is little to be envied who can pass through this room without having his spirits refreshed by this touching representation of the innocence, the purity, and the piety of childhood.'

He pointed to *My First Sermon*, and the audience cheered. The creator of *The Carpenter's Shop* had become a role model commended by the Archbishop of Canterbury.

While he spoke, a Berners Street gallery was highlighting that formerly scandalous thirteen-year-old picture which the *Athenaeum* now called 'a noble work which comes without a shock before the public eye'.

Almost everyone was captivated by *My First Sermon*. The *Art Journal* called it 'one of the happiest works Mr Millais ever painted'. The *Morning Post* said that 'it could make the reputation of any painter in the world'. *The Times* judged that 'no more delicious or unaffected picture of childhood was ever painted'.

Millais was now London's most sought-after artist. In August, he told Effie, again with her parents, 'Colls has sold all my drawings, and Watson also. Each has given me a commission of 12 more . . . I will now get £30 a drawing instead of 20. I nearly finished the little replica of the First Sermon which White wanted for £100. I will finish it today. I also have to finish a drawing for Watson, as he calls this morning. I called on Mrs Norton, who didn't know I am to make an illustration to her novel, which I am just finishing . . . There is no reason why I shouldn't make 5000 this year.'

A few days later he wrote, 'They have risen the price of the engraving of "The First Sermon" as they can't print fast enough. I wish I could have an interest in these publications. I think in a few years I shall make a good fortune independent of my painting.'

* * *

While the Exhibition was still on, Effie advised her husband to be circumspect in behaviour and speech. 'It does no good,' she told her mother, 'to speak one's mind as he did last month about the RA elections.' She referred to the vacancy to be filled in December. It was important not to say or do anything that might threaten his near-certain elevation.

He did mind his manners, and on 23 December he became a Royal Academician. Ten years earlier he had been named an Associate. He had waited too long, he thought, sometimes aloud. Even so, only eleven RAs had been younger than he, aged thirty-four years and six months.

CHAPTER 19

1864–65

Four days after her husband's promotion, Effie was off to Perth, leaving the children behind with their father. She stayed for nearly a month. Back home, Millais was, or professed to be, miserable:

> *5 January.* I cannot tell you how glad I shall be when you return. You know what a terrible discomfort it is. Every day I suffer and feel irritable and wretched.
> *11 January.* I am really quite out of my mind to come to you and I can do *nothing*. I am just now up from bed, *a quarter to 12.* I am so sleepy and dull. I cannot get up or do anything.
> *15 January.* I am in a fever all day and night and feel that I can't stay away from you any longer.
> *20 January.* I find the strain greater every day, and really *my sleep* [underlined twice] is affected. I am afraid at this year's exhibition I can't have very much as the time is short.

One might have thought that he would enjoy his children. There were now six. Geoffroy was born in 1863. But in only one letter did he mention them: 'The children are well, but I scarcely ever see them. I have no time for them. Directly my work is done I rush out and never return till the small hours, and I have no time for them in the morning.'

Later in the year, when Effie and her husband were in Paris, she wrote to her mother in familiar tones: 'The shops are most tempting, and if I had any money, I would buy you all lots of things . . . I shall, I hope, select something pretty for poor little Geoffroy. Everett declares that nothing will induce him to spend a farthing on any of the children. I have seen delightful, soft looking flannel jackets and hoods for the little girls, and I wish I could persuade Everett to let me get two for Mary and Effie for going out at night in the winter. But Everett keeps the money and says we won't have enough to go back.'

Two days later she wrote, 'I cannot get poor Geoffroy a hat without Everett's leave, and he thinks it so useless to get anything for so young a creature. I don't believe he will let me.'

This was the man who had become his nation's favourite painter of children. I am reminded of Jean Jacques Rousseau, author of *Émile*, that great booklet on children's rights, whose own infants were abandoned and taken in by a foundling home.

* * *

Seven years passed before Millais did a second *Huguenot*, but his fans didn't wait long for *My Second Sermon*. It was exhibited in 1864. The same girl in the same clothes in the same pew was sound asleep. This was his first, and almost only, painting with even a trace of humour.

The Archbishop of Canterbury again referred to this little girl: 'I have this evening learnt a very wholesome lesson which may be usefully studied by my right reverend brethren. I see a young lady there (pointing to *My Second Sermon*) who has by the eloquence of her silent slumber (cheers and laughter) given us a grave warning of the evil of lengthy sermons and drowsy discourse (loud cheers). Sorry indeed should I be to disturb that sweet, peaceful slumber.'

Everyone, it seems, agreed with the Archbishop. As the *Art Journal* said, 'We are all rejoiced to recognise the little girl dear to many a heart now grown into a naughty little girl . . . fast asleep in church. Yet no one loves her a whit the less.'

My Second Sermon, less a sequel than an extension, reminiscent of Hogarth, was one of four Millais paintings of children at the Exhibition. Another, with a fancy title, *Leisure Hours*, showed two young sisters in red velvet dresses playing with flowers on a carpeted floor. The others were full-length portraits.

Although he had said he wouldn't have 'very much' to exhibit, five of his pictures were at the show. The fifth, akin to *Trust Me*, was another ambiguously titled work, *Charlie is My Darling*. It showed a young woman in dark green riding clothes standing and awaiting her mount. Who is she? Who is Charlie? Her beau? Her horse? Or is the picture somehow related to the Jacobite song 'Charlie is My Darling'? It was intentionally enigmatic.

In his debut as a Royal Academician, Millais showed four portraits of children and a conundrum. Was he doing the right thing? Or was he underrating his talent?

A year earlier, despite the overwhelmingly favourable response to *My First Sermon* and *The Wolf's Den*, these questions had been tentatively asked in two or three papers, including the *Daily News*: 'We may feel in looking at these pictures of children a certain regret at the lavish bestowment of so much power on such homely subjects.' Now in 1864 even William Rossetti mildly objected to what his former Brother was doing. He had become an art critic for *Fraser's Magazine*, and his mostly complimentary notice contained this sentence: '"My Second Sermon" is an excellent painting, but it is rather exasperating to find a man of such pictorial power and command of expressions knocking off picture after picture of little girls and boys.'

On his own initiative, William Rossetti would never have said this. He must have talked it over with Millais, who was defensive about what he had been doing.

'I can't help it,' he told a friend. 'I am pestered morning, noon and night by people telling me that they have found the most beautiful child that ever was seen and asking me to paint her.' And to name the price.

Because of self-doubts, he backtracked in 1865. Not one child appeared among his five Exhibition entries. Nor were there any contemporary pictures. He had two depictions of ordinary incidents, based upon Tennyson and the New Testament. He also had two portraits – of Joan of Arc and the Old Testament's Esther.

Millais's fifth painting of the year was a throwback to the Pre-Raphaelite days, a scene from ancient history of a couple at a powerful moment. Called *The Romans Leaving Britain*, it evolved from a sentence in Raphael Holinshed's sixteenth-century chronicle, *Historie of England*: 'The Romans bade the Britaynes farewell, as not minding to return hither again.' Typically, Millais saw the human side of a momentous historical event, the departure of an army after four centuries of occupation. On a grassy slope overlooking a sandy beach, a Roman soldier is taking tearful leave of his native lover.

It had been a long time since he had prepared so carefully for or worked so hard upon a painting. He spent days looking for the proper site. From Folkestone, he wrote to Mrs Gray, 'I took a long walk on the beach to discover a likely background for my picture, but I have nearly determined to go to Jersey, where I know I shall find the right thing.' Actually he settled on the Dorset seashore and suffered through a bitterly cold January and February. It was very slow going and, in late February, Effie wrote to her sister Sophia, 'Everett is making scant progress on his picture. I despair of ever seeing it get on.'

It was in fact finished just ahead of the deadline. Was it worth the effort? Yes and no. As a dramatic scene it is disappointing, with none of the emotional fervour of Millais's best early pictures. It couldn't be compared to *A Huguenot* or *The Order of Release*. Yet it had to be done. Millais needed to get it out of his system.

The portraits are also unsatisfactory. Esther and Joan are less notable for themselves than for Esther's elaborate yellow robe and Joan's shiny sword. Clearly Millais had lost his enthusiasm for costume pieces and did them only because he had been accused of painting trivia. Implicit in this charge is the idea, once expressed by Ruskin, that a fine picture must have a noble subject. Now most of us would agree that the subject itself is less important than its treatment. By this criterion, *Trust Me* is better than *The Romans Leaving Britain*, and *Charlie is My Darling* and *My First Sermon* are superior to *Esther* and *Joan of Arc*.

Millais had been coming around to this view, but he was not convinced until after the Exhibition of 1865. In 1866 he would abstain from the show, and then in 1867 he would return triumphantly with four portraits of small children. He would paint for another thirty years. The historic pictures could be counted on the fingers of one hand.

* * *

During the summer of 1865, bogged down with commissions, more than ever Millais wanted his wife nearby. In July for the umpteenth time she went to Perth. After several weeks, he wrote, 'It is such an awful discomfort your being away that I am always sick.' A week later he told her, 'It is quite impossible for me to do this alone as I cannot stand it. If you cd. join me I would work twice as fast . . . and I think I then could have made so much money we might enjoy ourselves in great comfort.'

Again I am drawn back to Browning's Andrea del Sarto pleading with Lucrezia:

> If you would sit thus by me every night
> I should work better, do you comprehend?
> I mean that I should earn more, give you more.

In his letter he said, 'I don't think you shd. look upon it as a hardship to return to yr. house. Indeed very many women wouldn't remain away. I would work my hands off to get through if I was made happy with someone near me . . . It is very hard working without a soul to speak to.'

A bad habit grew worse: 'I smoke all day, but it makes no difference.' And he was ready to do more than smoke. On 4 September he wrote, 'I don't feel the least [illegible word] to get about my work, and it is already twelve o'clock. I can scarcely stand it. I would get on *Real* better if you were with me. But I must not go to Cremorne.'

This is intriguing. Cremorne, which had opened in 1846, was a twelve-acre pleasure garden in Chelsea, west of Battersea Bridge between the river and the King's Road. In the words of a contemporary novelist, it was a 'perfectly entrancing scene, with coloured lamps, well-kept walks, lovely flowers, brilliantly illuminated temples, splendid conservatories, unrivalled ballets, and a platform with a thousand mirrors and a magic orchestra, which may well recall the glowing pages of the "Arabian Nights"'.

This description, one might say, was of Cremorne seen for the first time. Looked at more closely, it was not as innocuous as it may have appeared. As William Rossetti said, Cremorne was 'a place of demi-reputable entertainment and assignations, with all their accompaniments and sequels'. According to a popular slogan, it was known for 'dancing, smoking, flirting', or, as sometimes said, 'the three D's – dancing, drinking, and deviltry'. Inevitably it became associated with rowdyism, which was so widespread in the late 'fifties and 'sixties that police reports constantly included altercations at Cremorne. In the early 'seventies a pamphleteer called it 'a nursery for every kind of vice'. Finally in 1877 the Chelsea Vestry forced it to close down for good.

Cremorne was an artistic magnet for several painters, most notably James Whistler. His interpretation of its fireworks, *The Falling Rocket*, was the subject of his libel suit against Ruskin. Millais, however, never drew or painted anything at Cremorne. He could only have gone there for the reason that many other men, including Gabriel Rossetti and Holman Hunt, were drawn to it, to find and enjoy female companionship. Ladies, in the Victorian sense of the word, did not go to Cremorne, unless disguised or on the sly, but there was no shortage of unattached women looking for fun.

John Everett's oblique mention of Cremorne suggests that Effie knew about, and was undisturbed by, his visits. She was not persuaded to return home. Instead, she apparently told him to stop complaining, finish his pictures, and join her in Scotland. 'It is all very well your saying to get the work done and come north,' he replied, 'But the work won't get done, and today I have been in bed all day with a headache . . . I feel quite incapable of working with such a headache. I have simply been sitting and doing nothing as I feel so uncomfortable . . . If you were here I could get my work done, but as it is, I don't know when I will get it done.'

Finally this normally parsimonious man wrote, 'It is absurd to offer inducement, but when all is done I meant to buy you a really fine £40 bracelet. I might get it all done within the month if you will keep me company.'

A few days later Effie was in London.

*   *   *

By themselves these letters might make Effie appear to be heartless and selfish. But they don't tell the whole story.

In the autumn of 1864, she had been suffering from a puzzling ailment, reminiscent of the last days of her first marriage. After resting in Perth, she went to Edinburgh to confer with the Grays' family physician Dr Simpson. She reported back to her father, 'I found *50* [underlined three times] people waiting to see him, many having been there since nine in the morning.' Treated preferentially, she waited for only an hour.

I always find him kind and judicious [she wrote] and I had a very satisfactory talk until I thought I had quite my share of his time and came away. He gave me a bundle of prescriptions and told me to try one after the other, and go on with any that suited best, that he could only alleviate my distress, not cure it, but that although such great want of rest was wearing, it was not dangerous and proceeded entirely from my nervous system being rather worn out . . . He did not think I ought to travel, but go to the seaside or mountain air, both of which tend to sleep. [Effie was an insomniac.] I told him I thought the sea would suit Mr Millais best as he was going to paint the Romans leaving Britain. Dr Simpson was immensely interested, as he is an antiquarian. He gave me the names of the best books on Roman costumes.

Effie wanted to join her husband in Dorset, but she was blocked by her health. When he was painting his background, she was home alone, feeling miserable. For a time she feared for her life. In addition to being sick, she was in an advanced state of still another pregnancy. She told her mother, 'I would rather have you and Alice [her nineteen-year-old sister] coming just before my illness instead of after it as I would like to see you in case anything happened to me.'

She fully described her plight on 2 February in a letter to her father: 'I cannot help at times being very anxious about my health as I feel the constant strain of suffering now so endless. Just now I suffer from cough, toothache, and cold. I have no disease, but my doctor says I am in a feverish and shattered state and not fit to take change of air. I have not had one night's natural sleep without the aid of drug or stimulant for six months.' Then she referred to something that surely was a major cause of her weakened condition: 'I am getting worn out with having children so fast, and I have had no chance of a healthy life for years now.'

Her husband, she noted, had returned from Dorset, but 'is away every day at 5 to the Academy and keeps very late hours, night and morning'. It was his turn to teach in the Life School, and he was a fine instructor. The art critic Cosmo Monkhouse wrote, 'Mr G.H. Boughton tells me that Millais helped not as others would, with a word of advice only, but would seize a piece of paper and rapidly draw a hand or foot in perfect lines, and leave it with the student, saying "That's what you want."' The *Athenaeum* reported, 'Mr Millais has attended to his duties with so much zeal and has proved so excellent a teacher, whether with regard to courtesy of demeanour or technical power that the students were only deterred from presenting him a written expression of thanks by the lack of a precedent to that effect.'

He showed considerably more concern for his students than for his wife. At about the time that the *Athenaeum* note appeared, Effie wrote to her twenty-one-year-old unmarried sister Sophia, 'You are not half as quiet at Bowerswell as I am here, as I never see anybody from five o'clock one day till eleven the next forenoon, and I always dine alone . . . I am thankful when bedtime comes. My only excitement in prospect is a visit to the dentist. Alice and you should be thankful at home to be able to read and work and do what you like. You don't know anything yet of prolonged bodily suffering and the frightful strain it is to mind and body, continual pain, irritation, and want of sleep.'

Her fourth son, and seventh child, John Guille, was born in March. At the moment of his birth, John Everett was in a Trafalgar Square classroom.

Autumn Leaves

Sir Isumbras

The Vale of Rest

Apple Blossoms

My First Sermon

My Second Sermon

Chill October

Hearts Are Trumps

Effie Deans

CHAPTER 20

1865–67

EVEN when she was not well, Effie loved to travel. She had a thirst for adventure. She enjoyed meeting people and seeing new things. John Everett, on the other hand, a friend said, 'was one of those who have no delight in travel, or, rather, one of those to whom the irksomeness of catching trains, of being immured in trains, and bounding into and out of hotels, appears in the light of a prohibitive price'.

Their dissimilarities came out in short trips, as when visiting Paris for a week in the autumn of 1864. After a day in Le Havre, Effie wrote to her mother from Paris:

> I had a delightful sea bath at Havre, where Everett might have had the same in a fresh or salt plunge, hot or cold, just below our bed room, but he won't go the least out of his way to go down a stair where the baths were beautifully clean and cheap. He even groans over a foot bath . . . If I was stronger and able to go about, I should like to see many things I have never seen – Père la Chaise, the Hotel Dieu, the Jardin des Plantes, the Markets, etc., but Everett dislikes sightseeing unless I manage it all for him, and I am not able to do much . . . Although I am often unwell, what I do see I enjoy very much indeed.

One year later they took their longest journey, a Continental holiday.

They stopped first in Chamonix. Effie wrote to her mother, 'Everything now is most comfortable, and the hotels have all the comfortable modern appliances except large bath towels. Evidently the days for roughing it are gone.' When she and Ruskin travelled, they were often the only British guests at a Swiss hotel, but now, she said, 'We meet plenty of English of the most vulgar description who don't know a word of any European tongue and are always calling for Allsops pale ale and making themselves at home everywhere.' As for her husband, he was 'delighted' with the scenery, which he viewed from the hotel veranda, a drink by his side.

From Chamonix they went to Milan. Effie reported that John Everett was 'much happier in a town. He is delighted with our hotel, a new one with a lovely white staircase.'

Milan was followed by the trip's highlight for Effie, a return to Venice. One would have thought that any artist would be excited by a first visit to this city, but Effie wrote to her sister Sophia:

If you and Alice ever marry people who will bring you to Europe, I do hope you may enjoy all these wonderful places as they deserve. With Everett it would be impossible to do so or not to be immensely influenced by his perpetual fault finding at everything and his fretted temper. I am extremely thankful that neither you nor Alice are with me, for you would not be allowed to admire anything in a natural way, and the impressions left on your minds would not be the true ones. We have beautiful rooms, our butter iced and snails and other delicacies, with the beautiful moon on the square and the air soft. The mosquitoes are all dead, and there was nothing to prevent us from enjoying ourselves very much indeed if only Everett would. Fortunately he does not scold me personally, but I have to listen to all his complaints. So I have let Val Prinsep take him this morning to the pictures as I wanted to rest.

Val Prinsep was another British artist in Venice for the first time. Millais came upon him in a café. They spent the entire morning together, playing billiards.

After six days in Venice, Millais told his mother-in-law, 'I saw *every-thing* [underlined twice].' The pictures were 'splendid,' but the city was 'so much on the decline that one cannot be in good spirits amongst such universal ruin'. He was 'glad to be out of it as I am with every new place I see'. This was his first letter from Europe. He hadn't posted anything earlier because:

I haven't felt disposed to write as the constant travelling takes the joke [sic] out of one completely. Breaking one's neck over churches and galleries is bad enough by itself, but in the company of people who exact unlimited praise of everything they take you to is still more exhausting.

Then there were the encounters with other British tourists:

We meet many country men and women who might be acquainted with a friend or acquaintance or know a party who met us they forgot where, and so a sort of understanding takes place, which in the desolation of continental travel ends in a mutual exchange of cards and a general invitation to spend the rest of our lives at each other's houses. This has happened so often that I must seriously consider the purchase of the whole of Cromwell Place for accommodations.

He admitted to being 'a grumbler abroad', but not at home, where 'I am satisfied with my bed, board, and especially my painting room. As for the noises of London they are a Jew's harp to a trombone here, for every Italian howls his Rigoletto to the moon, and dogs delight to bark all night from nine o'clock till two, when bells begin, a ceaseless din.' He also complained about mosquitoes, attracted to his 'sweetness' with 'nocturnal visits'.

The letter was posted in Bologna, where he had been 'overcharged in everything'.

With Effie, there was just one problem, insomnia. 'She is sleeping *very badly* [underlined four times],' John Everett told her mother. 'Indeed she never closes her eyes as a rule. And she's so nervous that the least noise puts her off. My breathing last night being heavier than usual kept her awake all night.'

Despite her insomnia, she was having a great time. From Florence, which followed Bologna, she wrote to her mother, 'Although I did not sleep all night but an hour, I have enjoyed the day immensely . . . The town is so full of life and really most beautiful . . . I get on somehow, and it is wonderful with sleep every two days what one can do.'

While in Florence, Millais, the opera-lover, missed a chance to hear the legendary soprano Adelina Patti. Effie told her sister Alice, 'Everett had a stall to hear Patti, her first night, but there was a confusion about it, as he does not take time to understand a thing thoroughly sometimes, and there it was, empty through the performance, waiting for him.'

In Florence, as in Venice, John Everett lamented, 'the mosquitoes are horrible'.

After Florence, they stopped briefly in Pisa, with a visit to Campo Santo. Then they went on to Rome.

Effie was exhilarated to be in this most historic of cities. 'I shall enjoy these ruins immensely,' she told her mother. 'I wish I had read a history of Rome before I came.' She saw a great deal, usually 'by herself. She went alone to the Catacombs because 'Everett feels nothing in the world worth seeing at 9 or 10 o'clock.' At the Vatican she 'saw the Pope and his attendants going out on a drive, two carriages and four, and Swiss guards in middle age costume . . . The Pope walked down close to me . . . Everett would not come with me, which I thought very stupid as he may never have another chance.'

While Effie was watching the Pope, her husband was back at the hotel with several other English tourists, in a public room playing whist.

After Rome came Leghorn, Geneva, and, finally, Paris.

In Paris, Effie was again lured by shop windows and was again frustrated. Two weeks before Christmas, she wrote to her mother, 'I have not bought anything since I left except the terra cotta and a bas relief at Florence. I have much need of a bonnet as I went away with my hat and return with it in a very shady state, but Everett says I can make up my old one. I am much tempted with little hats and things that would suit Geoffroy and [John] Guille, but as I have not had a sou for a month past I can only admire.'

After two months abroad, they returned almost empty-handed.

*   *   *

Waiting at Cromwell Place was an invitation for Millais to become the Royal Academy's Professor of Painting. His principal duty would be to deliver two or three lectures a year. He declined, Effie told her father, because 'it would take up too much of his time . . . It is a pity.' She would have enjoyed being a professor's wife, especially since John Ruskin wouldn't get *his* professorship, at Oxford, until 1869.

He really *didn't* have time to be a professor, nor to paint pictures that were demanding. Because of recent expenditures on travel, for many months he would do only what could be completed, and sold, quickly. During all of 1866, he turned out nothing worthy of mention. Artistically the year was a blank.

* * *

Never did, or could, Millais stay away from the big Summer Show for two years running. In 1867, he exhibited five paintings, including four portraits of children. *Sleeping* and *Waking* were glimpses of five-year-old Effie in bed. *The Minuet* showed a ten-year-old girl 'standing up' to start her dance. *Master Cayley* was the head and shoulders of a small boy.

Millais wasn't apologetic about these pictures, nor should he have been. They were extremely well done without signs of carelessness, and his work was properly appreciated. *The Times* called *Sleeping* 'the most beautiful picture Mr Millais ever painted'. The *Art Journal* proclaimed *Sleeping* and its pendant to be 'two of the most delightful pictures ever seen in the Academy'. The *Morning Chronicle* said that *Master Cayley* was 'a beautiful little head which Vandyke would have been proud to father'. The *Saturday Review* referred to *The Minuet* as 'one of the sweetest little faces ever painted . . . exactly the kind of picture Mr Millais can paint better than any other painter who ever lived'. *Blackwood's* judged the portraits as a whole to be 'the glory of the Academy'.

Millais's fifth picture also featured a child, from the distant past. This was *Jephthah*, based on the Old Testament narrative of the warrior who went to battle after vowing to 'offer up for a burnt offering whatsoever cometh out of the doors of my house to greet me when I return'. The painting depicts the aftermath of his homecoming to be greeted by his daughter. Jephthah sits grief-striken, his daughter clings to him, her nurse wrings her hands, and attendants stand by helplessly.

Jephthah, large and spectacular, stood apart from the other pictures.

It gained respect because of the work that had gone into it, but it created no excitement. A potentially poignant scene unfortunately lacked poignancy. Earlier he had written about it to Hunt: 'I am working and alone knowing my bitterness over the difficulties of the painting.' These difficulties were due in part to a lack of enthusiasm. He did the picture only because he couldn't yet completely turn his back on historical and literary subjects. But his real artistic interest was centered on contemporary life.

* * *

During the summer of 1867 Millais started work every day after finishing breakfast and continued without cessation until seven in the evening. He was, he told Effie, 'making a hundred a day,' six days a week. (At that time, £100 equalled $500.) He had so many commissions that he turned down or postponed one offer after another. Early in June, when Effie was briefly out of town, he told her of a typical offer: 'A Mr Fisher brought his wife (a very pretty creature) begging me to paint her and to name the price. I had to postpone a reply till the winter.'

Along with routine commissioned work, he was doing what he hoped would be his principal painting of 1868. This work, *Rosalind and Celia*, was a rural scene from Shakespeare, but it wasn't like his Shakespearean pictures of the early 'fifties. With *Ferdinand Lured by Ariel* and *Ophelia*, he was guided by an exact text. Now he was imagining a scene. In Act 2, Scene 4, of *As You Like It*, Rosalind and Celia, with the clown Touchstone, wandering in the Forest of Arden, become quite tired. Celia says, 'I pray you bear with me. I cannot go no further.' (Double negatives are common in Shakespeare.) At this point Millais imagines the trio stopping to rest and shows them sitting under a tree.

Perhaps because he was depicting something that doesn't actually occur in the play, this picture was almost unbelievably difficult. He came to hate it. 'I would rather do anything almost,' he told Effie, 'than have to return to the "Rosalind".'

When he wrote this, in August, Effie was, as usual, in Scotland. But not in Perth. She was taking an extended holiday at fashionable St Andrews, mainly on the sandy beach. (In one letter, John Everett wrote, 'I am glad you are enjoying yourself with what appears to be your greatest pleasure in life, sea bathing.')

While she swam and sun-bathed, he slaved away in London, bewailing, as ever, their separation, the state of his health and the pressure of work. Then on Tuesday, 27 August, he had great news: 'I have at last got both heads of "Rosalind" to my satisfaction, and they are really good, so I can leave this picture and return to it and finish at once! I purpose leaving Saturday morning or Friday night, so please meet me at Perth, for I am dying to hug you.'

Effie's response came immediately. She could not meet him at Perth, presumably because she would not interrupt her seaside holiday.

* * *

In this month of August 1867, Effie and John Everett reached an irreversible turning point in their relationship.

His letter of 29 August began, for the first time, 'Dear Effie.' His mood was rather restrained: 'Yesterday the little pictures were fetched, so there is nothing more to do . . . I will come directly I have sent away the illustrations for Trollope. Smith wants me to illustrate a paper of Charles Collins [who had gone from painting to writing] which is to appear in the Cornhill . . . I had hoped to have got the "Rosalind" finished, but it is no nearer than when you left . . . I am in a perfect fever this morning and have a headache. I shall most likely start Sunday morning or night and be at Bowerswell to receive you when you return from St Andrews.'

As a diversion Millais once wrote:

> What though you're soundly execrated,
> Such is the common lot of strife.
> Be sure of this, although you're hated,
> One will believe in you, your wife.
>
> There rest, and live a life of ease,
> Forgetful of all bygone strife,
> But not of her who on her knees
> Has alone worshipped you, your wife.

If John Millais wanted his wife to fall to her knees and 'worship' him, we might excuse Effie Millais for her recent behaviour.

CHAPTER 21

1867–69

JOHN EVERETT'S last passionate letter to his wife was dated 27 August 1867. The nature of their new relationship may be inferred from his subsequent correspondence:

> *27 October 1867*. I am in receipt of your last letter. If I don't hear from you I will be at the Great Northern Station to meet you Tuesday night.
> *23 March 1868*. The Arthur Lewises ask us for dinner the 30th. I have accepted for myself only as I don't suppose you will be back, but if you can go write and say so at once.
> *23 July 1868*. I don't look forward to coming North and I am not at all sure that I shall come.
> *5 August 1868*. I suppose you are at St Andrews by this time bobbing under sea water in a bathing gown, and I suppose you will let me know your address.
> *19 August 1868*. I look forward to seeing you and I hope we shall enjoy ourselves together.

What brought about this strikingly altered relationship between John Everett and Effie?

Although Effie's health may have been a factor in the change, it could not have been a major cause. I can only speculate, but it seems to me that the fundamental reason for the transformation lay in their contrasting attitudes toward sex. As his letters indicate, John Everett was exceedingly passionate. Effie, I am convinced, partly because of hints in her husband's correspondence, was decidedly unenthusiastic about sex.

When she was young, Effie amused herself with men, but she never became seriously involved with any of them. When she married, she chose a considerably older man for whom sex was of little or no importance. And she appears to have been perfectly satisfied with a sexless marriage until she met John Millais. Bored by her pedantic husband, she was attracted to the most popular, most famous, and perhaps most handsome painter in Great Britain. After becoming Mrs John Millais, for a time she faithfully performed her marital duties, but probably without much exuberance. When she said 'Basta!' to Rawdon Brown, after the birth of her fourth child, she was, I think, referring not only to children but to the process by which children are created.

It might not have been necessary to resort to conjecture if Effie's letters to John Everett had survived. But, as I have noted, although the Millais family correspondence (except for Effie's letters from the Trossachs to her parents) was generally well preserved, almost everything that Effie wrote to her husband has mysteriously disappeared. It can only have been destroyed by one or more of her descendants. Why? Because they would have revealed a coolness, conspicuously contrasting with John Everett's warmth? I have already likened Effie in this regard to her contemporary Sue Bridehead, in Hardy's *Jude the Obscure*, and I repeat that a distaste for physical love was not uncommon among so-called Victorian 'modern women'.

This aversion was not, I think, an indication of frigidity. It came about, at a time when family planning was almost nonexistent, because sex was inextricably linked to childbearing, which entailed great restrictions on the childbearer's personal freedom. For a woman like Effie there was much more to life than never-ending bearing of children. Unfortunately, this way of thinking was beyond the comprehension of most Victorian men, even those who, like John Millais, were comparatively enlightened. (As an American, I am reminded of Thomas Jefferson, one of the most brilliant of my countrymen, who owned slaves and was convinced of the innate inferiority of black persons.)

And so after much thought on the subject, I cannot escape from the conclusion that the principal reason for the end of all intimacies between Mr and Mrs John Everett Millais was Effie's wish to be an independent human being rather than the perpetual sex object of her husband. (The final break occurred about ten years before Nora Helmer's celebrated slamming of the door in Ibsen's *Doll's House*.)

* * *

Conceived about six weeks before John Everett's aforementioned 'last passionate letter' of 27 August 1867, the eighth and last Millais child, Sophie, was born in March 1868.

John Everett was doing so well financially that he no longer haggled over prices. He told Effie about a painting that he had hoped to sell for £750: 'Agnew won't give me more than 700, which I have accepted as I can't be bothered.'

The eldest Millais daughters, Effie and Mary, attended an exclusive boarding school. The two senior sons, Everett and George, were enrolled in a preparatory academy for Rugby School, one of the traditional grounds for English gentlemen. Some years earlier the most famous British head master, Thomas Arnold, had broadened Rugby's curriculum beyond that of its rivals. It was, for example, the first to include as required subjects modern history and modern languages. This perhaps explains why John Millais passed over Eton and Harrow in favour of the more progressive institution.

One of the boys was not very serious about his schooling. Late in July 1868, when Everett was twelve and George was eleven, John Everett wrote to Effie, in Scotland:

The report cards have come, and Evie's is really bad – *careless*, *idle*, and *disobedient* [underlined three times]. If he defies his masters I hope they will thrash him well. George's is altogether as good as Everett's is bad. If the reports aren't better next term I will send Everett to a commoner school. I hope you will speak very seriously to him as none of his reports have been what they ought to be . . . I cannot overlook a really bad series of reports. When I think how little trouble I gave my parents and how I slaved as a boy, I feel quite frightened that Everett may be a real trouble to us if not checked while he is young. [It will be remembered that Millais had refused to attend school and was educated by his mother.] I am *quite* delighted with George.

In 1871, George would enter Rugby, but Everett would never enroll there or in any other public school.

Everett's academic record was one of two disquieting matters for John Everett. The other was Effie's continuing insomnia, about which he was not notably solicitous. Sometimes he would refer to it perfunctorily in a letter and then go to some other topic. At least once he implied that her problem was psychosomatic: 'Your enduring sleeplessness is so chronic with you that there may be no chance for you but the stillness of a mountain top. There is no Highland cot without a dog to bark or cock to crow, and generally both, and either will destroy the possibility of sleep in one so nervously constituted as you are.' (Did he forget how he couldn't sleep in Italy because of barking dogs and church bells?)

* * *

The by-laws of the Royal Academy stipulate that a new Academician 'shall not receive his Letter of Admission till he hath deposited . . . a Picture, Bas-relief, or other specimen of his abilities, approved of by the sitting Council of the Academy'. This Letter of Admission, signed by the Sovereign, is the Academician's 'diploma'. The 'specimen' is his or her 'diploma work'.

Millais's 'diploma picture' hung at the Academy's last Trafalgar Square show, in 1868. Called *Souvenir of Velasquez,* it showed a little blonde girl in a black velvet dress sitting on the ground with a sprig of orange in her hand, obviously a reminder of Velasquez's *Infanta Marguerite* in the Louvre. Actually it was a clever tour de force superficially resembling the work of the nineteenth century's favourite Old Master.

Also exhibited in 1868 was the vexatious *Rosalind and Celia,* Millais's last picture to draw from reviewers the term 'Pre-Raphaelite', if only to point out why it *wasn't* a Pre-Raphaelite picture. As the *Art Journal* said, 'It contains not a suspicion of Pre-Raphaelitism. On the contrary, it is all painted with dash, mastery, and off-hand facility.' After his ordeal with this work, Millais may have been surprised to learn that it had been painted with 'off-hand facility'. Is it any wonder that he felt as he did about art critics?

* * *

In 1869, exactly one hundred years after its founding, the Royal Academy moved into its present home in Burlington House, Piccadilly. At last the Exhibition would be held in galleries where everything would be properly seen. Pictures would no longer be jammed together. Never again would a *Pizarro* hang under the ceiling, and nothing in the new building resembled the infamous Octagon Room. Burlington House began a new era for the RA. It also vitalised a new development for John Millais. The portrait of Mrs Freeman in 1862 had been followed in 1864 by portraits of two children, and in 1867 by *Master Cayley*. Now in 1869 three of six entries were portraits. And during the rest of his life nearly two-thirds of his exhibited paintings would be portraits.

It has been said that Millais did portrait work because of what he could earn from it. His income was indeed high, and it was needed to maintain his family life style. But the primary motivation was not, I think, financial. 'The real happiness of an artist,' he once wrote, 'is mainly from his labour, the construing of the enigmatic, and the attempt to embody his ideas. The word of congratulation which the outside world bestows on him is very flattering to his vanity but is worthless if he does not himself believe it is deserved.' This, I believe, is a sincere statement and is relevant to his work in the portrait genre, the importance of which he came to recognise in his maturity.

As a portraitist, Millais was every bit as realistic as in his other paintings, but now he was no rebel. He was quite happy to become part of a long-standing tradition, one that included such masters as Titian, Veronese, Velasquez, Rembrandt and, yes, Raphael.

In remarks delivered at the Royal Academy's Life School, he made it perfectly clear where he stood:

In Titian's *Bacchus and Ariadne* (the finest oil picture I know of), except for the leopards, which the artist had not the opportunity of studying, there is no idealising of form. I can see the people who sat for him. There is a distinct individuality in each figure in spite of the broad or grand treatment . . . The same may be said of the Louvre Veronese Feast [*The Wedding Feast at Cana*], where the individuality is even more striking, many of the figures being absolutely portraits. Titian and Veronese partook of the same spring that Phidias and Praxitiles drank of. Rembrandt, Velasquez, Vandyke, and Murillo are also all truthful students of nature . . . and there is the same faculty in these men of *fidelity* and no marked intentional departure from the object portrayed to make it better.

Contrary to what some critics have asserted, Millais's portraits do not demonstrate a decline in the quality of his work. In his Pre-Raphaelite subject pictures, beginning with *Isabella*, he had taken great care with the faces of his figures. To go from them to his later portraits was a logical development.

* * *

One of the portraits of 1869 was of a prominent fifty-one-year-old civil engineer, John Fowler, later Sir John. He had just supervised construction of the world's first subterranean rail system, now the Metropolitan Line of the London Underground. He is seated at a desk in his office. Another subject was Nina Lehmann, a strikingly beautiful fifteen-year-old girl from an affluent family. In a white dress, she sits casually on a garden stool, amidst camellia bushes.

These portraits showed how skillfully Millais could discern the essence of a subject's character and individuality. Extravagantly praised, each was more than once characterised as the best picture in the show. This is from *The Times*:

The full-length of Miss Nina Lehmann is an extraordinarily daring achievement . . . No other living painter would have ventured on a juxtaposition of the pale blue of a curtain and the vivid metallic green of camellia leaves, or could have brought out the shell-like flesh tones of the face and the pale gold of the hair against such a background . . . The picture is a complete justification of Mr Millais's change of method and manner. He learnt all that mature study and painstaking imitation could teach him in the [Pre-Raphaelite] school. This masterly representation is the fruit of the lesson.

[227]

If 'Nina Lehmann' be Mr Millais's triumph of power, his half-length of Mr Fowler is very decidedly the best portrait of the year. It might be a lesson to our professional portrait painters. Here sits a man as he is – as true a translation on canvas as ever Titian accomplished, the uncompromising truth. Mr Millais has been true to his art and his subject. It is not his business to make people fall in love with his subjects; he has no need to attract sitters . . . If people come to him to be painted, they must be painted as he chooses. Only people willing to be painted on these conditions will come. All the better for him and them. They are likely to be the best worth painting.

The writer concluded, 'In his portraits, Mr Millais is the most uncompromising of realists.'

This uncompromising realism was particularly striking in his third portrait of the year. This one tells a story. It is called *The Gambler's Wife*, and was a commentary on an acute contemporary social problem, self-destruction by gambling. This topic was repeatedly touched on in Victorian novels, focused usually on 'fast young men', who, particularly after over-indulging in wine, would wager far more than they could afford to lose in a billiard room or at a card table. But it was not from a work of fiction that Millais got his idea. He was himself an inveterate card player. He once told Mrs Gray, 'I go nearly every night to the Garrick to play a rubber of *that awful game* [whist].' Although his own losses were never excessive, he had seen others ruined. His painting was inspired by his observations.

The story underlying *The Gambler's Wife* is clear even without the title. An attractive young woman in a plain black dress stands near a table with scattered playing cards. She holds one and contemplates it sadly. The expression on her face tells it all. Her life has been destroyed by that card and others like it. Millais surely felt the poignancy of his scene, and as in *A Huguenot*, he shows an eloquent restraint. The picture is sad but not didactic or melodramatic. He was not a preacher; he was a compassionate observer. In its presentation of a contemporary predicament, *The Gambler's Wife* might properly be compared to the work of Hogarth.

* * *

On 8 June 1869, John Millais reached the age of forty. This alone might have induced thoughts on mortality, but a few days earlier he had a more persuasive reminder. His friend and exact contemporary Mike Halliday, his companion in the Highlands in 1854 when Effie was obtaining her decree of separation, died unexpectedly from natural causes. 'I was so shocked,' he told Effie, 'for the news was so sudden. I didn't even know he was ill . . . I never leave town, I have noticed, without one of my friends dying during the interval.'

For the first time he had a solicitor draw up a last will and testament.

*　*　*

Perhaps this chapter should have ended with the preceding sentence, but I cannot overlook an unpleasant peripheral episode which reached a climax at this time. It involved John Ruskin and one Rose La Touche. I shall not delve into this affair, which has been discussed by most of Ruskin's biographers. I will deal only with the role played by John Millais and, more directly, Effie Millais.

In 1858, the thirty-nine-year-old Ruskin began to give drawing lessons to ten-year-old Rose. By 1864 the teacher had fallen in love with his pupil. She was, he told a friend, 'the only living thing in the world I care for'. On her eighteenth birthday, Ruskin proposed to Rose; because of parental objections she deferred her answer until she was twenty-one. It seems clear that she loved him, and there can be no doubt about his feelings. This was the only real love of his life.

When her twenty-first birthday drew near, Mrs La Touche, uncomfortable about the situation, wrote a letter of inquiry to Effie. This letter and Effie's reply have not survived, but the gist of Effie's response may be inferred from Mrs La Touche's second letter to her, dated 21 May 1868: 'my daughter earnestly begs me to express to you her deep gratitude for your generosity in granting the information that saved her, and us all, from so much misery.'

Effie's words actually intensified Rose's misery, and because of her continuing feelings toward Ruskin, Mrs La Touche wrote once again to Effie in 1870. Even at this late date John Everett could not remain silent, and he sent Mr La Touche a letter with this sentence: 'When called upon to answer the charge [of impotence] he decamped to Switzerland, neither he nor his family making any answer to the Court.' Millais of course knew that Ruskin had left for Europe two weeks after the citation had been served on the date that had been fixed four months earlier.

After Millais's letter had arrived, Mrs La Touche asked Ruskin about his earlier marriage. He unequivocally denied that he was impotent. On 8 October Mrs La Touche wrote again to Effie, informing her that Ruskin 'states that you were never his wife . . . that your tastes and his were from the beginning incompatible; that he respected you too much to be anything but a protector and companion to you – that he made every possible effort to make you happy; and that failing to do so, and finding you desired your liberty, he resolved to retire altogether and make no reply to the citation . . . in order to secure your freedom and happiness at the cost of his own reputation.'

John Everett and Effie both replied. Writing to Mr La Touche, John Everett said, 'Mr Ruskin is open to assert what he pleases to his few credulous admirers as far as we are concerned . . . His conduct was simply infamous; and to this day my wife suffers from the suppressed misery she endured with him.'

Effie sent Mrs la Touche a truly remarkable letter:

Mr Ruskin took exactly the same course with me as with your daughter . . . and immediately after the wedding ceremony he proceeded to inform me that he did not intend to marry me. Afterwards he excused himself from doing so by saying that I had an infernal disease. His father tried to induce him to believe me insane, and his whole conduct was as monstrous as his present statements are falsehoods . . .

Now that I am a married woman and happy with a family I think his conduct can only be excused on the score of madness, and his wickedness in trying his dreadful influence over your daughter is terrible to think of.

I can easily understand the hold he has acquired, as it was exactly the same over myself. His conduct to me was impure in the highest degree, discreditable, and so dishonourable that I submitted to it for years not knowing what to do, although I would have often been thankful to have run away, and I envied people sweeping the crossings . . .

From his peculiar nature he is utterly incapable of making a woman happy. He is quite unnatural, and in that one thing all the rest is embraced.

He always pretended to me to the last that he was the purest and holiest of men, and he had a peculiar influence over a young mind in making himself believed . . .

He once years before [their separation] offered me £800 a year to allow him to retire into a monastery and retain his name – that I declined to do. He was then under the influence of Manning.

I think if your daughter went through the ceremony with him her health would give way after a time and she would be submitting to the same kind of treatment as I was.

It is very painful to write all this and be again obliged to recall all those years of distress and suffering, of which I nearly died. But I hope your daughter may be saved.

This letter reminds me of how a certain American writer once characterised a statement by another American writer: Every word is a lie, including 'and' and 'the'.

The dispatch from Effie, characterised by Ruskin as 'that accursed woman of Perth', had its desired effect. It brought about a permanent separation of Ruskin and Rose. It was also perhaps a contributing cause of Rose's death in 1875 at the age of twenty-seven. Since the death certificate disappeared, there is no certainty of the cause of her death. Some have suggested that she committed suicide.

CHAPTER 22

1870–77

In his forty-first year John Millais was recognised as his nation's foremost painter. But he didn't rest on his laurels. He was never more industrious than in the 1870s. And, despite his resolution to the contrary, he continued to do new things.

In the 1870 Exhibition he had six entries, once again demonstrating his unending versatility. There were two portraits, one of which, of the Marchioness of Huntley, had already been sold for £2000. There was a contemporary scene, a young dressmaker leaving an offering in a box at London's Hospital for Consumption, with a title already used for an earlier gigantic work, *A Widow's Mite*. There was a historical work, *The Boyhood of Raleigh*, showing the future explorer as a child sitting by a sea-wall and listening intently to a well-travelled mariner.

There were also two paintings which were the first of a kind.

Never had Millais based a picture on a contemporary news event. Now came *A Flood*, stimulated by a calamitous inundation of Sheffield after a dam guarding the town reservoir had burst. The rushing water totally or partially destroyed 4500 buildings and caused 240 drownings. The painting looked at the disaster from a fresh vantage point. Millais got the idea from Charles Reade's recent novel *Put Yourself in His Place*, which contains a detailed account of the deluge, including an incident that Reade had come upon in a newspaper:

> In the large fish-pond, now much fuller than usual, floated a wheelbarrow, a hair mattress, an old wooden cradle, and an enormous box.

Little [a character in the novel] went splashing through the water to examine the cradle: he was rightly rewarded. He found a little child in it awake, perfectly happy enjoying the fluttering birds above and the buoyant bed below.

Millais showed a cradle floating peacefully in a quiescent pool, the occupant stretching its arms, happily oblivious of danger. The baby, unlike its prototype, is not alone. Perched on an edge of the cradle is a terrified black kitten, well painted but smacking of claptrap.

Most viewers didn't object to the cat or anything else in the picture, which, the *Art Journal* reported, was a 'sensation'. The *Illustrated London News* found it 'impossible to find fault with this painting; in its way it is perfect.' But it was a one-shot effort. This was his only plunge into a newsworthy current occurrence.

Hanging alongside *A Flood* was *The Knight Errant*, with Millais's first full nude. She was not, despite his principal current interest, a present-day woman. Far from it. The painting takes us back to the days when knights rescued damsels in distress. And it is very, very proper. The title character is untying the bonds of a young woman stripped by robbers and tied to a tree. Nothing is titillating. The victim is devoid of expression or individuality. Millais was a great painter of flesh, but this woman's flesh is singularly unlifelike. The knight stands discreetly behind her. They don't make eye contact. She looks to the right; he looks to the left. The *Saturday Review*, noted for propriety, observed, 'On the score of morals and good taste, the work is unexceptionable.'

Actually it was not at all exceptional. The *Manchester Guardian* put it all in a nutshell: 'Having painted a great many other things, Mr Millais has apparently decided to paint the nude – lashed most methodically to the stem of a silver birch by an arrangement of ropes worthy of a sailor. The knight is cutting the ropes as if he were carving a joint of beef. This is an absurd work, destitute of any rational motive.'

Almost unheard of for Millais at this time, the picture remained unsold for four years. He would never paint a second nude.

* * *

At the Exhibition of 1871 Millais unveiled the most fatiguing work of his career, begun in 1863. It is known as *Moses*, but the catalogue contained only a passage from the Book of Exodus: 'So Joshua did as Moses said unto him, and fought with Amalek, and Moses, Aaron, and Hur went up to the top of a high hill. And it came to pass when Moses held up his hand that Israel prevailed: and when he let down his hand Amalek prevailed.' Moses is shown seated on a hilltop watching the battle with Aaron and Hur, on either side, holding up his hands.

It was not, and could not have been, a total success. Critics felt that the concept was too demanding. The *Art Journal*'s reviewer said, 'the difficulties of the subject are almost insurmountable.' I disagree. This picture wasn't much more difficult, if at all, than some of the early works, *Isabella*, for example, completed in a few months. Millais really no longer enjoyed doing big pictures with big subjects. By now he had just about had his fill of multi-figure scenes from the past. During the remaining twenty-five years of his career he would exhibit only two, none at all until 1884.

At the 1871 show, he was much more interested in his other entries, an excellent portrait of George Grote, Vice-Chancellor of the University of London, and a highlight of his career, *Chill October*.

Reviewers admired and were amazed by *Chill October*. The *Saturday Review* called it 'the novelty of the year.' The *Illustrated London News* critic said, 'Mr Millais surprises us more than ever.' *Punch* concluded that its 'moral' was that 'a man of genius can do what he likes.'

The reason for the astonishment was that in his forty-second year Millais was exhibiting his first pure landscape.

Why had the creator of superb backgrounds for figure paintings not done this earlier? Because he and many other figure painters felt that landscape art was beneath them. As the noted art critic Philip Hamerton wrote in 1866, 'It is the commonly received doctrine amongst painters of history and genre that figure painting represents *mind*, whereas landscape painting represents matter.' Since the mind is superior to matter, the portrayer of human beings must be above '*un simple paysagiste*', as he was often called, 'a mere landscape painter'.

Why then did Millais exhibit a landscape now? For the same reason, I believe, that he had painted a moonlight picture. He had been encouraged to do it by Effie. The two of them maintained a civil, properly formal relationship, and she continued to show interest in his work. It was only natural for the former wife of John Ruskin to suggest a foray into landscape art. This is not just speculation. One of Effie's few surviving letters to John Everett, dated 29 September 1869, contains this sentence: 'I wish you could do a landscape yet, but I am afraid it is too late in the year and getting too cold and windy for you to sit out.' Millais was in Scotland, and it *was* too late to begin a picture outdoors. He put it off until the following summer.

Some time later he recalled, '"Chill October" was painted from a backwater of the Tay near Perth, a simple scene. The traveller between Perth and Dundee passes the spot where I stood. Danger on either side – the tide, which once carried away my platform, and the trains, which threatened to blow my work into the river. Many of my friends were at a loss to understand what I saw in such a scene. I made no sketch for it, but painted every touch from Nature, on the canvas itself, under irritating trials of wind and rain. The only studio work was in connection with the effect.'

Millais was following to the letter Ruskin's famous exhortation to painters to 'go to Nature in all singleness of heart and walk with her laboriously and trustingly, having no other thoughts but how best to penetrate her meaning . . . neither to choose, nor compose, nor imagine, nor experimentalise, but to be humble and earnest in follow- ing the steps of Nature.'

The finished picture presents just what Millais saw: a thick bed of reeds in the foreground, willows and alders in the middle, and the backwater receding into the distance. It is a faithful transcription and also a lonely, foreboding vision of a Scottish autumn, a fine mood piece.

* * *

It was at the private view in 1871 that I first saw Millais. I was walking with Val Prinsep.

'Here comes Millais,' he said.

I was tremendously excited at having the chance of seeing the great man, and I gazed with respectful admiration.

Val said in passing, 'Good show of Old Masters.'

'Old masters be damned!' riposted Millais as, with twinkling eyes, he looked at me. 'I prefer the young Mistresses!'

Val roared with laughter.

'Only Johnny Millais would dare to make a remark like that,' he said.

I thought Millais strikingly handsome; good features and splendid figure. I don't remember any of the pictures I saw. I remember only Millais.

This is from the memoirs of the extremely attractive Louise Jopling, a fine painter, mainly of portraits. In 1871 she was Louise Rose, twenty-seven years old and married to a civil servant. In the 'seventies she and Millais were close, if not intimate, friends. Her husband died in 1872, and in January 1874 she married a painter, Joseph Jopling. In her memoirs, she wrote: 'Ours was a very quiet wedding in the church at the Boltons, South Kensington. Millais came and was full of fun. He was struck by the good looks of my sister, and putting her arm under his, he said, "We are the best-looking couple here, so we must walk arm in arm."'

John Millais is frequently mentioned in Louise Jopling's book, but nowhere is there an allusion to Effie. Perhaps she had reasons for not speaking of Effie. Then again, perhaps Millais was alone when she saw him socially. In the 'seventies Effie and John Everett often went their separate ways.

His letters began 'Dear Effie' and ended 'Yrs. J.E. Millais'. No longer did he complain about working apart from her. On the contrary, he was often content to have her gone. Thus on 31 December 1872, he wrote, 'Unless you return in a very different frame of mind, it will be better for you to keep away as I cannot have my work hindered.'

When this was written, the children had come home from school for the winter recess. It didn't bother Effie that she had not yet seen them. On 7 January he wrote, 'I have not written about domestic affairs as they wd. not conduce to your comfort. The girls and boys have been very good of late, but at first (upon their arrival) I was almost driven mad – having such continual interruptions to my work. However we are in working order now . . . and there is no need for you to come home as I can manage till the holidays are over. Next door they are repainting and *continually* knocking early in the morning, and as long as that continues you are better away.'

[236]

Effie and John Everett were not with their children often enough to have many disagreements on how to raise them. On one point, however, they were at odds. Effie was a 'modern' woman, and John Everett was a prototypical Victorian male. This brought on a minor conflict. 'It occurs to me,' he wrote to her in August of 1870, referring to young Effie and Mary, twelve and ten years old, 'to write a line to say that I think you should not allow the little girls to go out so much in the evening. When they are so exempt from supervision they become wild with their companions, they lose all control, and they are not like the boys, whom I have perfect confidence in.'

Nothing would suggest that Effie followed her husband's advice.

*   *   *

There was one personal experience that Effie and John Everett shared. It took place in 1874 and was traumatic for both of them.

Because of his standing, John Millais thought that his wife should be presented to the Queen. (It would not be her first royal presentation. She had had the experience as Mrs John Ruskin.) In May they broached the matter with persons close to the court, who felt confident of obtaining an invitation. Then Effie received a bombshell from her close friend the Duchess of Sutherland:

> I hardly know how to tell you what it pains me so much to write. Yesterday exception was taken by the Lord Chamberlain to your being presented on my sending the card into his office. I at once wrote to the Queen, urging an exception be made ... to the rule against any one being presented to the Queen who has been divorced.
>
> I have just had the Queen's answer, and I am grieved to say that without in any way implying blame in your case, Her Majesty sees too many difficulties in acting contrary to the usual custom, to advise it.

Effie at once replied.

> I am distressed and shocked beyond measure ... I am satisfied that Her Majesty would not do an act of injustice to any of her subjects, and would not if correctly informed of my case have denied me the

privilege of a presentation. I have never been *divorced*, nor did I divorce Mr Ruskin. By the Ecclesiastical Law of England, the Church of which Her Majesty is the head, and the civil law of the country, I was given my freedom, the ceremony of marriage through which I had passed being declared null and void . . . I was blameless and free to contract marriage as a spinster, and I was not married to Mr Millais for more than a year afterward. Mr Millais and I are satisfied if Her Majesty was cognisant of the fact no exception could be taken by the Lord Chamberlain.

The Duchess agreed that Effie was being treated unfairly, and the Duke of Sutherland told Millais that efforts were under way to persuade the Lord Chamberlain to change his ruling. But when the Duchess again wrote to Effie, she said, 'I cannot tell you how grieved I am to have had a second letter from Her Majesty in answer to my last, saying that on account of the difficulty it would make with *others*, the presentation is impossible.'

Now John Everett wrote to the Duchess: '*Injustice to my wife is not defensible on the score of her misfortune proving an awkward precedent.* Think what the prohibition carries. Everyone, even her own children, will conclude there must be something against her character. Then again, if she is not considered worthy of passing before Her Majesty, how is she fit to mix in the society in which we move?'

Millais heard from Sir Robert Collier, Sir Arthur Helps, and the Duke of Westminster, each of whom had tried to persuade the Queen to soften her decree. But she was inflexible. Finally one of the Queen's closest attendants, Sir Thomas Biddulph, informed Millais's friend Francis Knollys that 'the Queen decided that she could not receive Mrs Millais. It seems a hard case no doubt but I believe all precedent is against receiving a lady who has been the wife of another man still living, and the public might not understand the peculiar circumstances.'

This concluded the affair.

*   *   *

In the 'seventies John Millais painted three types of pictures – landscapes, contemporary scenes, and portraits. After finishing *Chill*

[238]

October Millais had no immediate plans for further landscapes. For all anyone knew at the time, it might have become, like the moonlight and the nude, a solitary foray. In reality, *Chill October* was the first of a series. One reason for the subsequent landscapes was the response to the first one, an unqualified success. But there was more to it. Millais now believed in landscape art. Far from considering it inferior, he gave it his ultimate compliment. He compared it to music.

The concept that music is the purest of the arts, with the most direct impact, is ancient, going back at least to Aristotle. Early in the *Poetics*, Aristotle notes that while language is needed for the exposition of other arts, 'in music harmony and rhythm alone are employed.' This idea achieved its greatest recognition in the nineteenth century. The writings of Baudelaire and Ruskin contain references to the purity of music, and late in the century Joseph Conrad wrote his famous tribute to 'the magic suggestiveness of music – which is the art of arts'.

But it was Walter Pater whose name has been most closely associated with this doctrine. Probably his most original and influential essay was 'The School of Giorgione', published in 1877 in the *Fortnightly Review*, and included in 1888 in Pater's book *The Renaissance*. 'The School of Giorgione' contains Pater's most celebrated pronouncement: '*All art constantly aspires towards the condition of music.*' (The emphasis was his.) He then amplified this statement: 'The art of music most completely realises the artistic ideal, the perfect identification of matter and form. In music is found the true type or measure of perfected art . . . The arts may be represented as continually struggling after the principle of music, to a condition which music alone realises.'

In a later essay, 'Style', Pater said, 'Music is the ideal of all art precisely because in music it is impossible to distinguish form from substance, the subject from the expression.' Because of these and other similar remarks, Pater has been hailed as the inventor of this principle which he popularised.

I should like, however, to call attention to some thoughts of Millais jotted down between 1872 and 1875 – that is, at least two years before the publication of 'The School of Giorgione' – on sheets of paper which have become part of the archives of the Pierpont Morgan Library and until now have been unpublished:

However strong words may be, they are found wanting and are limited, appealing only to that section of mankind who understand the language . . . Music all the world may enjoy to the full. Words leave off when the grandest music begins.

Handel has given us a further insight into Heaven in his oratorios than words can ever hope to give. The medium of sound is profoundest.

As an artist I would like to pay a humble tribute to the power of music over those who are fortunate enough to feel its language. It has more of Heaven in its composition than poetry or painting, and if less human it is more divine. Words are admittedly weak to convey thought.

Then he explicitly brought landscape art into the equation: 'Land and seascapes under conditions of light and shadow may possess a practical sentiment which will speak to the spectators as music does, and excite in us a higher devotion for nature herself.'

In light of these feelings, it is not surprising that *Chill October* was followed by two landscapes in 1872, two in 1874, and single pictures in 1875, 1876, and 1877. 'We have learned,' the *Graphic*'s reviewer wrote in 1877, 'to expect a landscape as an annual contribution by Mr Millais.'

During this spree, on 27 May 1875, he laid open his feelings in a letter to a friend:

In my opinion the fundamental principle of all durable work is that it should be humbly approached and simply and unaffectedly painted – never deviating from the nature before you, except to obtain that impression or statement which is fleeting and which the artist has to render almost as quickly as it passes before him.

In my opinion the pictures that will stand must process in the highest degree the fundamental qualities of fine drawing and modest colour rendered in the simplest possible manner. We should have no care beyond this . . . I would advise a young artist to approach whatever he undertakes reverentially, never permitting an idle touch in the progress of his work, to disabuse his mind of all dodges or artifice.

He practised what he preached. Each landscape was painted in Scotland, in the midst of what he knew and loved. Each was done completely on location. (He could not, or would not, emulate Turner and other landscapists, who often did a sketch at the scene and painted the picture in a studio.) Everything he saw was faithfully replicated. The fine Liverpool landscapist Alfred Hunt called these pictures 'wonderful transcripts of the plain fact'. The *Graphic*'s critic said they were 'the *ne plus ultra* of literal landscape'.

It wasn't easy to be an artistic literalist. In 1876, working on *The Sound of Many Waters*, he wrote to Holman Hunt, 'I am now in a Highland cottage . . . I have commenced a landscape which is a beautiful scene of rushing water between rocks and autumn foliage forming a crescent above . . . It is a diabolical subject as it is so full of detail.' A few days later, he told Effie, 'The labour in this painting is certainly *much greater* than in any I have yet done, but it will be very thoroughly carried out. I am sure no sledge-harnessed mariner of Nares's crew worked harder than I have at this North Pole of a picture. [Sir George Nares had lately led an expedition into the Arctic.] I stand until I am ready to drop, and drink enough whiskey and water to make an ordinary man quite giddy, but without feeling it.'

In addition to the arduousness of the picture, he had to walk eight miles each day to and from the site. This was too much for a man approaching his fiftieth year. And there was another problem. He told Hunt, 'My sight is so indifferent for small print that I use glasses and am writing this with goggles.'

What he had been doing requires good eyesight. And so *The Sound of Many Waters*, exhibited at the Academy in 1877, ended what might be called his second burst of Pre-Raphaelitism.

It was a good ending. After visiting the 1877 Summer Show, Gabriel Rossetti wrote to a friend, 'Millais has greater force in the rendering of nature than any painter in the world.'

* * *

Although he became a dedicated landscapist, Millais was still at his best with human beings. During the 'seventies his pictures of people were contemporary scenes with one or two characters and portraits.

One of them, appearing in 1874, had a 'big subject', *The Northwest*

Passage. Lately the Northwest Passage had been in the news. In the early 1850s, after three hundred years of exploration, it had finally been discovered by a British expedition commanded by Captain Robert McClure. Now it remained for someone to navigate it. Millais had this in mind when beneath the title in the Exhibition catalogue he put this sentence: 'It might be done, and England should do it.'

The picture shows an ancient mariner's living room, replete with charts and other maritime accessories. The old man and a young woman, probably his granddaughter, sit near a table as she reads aloud from an account of Arctic exploration. Apparently he will speak the line placed in the catalogue. (The passage would be made thirty years later, by Norwegians.)

Millais's other current subject pictures were smaller, in size and in scope. There were, of course, pictures of children. *Getting Better* shows a boy lying in bed with two young friends by his side. *Forbidden Fruit* has a little girl looking wistfully at an apple in her lap, which, for some reason, she must not eat.

More original was *A Somnambulist*. A young woman in a nightgown carrying a candle sleepwalks perilously close to the edge of a cliff and approaches a break in the path. Will she fall to her death, or will she somehow be rescued? This sounds like cheap melodrama, but actually it was well done. As the *Illustrated London News* said, it 'demonstrates unrivalled powers of observation with not the least approach to sensationalism'.

Then there was a popular trio of pictures exhibited in 1871, 1875, and 1877. The first was *Yes or No?* It shows an attractive, vivacious young upper-middle-class woman holding a letter and a man's photograph. She is apparently wondering how to answer the letter-writer, presumably the man in the photograph. But what is his question? A marriage proposal? Or an invitation to a dance? This was another scene of ambiguity.

The picture of 1875 was called *No!* A different young woman, in a black dress, holds a letter and a quill pen, indicating that the letter is hers. The title says that it is a negative response to her correspondent. Her expression is half-sad and half-firm. She evidently had to reject him, but she doesn't want to hurt him too much.

Terminating the series was, naturally, *'Yes.'* A third young woman, obviously happy, is joined by a young man. There is no ambiguity here. She has accepted his proposal of marriage.

It would be a mistake to regard these pictures as trivial. The probable question underlying each of them was for most middle-class women, and their parents, a matter of the greatest importance. Millais treated it as seriously as the women themselves would have. The public responded with enthusiasm.

Because of the fine portraits in his scenes of modern life, the dividing line between them and the straight portraits was often fine-drawn. Sometimes it is difficult to determine the category in which a painting belongs. A conspicuous example of this was *Hearts Are Trumps*, of 1872, Millais's best group portrait. It is also a glimpse into one of nineteenth-century Britain's most popular diversions.

In August 1871, he wrote to Effie, 'I dine with a Mr Armstrong this evening who from seeing the "Sisters" [a group portrait of 1868] wants me to paint his three [adult] daughters. They know the price and are prepared to give anything I ask. I go to see the girls this evening. The mother is handsome, and I think the children must be also.' Three days later he said, 'I have accepted the commission for painting the three girls.' In his hagiography of his father, John Guille Millais identified them as daughters of Sir William Armstrong, the celebrated engineer-inventor who created the Armstrong gun. In point of fact, Sir William Armstrong died unmarried and childless.

Millais patterned his work after a well-known picture by Sir Joshua Reynolds. In *The Ladies Waldgrave*, Reynolds shows three adult sisters in white dresses sitting around a table. One is winding a skein of silk; another holds the skein; the third is playing a tambourine. Millais confidently invited a comparison by positioning the Armstrongs around a table exactly like the Waldgraves. Beautifully dressed, they are in a conservatory, with sunshine pouring in. They are not just sitting. They are playing the game which for Millais was obsessive, the three-handed version known as 'dummy whist', with the 'dummy's' hand exposed in the foreground.

Millais probably talked about it to William Rossetti, whose anonymous review in *Fraser's Magazine* contained this observation: 'The attitudes of the three young ladies are marvellously expressive of the fortunes of each. The girl on our right, with calm triumph in her eyes and on her lips, turns her cards towards us and reveals that she holds nearly all the court cards in trumps. Her neighbour, with fewer chances, waits the luck of her opponent. The third in half contempt of fortune, relying on her partner's cards, surveys her barren hand.'

At the Exhibition, a representative response was that of the art critic for the *Academy*, who called the painting 'a splendid tour de force', and said that 'nothing could be more startlingly real than the effect produced by this painting . . . The girls playing cards are more real, more alive, than the living men and women who gaze on them.'

This last sentence provides the key to Millais's success as a portrait painter. His men, women and children were distinct, individualised, living, breathing human beings. In their totality, they depict an entire society.

His striking diversity in this genre was particularly well shown at the Exhibition of 1873, the high point of his career as a portraitist. In 1873, everyone used superlatives. 'The main strength of this Exhibition,' the *Spectator* said, 'consists in the portraiture, where Mr Millais stands pre-eminent.' The *Saturday Review* concluded that he was 'the most fertile in resources of any painter now living'. The *Illustrated London News* and *The Times* spoke with one voice. These portraits, according to the *Illustrated London News*, were 'the most remarkable work in the Exhibition'. The writer for *The Times* said that 'the most remarkable work of the year is among the portraiture of Millais.'

Five of his six entries were portraits. They ran the gamut from a five-year-old girl to a ninety-four-year-old woman. The little rose-cheeked girl appeared in the delightfully simple *Early Days*, sitting in a garden, a black kitten in her lap. In *New-laid Eggs*, a captivating young country woman in a Dolly Varden outfit has a basket of eggs hanging down from her arm. Alongside *New-laid Eggs* was the half-length of an aristocratic middle-aged man wearing the robes of a Doctor of Music, seated at a table and looking up from a musical score. He was the eminent composer and professor of music Sir William Sterndale Bennett. *Mrs Bischoffsheim* epitomised the fashionable *grande dame*, presented in profile, bejewelled in an antique chintz gown, with a facial expression combining alertness, intelligence and defiance. This was one of the two most talked-about pictures at the show. The other was Millais's profile portrait of ninety-four-year-old Mrs Heugh.

Mrs Heugh is at once reminiscent of Whistler's portrait of his mother, shown at the Academy a year earlier. Like Mrs Whistler, Mrs Heugh sits in an ordinary house dress, hands folded in her lap. Millais admired Whistler's work and may have been influenced by the earlier portrait. If any reviewers detected the similarity, they did not mention it. The *Art Journal*'s critic, who called *Mrs Heugh* 'the most powerful work Mr Millais has ever painted', compared it not to Whistler's mother, but to a Tintoretto portrait in Florence's Pitti Palace. Even *Punch* took note of Mrs Heugh. Its 'Academic Rhymes,' referring to a few of the pictures, contains these lines:

> HEUGH! Eheu! – No! Time, by this hand is stayed:
>   Painter and sitter worthy of each other,
> Smile, REMBRANDT's ghost! approve, VELASQUEZ's shade!

Punch's poet was not alone in thinking of Rembrandt and Velasquez. *Mrs Heugh* reminded numerous viewers of Rembrandt, and the *Athenaeum* said that 'Velasquez wouldn't be ashamed of *Mrs Bischoffsheim*.'

Others, however, while acknowledging its quality, lamented the time that he was giving to this work. The most eloquent of these critics, highly talented Margaret Oliphant, voiced her opinions in two unsigned articles for *Blackwood's Magazine*.

In reviewing the 1875 Exhibition, Oliphant wrote:

> Mr Millais, for whom, twenty years ago, we were wont to look eagerly as the poet, the glorious young revolutionary, the rebellious yet beloved hope and favourite of the Academy. What has come to the daring and splendid youth who once took us by storm? Mr Millais has resigned himself to mammon, or what is the same thing, to portrait-painting.

She returned to this point in the 1876 show, when four more Millais portraits hung in Piccadilly:

> Look at him now: he could once touch those higher strings which vibrate through the very soul. Once he could show us how hearts

work, how they struggle, and by what means they get the mastery. Who does not remember the tenderness of love in the Huguenot, grieved only to disappoint the poor girl's fond expedient of anguish, not to risk his life; and that hard self-repression of the weary wife, all work with the labour of her mission, thrusting her order of release into the jailer's eye, almost insolent in intense self-restraint of that love, and joy, and woe, which were ready to burst out in passionate floods if but the danger were over? Look at him now. A painter of portraits . . . And this is what his genius has come to – genius which was revolutionary in its youth, and carried the very standard of vague rebellion!

These remarks disturbed Millais. In the autumn of 1876, he defended himself in a letter to Holman Hunt: 'I think more than ever of my profession and take infinite precautions, and I am never careless in anything I paint. I know many men say Millais has become rich and paints to make more and doesn't take the pains he used to take, but the fact is that I am more alive than I ever was to the necessity of *thoroughness for Art's sake*, and nothing comes between art and me and my work. I am painting now in bitter weather, up at six, at my work at eight and only cease at dusk, but my notions of completeness are different to the Huguenot and pictures of that time.'

No one could legitimately entertain doubts about his conscientiousness in doing portraits. For one thing, he would not accept as a subject anybody with a well-filled pocketbook. Louise Jopling recalled that 'he used to say, "It always takes two to paint a portrait – the artist and the sitter."' Because he was besieged by prospective sitters, he could be and was discriminating.

Once selected, a sitter seldom found it easy. The experience of one, the writer-sculptor-critic Lord Ronald Gower was representative. This is from his diary for 1877: 'April 6. To Millais's studio at eleven o'clock. He works *con amore*, and he makes much use of a pier looking-glass. He makes one stand up all the time, with very little time for rest. However, he does let one converse and even smoke.'

Millais was as painstaking and personally involved with portraits as with any other type of picture. In the spring of 1876, about three-quarters done with the portrait of a society woman, Mrs Sebastian

Schlesinger, he learned that she was about to take an Italian holiday. Immediately he wrote to Mr Schlesinger: 'I have just received a thunderbolt. I am *distressed beyond expression* to hear that your wife leaves London on Thursday for Florence. If you have any regard for me or the picture please detain her. If I have two good days I can make a good picture, but with only one more sitting it must remain a sketch. It has been a terrible blow to me, and if it is in your power like a good fellow let me complete my work creditably. My reputation and your advantage are surely worth considering for a matter of three days.'

Mrs Schlesinger delayed her departure. The picture was finished on time and exhibited in Burlington House.

Margaret Oliphant agreed that Millais took his portrait painting quite seriously and did good work. What she objected to was not that he did portraits but that he was neglecting other, more demanding, kinds of pictures. In a letter to Hunt, he candidly explained his professional conduct: 'I have long foreseen the uncertainty of *subject* work and have therefore devoted a great part of my time to portraiture.'

Despite his rationalising, he was affected by what people said and wrote, most particularly in the *Blackwood's* articles. Because of them, I believe, he did his finest painting of the decade and one of the best of his career, begun late in 1876 and exhibited in 1877. This picture marked Millais's return to that once cherished situation, the meeting of a couple at a moving moment. It was called *Effie Deans*.

Like *A Huguenot*, *Effie Deans* is an imagined scene. Its stimulus was Scott's *The Heart of Midlothian*. In the novel Effie, the beautiful daughter of a stern presbyterian farmer, is seduced and becomes pregnant, but she does not inform her lover, George Staunton, of her condition. Millais, however, has Effie telling him of her predicament in a scene that he envisions.

He must have wanted to awaken memories of *A Huguenot* because the meeting occurs by a stone garden wall. With her pet, a collie dog unmentioned by Scott, Effie is on the near side of the wall. The 'blue snood', which held together her hair, and was regarded as symbolic of virtue, hangs down loosely from her hand. She has informed Staunton, on the other side of the wall, of her condition. Her face beautifully suggests fear, sorrow, shame, and hopelessness. Her lover is a handsome knave who seems eager to conclude the discussion.

The title of the picture shows that Millais was not much interested in *him*.

Effie Deans was done in time for the RA Exhibition, but it did not go there. A dealer, Charles Marsden, bought it for £2500 prior to sending-in day, and he showed it in his own gallery in King Street, St James's. The regular reviewers made their way to King Street and loved what they saw. The almost unanimous response was epitomised by the critic for the weekly *Graphic*: 'This is Mr Millais at his very best. It is a picture not approached for interest since *A Huguenot*, but far beyond that group in composition and treatment of accessories, and with a pathos that goes far more directly home to English hearts.'

It is easy to agree that *Effie Deans* is indeed superior to *A Huguenot* and *The Order of Release*. Like those works, it has a superb setting and a great heroine, perhaps Millais's greatest, and it tells a compelling story entirely through facial expressions. What lifts *Effie Deans* above its predecessors is its universality. Viewers of *A Huguenot* or *The Order of Release* are outsiders. But with *Effie Deans* a spectator can easily become personally involved. Effie is not just someone from a novel. She is Everywoman. There but for the grace of God . . .

*   *   *

In the summer of 1877, Millais was represented in three places. Besides Burlington House and the Marsden Gallery, he had four pictures in Bond Street where it verges into Grosvenor Street, at the Grosvenor Gallery. This building was the brainchild of Sir Coutts Lindsay, a wealthy fifty-three-year-old connoisseur of the arts. Feeling that the Royal Academy needed some competition, he built his own gallery at a cost of £120,000 – a sizable amount at that time – and in the late 'seventies and 'eighties held shows that ran concurrently with those in Burlington House.

The grand opening of the Grosvenor on Monday, 7 May 1877 was a big event. The structure was lavish, one newspaper calling it 'the most superb building in London devoted to art'. The show, everyone agreed, was 'different'. It was particularly different from Britain's premier exhibition. As *The Times* observed, 'The most prominent pictures are those least likely to be seen at the Royal Academy.'

Sir Coutts didn't preside over a mainstay of the establishment. He welcomed rebels and outsiders with talent. His inaugural entrants with the most pictures were conspicuously non-establishment types, Edward Burne-Jones, with nine paintings, and James Whistler, with eight. One of Whistler's entries was the notorious *Falling Rocket*, of which Ruskin wrote, 'I have seen and heard much of Cockney impudence before now, but never expected to hear a coxcomb ask two hundred guineas for flinging a pot of paint in the public's face.'

Along with Whistler, Burne-Jones and assorted insurgents, Sir Coutts' entry list included a handful of Academicians – Frederick Leighton, Edward Poynter, George Frederick Watts and, most prominently, with four entries, John Everett Millais.

Millais's paintings were unlikely to stir up trouble. They were all portraits, and the subjects give some indication of the company he had been keeping: the Marchioness of Ormonde, Countess Grosvenor, Lady Beatrice Grosvenor, and Lord Ronald Gower. There was nothing second-rate about them. The *Art Journal* called them 'by far the best pictures in the Exhibition'. But they were portraits, as were two of his entries at the Academy. At the RA he was also exhibiting one subject picture. Six to one. That was about the ratio he would maintain for the rest of his career because of the 'uncertainty' about subject pictures. Portraits were commissioned and paid for in advance. And the prices were good. As George Du Maurier told his mother in the late 'seventies, 'If I were a portrait painter, my fortune would be made.'

Millais would need a fortune. Late in the year he and his family would undergo their last change of address by moving into a house constructed especially for them. Earlier he had mentioned the move to Hunt: 'My new home shall be a Palace such as the Italian painters commonly used but an eye opener to the public, as an attic is still associated with our craft.'

CHAPTER 23

1877–86

JOHN EVERETT's final residence was at 2 Palace Gate, Kensington. This is a portion of an illustrated essay that appeared in the *Magazine of Art* entitled 'Mr Millais's House at Palace Gate':

The face of the great red house is to the west. At the back stands the enormous first floor studio, with its tall window northward – a conspicuous object from the Kensington High Road. Northwards also looks part of a bow-window of the dining-room, its view sweeping up the broad walk of Kensington Gardens . . .

The entrance hall is of generous size, with a floor of black, white, and yellow marble, arranged in a bold design. A veined white marble dado, which recalls Genoa, runs round the hall, and grey marble pillars support the ceiling. On either side of a brass inlaid fireplace stands a clever negro bust.

From the hall, a flight of broad stone stairs leads up to the first floor, where plays a fountain spouting from the mouth of a black seal. The marble basin of clear water is lined with bright and beautiful shells. Tapestry covers the wall above, and several busts stand near.

From this pleasant resting-place lead the rooms of the first floor, the studio on one side, the drawing-room and dining-room on the other. The walls are of variegated whites – cream white, ivory white, milk white. Those accustomed to whiteness in a glowing climate . . . may be incredulous of the beauty of a background of whiteness in England, where the grey lights would seem to require some surface less dependent upon the colours of the atmosphere. Nevertheless Mr Millais's warm-white rooms have the merit of making the most of what light there is . . .

The furnishings must be described. The finely-sculptured old marble mantelpieces (white also) have panels of brass let in at the inner sides (where tiles are usually placed) with excellent effect. The mirrors are French and Italian, bright with gilding; and of the last century is an inlaid German cabinet having a great deal of beautiful workmanship. A wooden trellis-work screen and some silver work are from Burmah. The curtains are of ruby velvet embroidered in crewels, the crewel-work being from the Castle of Kenilworth. A brown parquet and large Indian rugs complete our notes of the more salient adornments of the stately double drawing-rooms.

The dining-room is quaintly and effectively decorated with dark old-masterish pictures of game and fruit, cocks and hens and fish.

The studio is a great, grand, massive, lofty room. Its Pompeian red walls are almost covered by Beauvais tapestry. Great oak pilasters rise to the ceiling, on either side of the tall window and the mantelpiece – a fine piece of old marble covering, above which hangs a Spanish portrait bearing proofs of Murillo's hand . . .

Below, on the ground floor, south of the hall, opens the breakfast-room. Its walls are covered with engravings and other things in black and white, such as numerous diplomas given to the great English artist . . . The engravings are the life of the room. Except for John Phillip's 'Gloria' and a small work of Mr Dante Rossetti's, they are all Mr Millais's own. They illustrate his career almost completely, beginning with 'The Carpenter's Shop'.

* * *

As soon as he was settled, John Millais started his first Palace Gate work of art, a portrait of eighty-two-year-old Thomas Carlyle. It was not surprising that his Palace Gate career began with a picture like this, in light of his recent sitters. His portrait subjects of the 'seventies had included the Vice-Chancellor of the University of London, George Grote; the distinguished surgeon Sir James Paget, Bart.; the Marquis of Westminster, Hugh Lupus Grosvenor; the eminent composer Sir William Sterndale Bennett; the famed financier the Hon.

Walter Rothschild; the Viceroy of India, Lord Lytton; and the versatile man of arts Lord Ronald Gower. He was creating his own contemporary national portrait gallery.

His position had become that of *the* fashionable portrait painter of London, comparable to a celebrity photographer of today. He didn't usually seek out subjects. They came to him, personally or through an emissary. For Thomas Carlyle, he was approached by Carlyle's long-time friend the historian James Froude.

After entering 2 Palace Gate, Carlyle is supposed to have said, 'Has paint done all this, Mr Millais? It only shows how many fools there are in the world.'

Again and again he returned for sittings. For a man of his age, it was fatiguing. At one point he wrote to a friend, 'Sunday is my only holiday from Millais, and I see not yet what will be the day of my deliverance. He seems to be in a state of almost frenzy about finishing with extremest perfection his surprising and difficult task.'

Finally Millais could say that it was nearly done and he would complete it on his own. Five minutes after Carlyle had departed for what he thought would be the last time, a handsome woman in her mid-thirties called at the house. She was Annabella Agnes Anstruther, known to intimates as 'AAA', a Scottish widow who was now Carlyle's closest friend and protector. She had arrived in her carriage to take him for a drive. When told by a servant that he had just left, she sent up her card with a request to see the portrait.

Completely satisfied with his work, Millais was pleased to have her visit his studio. In his shirt sleeves, he appeared to her like 'a handsome, spoiled puppy'. He proudly pointed to his depiction of her friend sitting and holding a walking stick while gazing directly at the viewer. 'He seemed to Mrs Anstruther,' Carlyle's principal biographer reported, 'to be demanding unqualified praise. "That of course," she said, "was quite out of my power to give. The features were all correctly given, and with great power of brush. But that was merely the mask; there was no soul or spirit behind it. I said that in fact I did not like it. This roused Millais, but I told him that it all depended on the standard one took. For my part, I maintained that Titian's beautiful portrait of the young man 'l'innominato', in Florence, was the finest type of what a portrait should be. Millais had the audacity to say,

'Titian could not paint a portrait!' and said that Reynolds was far better. But I said, 'Oh, no, *he* was a mere sketcher compared to Titian.'"

This unfortunate encounter was Millais's most humiliating experience since the Academy had rejected *Cymon and Iphigenia*. His reaction was extraordinary. He would not allow anyone else to see the portrait, and he sent word to Carlyle that he needed more sittings. He planned to do the whole thing over again from the beginning. Carlyle sat for a few more sessions, but the painting was never completed. And not until many years later was it seen in public.

But it did not disappear. It is very much alive, in London's National Portrait Gallery. Those who have seen it, and know of the circumstances surrounding its creation, have generally wondered what the fuss was all about.

* * *

Despite the Carlyle fiasco, the 1878 Exhibition season was a good one for Millais. Again he showed pictures in Burlington House, the Grosvenor, and the Marsden Gallery. Five were portraits, including two more entries for his personal British hall of fame. He couldn't, or thought he couldn't, bring out Thomas Carlyle, and so his man of distinction was the Earl of Shaftesbury.

Almost as old as Carlyle, Anthony Ashley Cooper had been since 1851 the seventh Earl of Shaftesbury. Of all holders of the title, he was the most illustrious, enjoying a career as a philanthropist, a social reformer, and a leader of the evangelical movement within the Church of England. The completed three-quarters-length seated figure of a man with a deeply lined face exemplified dignity and diligence. And it was one of Millais's best portraits.

Although he had become primarily a portraitist, he didn't abandon subject pictures. Two appeared in 1878.

After the success of *Effie Deans*, he returned to the Marsden Gallery with another painting inspired by Scott. This time it was an actual scene, from *The Bride of Lammermoor*, the early incident in which Edgar, the Master of Ravenswood, rescues Lucy Ashton from a charging bull. The picture shows Edgar and Lucy right after Edgar killed the bull, as he is about to take her to her father. As usual with

Millais, the facial expressions are effective. And the background of rocks and ferns is well done. But it can't be compared to its fore-runner. It could not possibly draw forth the feelings elicited by *Effie Deans*, requiring nothing from a spectator but a sympathetic under-standing. This scene from *The Bride of Lammermoor* presupposes a familiarity with the novel. A more salient reason for the pre-eminence of the former painting lies in Millais's motives for doing the works. He was moved by Margaret Oliphant's critical articles to paint *Effie Deans*. His incentive was to prove that he could still create the kind of picture that had made him famous. With *The Bride of Lammermoor*, he was simply cashing in on his earlier triumph.

Millais's other subject picture of 1878 hung in the Academy, and through the engraving it became one of his best known works. It was *The Princes in the Tower*.

The subject was the oft-told tale of the 1483 murder of twelve-year-old Edward V and his nine-year-old brother Richard. Millais showed the two boys in the Tower seconds before the arrival of their executioners. They are standing on a landing, frightened and clinging to one another. A shadow on the stairs in the rear denotes the impending arrival of the killers.

The external scene and the boys' clothing – short black velvet jackets and black stockings – are true-to-life. Millais did his research properly. And the scene contains a measure of pathos. But something is lacking. It is less convincing than most of the earlier pictures. For one thing, the two blond boys are improbably beautiful. It seems as if Millais had called Central Casting and said, 'Get me the two best-looking boys in Britain.' I am troubled by this picture, and so was *Punch*: '*The Princes in the Tower: Sanford and Merton*, in fancy costume are going to a ball without permission of their revered tutor, Mr Barlow. Hearing his step, they run down the kitchen stairs and hide in the cellar. Observe the shadow, which the coming event of Mr Barlow descending, with a supple cane in his hand, casts on the stone steps, and the terror depicted on the boys' countenances.'

The History of Sanford and Merton, by Thomas Day, was an extremely popular children's book in three volumes, published in 1783, 1787, and 1789. It is highly moral, completely humourless, Day's credo, under-lying almost every page, being that in the end virtue is always triumphant. An uproarious parody appeared in 1872, F.C. Burnand's *New History of Sanford and Merton.*

It is inconceivable that *Punch* would have lampooned *A Huguenot, The Order of Release, The Rescue,* or *The Gambler's Wife.* Its caricature of *The Princes in the Tower* was, I think, a significant commentary.

*   *   *

For some time John Everett and Effie had led independent lives, moving about separately, whether on holiday excursions or on visits to a theatre. Thus, on the last day of July in 1878, John Millais went alone to the Court Theatre in Sloane Square. This is not the present-day Royal Court Theatre, which opened in 1888, on the east side of the square. The earlier structure was on the south side. Millais attended a performance of *Olivia,* by the popular dramatist W.G. Wills, based on a section of Oliver Goldsmith's *Vicar of Wakefield. Olivia* was enormously successful because it was Ellen Terry's biggest hit thus far. Not everyone was happy about her playing in this very light vehicle. Twenty-two-year-old George Bernard Shaw said that Britain's greatest living actress was wasting her talents. This, of course, was what some people were saying about what Britain's greatest living painter had been doing.

On the day after taking in the play Millais wrote to his friend, the actor John Hare, 'I have not been so charmed with a play for many years. It was perfectly put on the stage and admirable all around. Ellen Terry's performance is quite perfect, and she looks lovely.'

Much time would pass before he would enjoy another evening in a theatre or anywhere else. On the day after he wrote this letter, his second son, George, now in his twenty-first year, suddenly took ill. Nine days later he died. The brightest of the eight Millais children, George was the particular apple of his father's eye. In 1876, after graduating with honours from Rugby, he became the first member of his family to enter either of England's great universities. He matriculated at Trinity College, Cambridge, and Millais told Hunt, 'He is studying to go into diplomacy. Lord Denby has promised him a nomination.' Millais was particularly pleased that his son enrolled in the college that had included among its students his favourite poet, Tennyson, and his favourite novelist, Thackeray. 'Fancy that!' he exulted in his letter to Hunt. Ironically, George Millais followed in the path of Tennyson and Thackeray by leaving without a degree.

Among the letters of condolence that Millais received, one came from Robert Browning, stopping in the village of Splügen, in the Swiss Alps. Browning sincerely sympathised with Millais, but he also had another, more personal reason for writing at once. It involved his own son, nine years older than George. The young Browning, known to everyone as Pen, had been a great disappointment to his father. (His mother died when he was twelve.) He had frittered away his early life, and when he was nineteen, Robert Browning said, 'He is unfit for anything but idleness and pleasure.' Soon thereafter, surprisingly, he was accepted as a student by Christ Church, Oxford. He didn't last long. He failed his first-year examination miserably, and in June 1870 he was sent down from Oxford. Later during that summer of 1870 Pen was in Scotland and met Millais. The young man loved outdoor sports, and he went grouse shooting, deer stalking, and salmon fishing with Millais.

There was something else, rather more important, that drew Pen to John Everett. Drawing was a hobby that Pen Browning took seriously, and when they were outdoors the two of them sketched a group of fir trees together. Millais was greatly impressed with Pen Browning's efforts, and after seeing more of his work, advised him to think about taking up painting as a career.

Pen responded enthusiastically to the suggestion, and for the first time he was industrious about something, his art. Sometimes he spent ten to twelve hours a day on his new vocation, and he continued to be strongly encouraged and assisted by Millais. He reached a climax in his efforts in this very summer of 1878 when one of his paintings, a street scene in Antwerp, was accepted by the Royal Academy for its Exhibition. (During the next six years, nine more of his pictures and one piece of sculpture would be shown in the Burlington House Summer Shows.)

'I was profoundly grieved,' Robert Browning wrote to Millais, 'to learn of your calamity. I know how little good any friends' sympathy can do in such a case, but you have rendered me such an inestimable service in helping to put my own boy in the right way that I feel it impossible to be quite silent now; besides I know the kind of heart

you have, Fortunately you are a strong man, and have proved yourself
such where strength is most tried – in prosperity. You will bear up,
even against this sorrow, for the sake of what is left you, and the great
course you have yet to run.'

For a couple of months Millais did not demonstrate much strength.
He could neither paint nor write. Not until 15 November did he send
the sad news to Fred Stephens: 'There is plenty to remind us that in
Burns's words, "Man is made to mourn." This summer we suffered a
great loss in my second son, and I have hardly touched any work
since.'

When he wrote to Stephens, he had snapped out of the doldrums,
brought back to life by the election of a new president of the Royal
Academy. The most recent president, Sir Francis Grant, had died in
October, and on the evening of 13 November, the Academicians
almost unanimously replaced him with Frederick Leighton. A dinner
in his honour was scheduled for mid-December, and Millais was asked
to speak at the affair. This revived him. At once he began to prepare
his speech.

Leighton was eighteen months younger than Millais. When he first
exhibited at the Summer Exhibition in 1855, Millais was already an
Associate of the Royal Academy. Leighton himself became an
Associate in 1864, a year after Millais had been elected an RA. But
Leighton, not Millais, was almost everyone's first choice for the top
position. As had been true of most of his predecessors, he was
elected for non-artistic as well as artistic reasons. He was extremely
cosmopolitan, having lived in Paris, Rome, Florence, and Berlin. He
had a wide and deep knowledge of foreign works of art. He was well
read in English and European literature. He was a fluent linguist. He
was an eloquent speaker. He had a warm, outgoing personality. He
was, in short, ideal for the presidency of the Royal Academy.

The dinner for Leighton was held at the Fine Arts Club, in Hanover
Square. After Millais had spoken, someone recalled later, his colleagues 'congratulated him, saying they had no idea he had a gift of
oratory and could speak so well and so spontaneously.
"Spontaneous!" he said. "Why, that wretched speech has kept me
awake for five weeks."'

This remark is suggestive of his success as a painter. What might seem to have been done effortlessly would in fact have resulted from much thought, planning, and reworking.

* * *

When Millais spoke at the Arts Club, he had just started what would be his principal work of 1879, a portrait of the Liberal Party leader, who had stepped down from his prime ministry in January of 1874, William Gladstone. He could not have been more dedicated to his task. 'I was at once struck,' Gladstone wrote in a personal letter, 'by a characteristic which marked him off from other artists to whom I have sat. It was the intensity with which he worked, which I have never seen equalled.'

After finishing it, Millais told Ronald Gower, 'I am happy that his family like the picture, and that I might provide posterity some of the characteristics of this great man.' Gower called the picture 'truly a majestic work, perhaps the finest portrait Millais has produced. The face is irreproachable, the expression lifelike, the eyes alive with mind and genius.'

Exhibited in Burlington House in 1879, it was a total success. Tom Taylor, in the *Manchester Guardian*, called it 'a national possession'. The *Illustrated London News* said that 'here we have the man himself'. *The Times* regarded it as 'a noble picture, in every respect the most noteworthy piece of portraiture in the exhibition'. The *Academy* saw it as 'the gem of the show, altogether unapproached by anything else in the galleries'.

Except for *Gladstone*, Millais's season of 1879 was an embarrassment. The *Academy*'s critic expressed the almost universal opinion of his other two entries in the Exhibition: 'Two portraits by Millais are truly sad to see.' One didn't even have a name. It was called *Portrait of a Lady*.

During the first fortnight of the show, Millais attended a Mayfair dinner party. One of the other guests, Louise Jopling, reported on a verbal exchange just before they entered the dining room:

It was May, and so the conversation turned to the Academy. A charmingly pretty woman said to him, 'Isn't Millais dreadful this year?' Before he could answer, she said, 'Oh, our hostess is looking daggers at me! I wonder why.'

'Well, drink a glass of sherry, and I will tell you,' said Millais, pouring out a glassful. 'It will help you to bear the shock.'

She laughed and drank it.

'Now tell me. I can bear anything.'

Millais said nothing. He just tapped himself on the chest, and it dawned upon her that he was the man of whose work she had spoken.

His delightful way of taking her adverse criticism put her completely at ease, and she was able to join him in his good-natured laugh at her expense.

* * *

After 1879, Millais had no more below-standard seasons. During the first six years of the 1880s, he painted sixty-nine major pictures. Sixty-three were portraits; twenty-seven men, nineteen women and seventeen children.

His male subjects included the orator and statesman John Bright; the president of the Royal College of Surgeons, Luther Holden; the vice-chancellor of the University of Glasgow, the Rev. John Caird; the world's foremost specialist in genito-urinary surgery, Sir Henry Thompson; the theologian-writer Cardinal John Henry Newman; the Royal Academician James Hook; the shipping magnate Thomas H. Ismay; the Bishop of Manchester, Dr James Fraser; the nation's best known sportsman, Sir John Astley; the actor Henry Irving; the poet laureate, Alfred Tennyson.

Two works in this genre deserve special attention; Millais's portrait of himself and his portrait of Benjamin Disraeli, the first Earl of Beaconsfield.

Some artists, often motivated by vanity, have painted numerous self-portraits. Millais was not one of them. His first serious painting of himself was done in response to an invitation. In 1879 Florence's Uffizi Gallery asked Millais and George Frederick Watts to join its Collection of Artists, Painted by Themselves. Both replied favourably, and with alacrity, and each portrait was shown at the 1880 Exhibition. These pictures were contrastingly self-revealing. The fine arts critic for the important architectural paper the *Builder* noted their differences:

'The two works are curiously representative of the artistic spirit and position of their painters. That of Mr Watts in a red skull-cap, with a background, on which is seen a painted ideal head, seems almost intended to have the appearance of an Italian master of the old school, and is quite removed from the style and character of modern English portraiture. That of Mr Millais, on the contrary, is a simple, unaffected painting of the head of a present day Englishman, a man of the world rather than an artist.'

The portrait of Disraeli was exhibited in 1881.

In the February of 1881, less than a year after Disraeli's administration had ended with his defeat by Gladstone and the Liberals, Millais wrote to ask the ex-prime minister if he might paint his portrait. On 2 March, Disraeli replied, 'I am a very bad sitter, but will not easily forego my chance of being renowned to posterity by your illustrious pencil. I am free on Tuesday and Wednesday, the 8th and 9th, and could on either be at your service. Choose the day. Would noon be a good hour?'

At noon on the 8th, the seventy-six-year-old statesman, in extremely poor health, appeared at 2 Palace Gate. With great difficulty he worked his way up to the studio. Like Gladstone, he would be depicted in a three-quarter-length standing pose. Wearing his familiar frock coat, arms folded, he would be shown as he addressed the House of Commons. After standing for only a minute or two, he sat down in a high-backed chair. While he stood, Millais hurriedly sketched his figure. Then more deliberately he did the face.

Twice the procedure was repeated. After the last sitting, Millais wrote to Effie, on 31 March, 'Unfortunately Lord Beaconsfield has been taken seriously ill, but I have got his likeness fairly well, if he is unable to sit again. Lord Barrington (his private secretary) told me that he is very anxious for his portrait to be in the Royal Academy and will get the Queen's command to admit it – the only way to get it in now.' (The sending-in day had passed.)

Five days later he told his daughter Mary, 'Poor Lord Beaconsfield I am afraid will never sit again, but I have a capital likeness and I believe the best that has been done of him.'

Despite the discomfort, Disraeli enjoyed his brief professional relationship with Millais, whom he playfully addressed as 'Apelles,' the ancient Greek painter whose portrait subjects had included Philip and Alexander.

On 19 April, Disraeli died. The Queen issued a command that, finished or not, the portrait should be shown at the Exhibition. Placed on an easel and bordered with crepe, it stood by itself before a railing in the centre of one of the galleries. Although incomplete, it was, everyone agreed, a fine likeness, as good as could reasonably have been expected. As the critic for the *Manchester Guardian* said, 'The circumstances under which Millais finished the picture were so disadvantageous that we cannot but wonder at its not ranking among Mr Millais's most successful works.' Nevertheless, this portrait was chosen for the frontispiece to the sixth and final volume of W.F. Monypenny's standard biography of the first Earl of Beaconsfield.

* * *

Among those desiring immortality through a portrait by Millais was seventy-six-year-old John Gould, the nation's foremost ornithologist, author of forty folio volumes on birds. Late in 1880, in response to Gould's invitation, Millais, with his son John Guille, visited him at his home in Charlotte Street, Bedford Square, the street of the Millais family's first London residence.

Gould, John Guille reported, 'sat propped up on his couch', surrounded by accoutrements of his profession. Millais 'was delighted with all that he saw, and on our way home he told me, "That's a fine subject. I shall paint it when I have time."' But Gould died in February 1881, and it was not until early 1885 that Millais began the painting. Sitting for Gould was the noted engraver, Thomas O. Barlow, who had worked with Millais on many paintings, and would himself appear in one of his portraits.

Since a model sat for Gould, this picture does not belong with Millais's other portraits. There is indeed some question as to whether it is even a portrait. It was the only one in the 'seventies and 'eighties with much of a background. Primarily interested in the persons themselves, Millais was disinclined to spend time on a detailed background. Many people, however, wanted more from the former star Pre-Raphaelite. With this painting he gave them more, a picture jam-packed with accessories. He took great pride in this work, which he regarded as of supreme importance. The position of the figure was precisely what he had seen four years earlier, reclining on a couch, propped up with cushions. He holds a brightly coloured blue bird and is talking about it to a woman and four children. Scattered about are stuffed birds and ornithological paraphernalia.

At first Millais called this painting *The Ornithologist*, but fearful that viewers would not know what an ornithologist is, he retitled it *The Ruling Passion*. Because John Gould was the type of person he had always admired, an unbending enthusiast, he enjoyed doing this work. But he was disappointed with the response. John Ruskin praised it highly, indeed too highly: 'I have never seen any work of modern art with more delight and admiration than this.' The mainstream critics, however, gave it mixed reviews. And it was difficult to sell.

Three days into the Exhibition, Millais wrote to Hunt, 'I have painted "The Ruling Passion" in fulfillment of a large commission from a wealthy gentleman. (I had commissions from *two patrons*, and now neither has signified a wish to possess it.) In short I have been thrown over, and if it were not for my *children pictures* and *portraits* I should be in a poor way.' Six months later he told Hunt, 'I still have not had an offer for my large picture, which is not encouraging to the painter, and except in portraiture I believe I will do very little for some time to come.'

Before the end of the year, in a letter to Dickens's daughter Kate, he said, 'I don't think I will trouble the critics and the public any more with "an important picture".' (Kate Dickens was now a widow. Her sexless marriage to Charles Collins had ended with his death from stomach cancer in 1873.)

*   *   *

Millais did not really enjoy painting children's pictures because although the father of eight he did not really enjoy children. And they were troublesome sitters, constantly fussing and fidgeting. But because of the compensation he had to do them. In the 1880s several were among his best known works. The first appeared in 1880, *Cherry Ripe*.

The starting point for this picture was a costume ball during the Christmas season of 1879, sponsored by the weekly illustrated *Graphic*. One of the youngest guests was the editor's niece, five-year-old Edie Ramage, who impersonated the figure in Joshua Reynolds's

Penelope Boothby. On the next morning, she again put on her costume. Her uncle took her to 2 Palace Gate and asked Millais to paint her portrait. The Reynolds attire alone would have won him over, but, additionally, she was uncommonly pretty. He did it for £1000.

For the third time, he was directly inspired by Reynolds. As a student in 1848, he had extended Reynolds's representation of Boccaccio's *Cymon and Iphigenia*. Twenty-four years later *The Ladies Waldgrave* was the prototype for *Hearts Are Trumps*. Now with *Cherry Ripe* he created almost a facsimile. *Penelope Boothby* shows a little girl sitting in a landscape setting, hands folded, gazing at the viewer. She is wearing a white dress with a black sash, white mittens, and, conspicuously, a mob cap with a black ribbon. Because of this last detail, the painting was often referred to as *The Mob Cap*.

Cherry Ripe shows a girl sitting in the midst of foliage on what seems to be a fallen tree trunk. Cherries are at her side. She is looking straight at the spectator. She is dressed in a white dress with a pink sash, with black mittens on her hands pressed together. On her head is a highly visible mob cap with a pink ribbon. This was no less than an audacious invitation to compare the two pictures. Millais was confident that he could weather the test.

He finished *Cherry Ripe* in less than a week and, beginning in February 1880, it was exhibited at the Grafton Gallery in Grafton Street, just off New Bond Street. It was exceedingly well received, but its celebrity was gained through the *Graphic*'s coloured reproduction of *Cherry Ripe*, which went everywhere. John G. Millais reported that it was seen by 'Australian miners, Canadian backwoodsmen, South African trekkers, and all sorts and conditions of colonial residents', who sent his father 'letters of warmest congratulation, some of which stirred his heart by the emotion they expressed'.

Having received £1000 for the work of less than a week, Millais was well recompensed. But he was not overpaid. Beatrix Potter reported in her journal that 'the *illustrated* editors made £12,000 by *Cherry Ripe*.'

More and more portraits of children followed *Cherry Ripe*, one after another. These were some of them:

Catherine Muriel Cowell Stepney (1880), a little blonde girl in a black velvet dress standing with a bouquet of flowers in her arms.

Cinderella (1881), the wistful fairy tale heroine seated in front of a kitchen fire, broom in one hand, a peacock feather in the other.

Dorothy Thorpe (1882), the title character kneeling and feeding two dogs from a silver cake tray.

Une Grande Dame (1883), a mob-capped five-year-old girl holding a parrot.

Lady Petty Primrose (1885), a young girl, hat hanging down from her neck, clasping flowers that she has gathered.

Orphans (1885), a little girl holding out an apron, upon which rests a rabbit. The plural title indicates that they had both lost their parents.

All of these portraits, and others unmentioned here, are of girls, because girls are generally more beautiful than boys. Millais's girls are all enchanting. He was indeed on the lookout for young charmers. The most beautiful of them may have been Beatrice Blackstone, granddaughter of the popular comedian J.B. Blackstone and twelve years old when she sat. John G. Millais told of how she was discovered: 'In the winter of 1880–81 one of my sisters went to the St James's Theatre and was so struck with the beauty of a child on the stage that she prevailed on our father to see her. He too was capitvated and wrote to her mother asking leave for her to sit for him. This granted, little Beatrice presently appeared in his studio, and we all agreed that we had never seen a more lovely child. The pictures for which she sat [*Cinderella* and two others] in no way exaggerated her beauty; they were portraits of herself.'

Although Millais's girls were all beautiful, they were not alike. They were individually characterised, and received rave reviews in which for comparative purposes Velasquez's name frequently and Reynolds's name repeatedly were injected. So often was Millais referred to as 'the Reynolds of the nineteenth century' that one writer called Reynolds 'the Millais of the eighteenth century'.

No one said that these portraits were not good. But some people objected to their repetitiveness. Echoes of Margaret Oliphant appeared in the papers. Writing about the 1883 Exhibition, *The Times*'s review said, 'Mr Millais might for a season let the little maids alone. A painter with his gifts should give us from time to time more imaginative works.' Also in 1883, the well-known critic Harry Quilter wrote, 'Mr Millais can, when he likes, produce pictures which have an almost unrivalled facility of touching our feelings. When we think of "A Huguenot", "The Vale of Rest", and "The Gambler's Wife", and consider that he now gives us babies, we are almost inclined to fancy that a truly paternal Government would hang him and his babies in a row, as an example to painters who could do great works and preferred to do little.'

Critics lamented that Millais had virtually abandoned subject pictures. In recent years he had done only two, *'Cuckoo!'* in 1880 and *The Grey Lady* in 1883, neither of which was important. *'Cuckoo!'* shows two young girls sitting in the woods listening to a bird. *The Grey Lady*, reminiscent of *A Somnambulist*, presents a ghostlike figure of a woman, eyes closed, ascending a night-time staircase.

These works are hardly momentous, but Quilter was unfair in saying that Millais 'preferred to do little'. In October 1883 he wrote to his daughter Mary, 'Really my powers (artistic) are on the wane.' Now in his fifties, he was probably incapable of doing what he had done as a young man. But clearly he was as diligent as ever, writing to Effie in the 'eighties, 'I am just fagged out and no wonder with what I have done since you left. I believe it is astounding the amount of work I have done.'

And just as in 1877 he had been prodded by Margaret Oliphant to do the superb *Effie Deans*, so in 1884 he was goaded by Harry Quilter to paint a subject picture of the type he had done when he was an active Pre-Raphaelite. It went to the Exhibition accompanied by *no pictures of children*. A multi-figured scene from the Second Jacobite Rebellion, it was called *An Idyll, 1745*. An English fifer-boy in Scotland with the regiment seeking to avenge the raid of the Young Pretender, Prince Charles Edward Stuart, sits against a tree playing his instrument. Three Highlander girls reclined on the grass are listening intently.

Unlike 1877, this time the response was devastating and no one was more stinging than Harry Quilter:

It is always sad to see a painter whose power is very great losing all the subtler qualities of his work, and the grace and charm of it being gone, only displaying the hard, naked faculty. That is what has been taking place with Mr Millais gradually during the last ten years, and now it has culminated. The power of painting and drawing is still there; the charm and beauty have disappeared. Look at 'An Idyll'. It is a thoroughly unreal and unpleasant piece of painting with little grasp of character and no idyllic character whatever . . . The picture is poor in colour, weakly humorous in conception, wooden and awkward in drawing, laboured and dull in painting, and utterly unworthy of a great artist.

In her journal, Beatrix Potter wrote, 'The papers criticise Millais's picture rather harshly, and I am afraid it is open to criticism. But he has sold it for £5000 to a Brewer. He doesn't complain of bad times, and he is in high spirits.' Five thousand pounds can soothe wounded feelings.

His main work of 1885 was the large and multi-figured ornithologist's portrait, *The Ruling Passion*, which, unlike *An Idyll*, for a long time remained unsold. Hence his resolve to abstain from 'important pictures'.

Actually for the first time he began to think about curtailing his work. Early in May, he told Hunt, '*Retirement* is written in very large letters on the wall of my own vision and I don't think it will be long before I paint for recreation alone.'

A few days later, he wrote to Mary, on her twenty-fifth birthday: 'Just one line to wish you many happiest returns. You will be glad to hear I am at my *work* although I cannot stick to it more than two hours a day . . . I am going into the Park to sit in the sun and smoke a pipe. I wish you were to be beside me as I feel very, very old.'

In three weeks' time he would celebrate his own birthday, his fifty-sixth.

* * *

During the early 'eighties Millais received numerous honours. The Académie des Beaux Arts elected him a Foreign Associate, and from Germany came the Order 'Pour le Mérite'. He got a particularly satisfying award in a city of fond memories. The *Art Journal* reported in August 1880, 'Mr John Everett Millais was presented with the

Honorary Degree of Doctor of Laws at the recent Oxford Commemoration. On his presentation by the Regius Professor of Civil Law, he was described as a colourist of so much truth *"ut in tabulis Venetum illud spirare saeculum videatur"*.'

The biggest prize came nearly five years later. He received a communication from William Gladstone, who had recently sat in Palace Gate for a second portrait: 'It is with a very lively satisfaction, personal and public, that I write, with the sanction of Her Majesty (and lawfully, though at the last gasp), to ask you to accept the honour of a hereditary title and take your place amongst the baronets of the United Kingdom.'

The letter was dated 24 June. The parenthetical words were there because Gladstone's second administration was ending. On that very day the third Marquis of Salisbury (whose portrait Millais had painted in 1883) became Prime Minister. Writing this letter may have been the last act of Gladstone's term.

The first English painter to receive a hereditary title, Millais at once wrote to his favourite daughter, briefly out of town, 'Oh, Mary, what a time you have lost here. With the Queen's approval, Mr Gladstone has made me a *baronet*. The delight of the house is [illegible word] to see.'

* * *

'Mr Millais is all the fashion this winter,' Beatrix Potter wrote in her journal in November 1885. 'He readily gets immense prices for his pictures. It seems impossible that such an unnatural rate of payment should continue.' Even *The Ruling Passion* fetched a good amount.

In December the *Art Journal* honoured him with the longest article it had ever published in its forty-eight years of existence. Written by Walter Armstrong, it covered his career in thirty-two large double-column pages, accompanied by forty-one illustrations.

A high point of his career came on 1 January 1886 with the opening of a retrospective exhibition. In the nineteenth century, one-person art shows were uncommon. When Gustave Courbet erected a pavilion on the Rue Montaigne in 1855 and unveiled forty-four of his pictures, he was doing something almost unheard of. It was still unusual in 1882 when Sir Coutts Lindsay sponsored at the Grosvenor Gallery a large comprehensive exhibition of pictures by one painter, George

Frederick Watts. The venture was a success, and in 1883 Lindsay did it again, honouring Lawrence Alma-Tadema. Then for a few years it became an annual event. In 1884 and 1885, Lindsay's subjects were the best of Britain's deceased artists, Reynolds and Gainsborough. For the exhibition of 1886 the obvious choice was the new painter-baronet.

The Times gave Sir Coutts's latest extravaganza two extended notices, the first appearing on opening day. (A private press view had been held.) At the start of his initial piece, *The Times*'s reviewer called Millais 'the most popular and, in general esimation, the greatest of our living English masters'. He was extremely well represented, with 130 paintings and thirty drawings, covering thirty-six years from *Isabella* to a couple of works that had been shown six months earlier.

The range was truly remarkable. Listed in alphabetical order, these were a few of the pictures: *Autumn Leaves*; Bischoffsheim, Mrs, portrait of; *The Black Brunswickers*; Bright, John, portrait of; *The Carpenter's Shop*; *Chill October*; *The Eve of St Agnes*; *Ferdinand Lured by Ariel*; *A Flood*; *The Gambler's Wife*; *Hearts Are Trumps*; *A Huguenot*; *Isabella*; *The Knight Errant*; *Mariana*; *My First Sermon*; *The Northwest Passage*; *The Proscribed Royalist*; *Sir Isumbras*; Tennyson, Alfred, portrait of.

'That so much masterly work came from one man's hand is a matter for wonder,' *The Times*'s reviewer said. 'That the hand is that of an Englishman of the present day is a matter for pride and rejoicing.'

It was also a matter for sadness and regret. On opening day, Holman Hunt recalled, 'an ardent appreciator of Millais's genius, Lady Constance Leslie, went to the exhibition. Ascending the stairs, she encountered the painter going out, with head bowed down. When he looked up, she saw tears in his eyes. "Ah, Lady Constance," he said, "you see me unmanned. Well, I'm not ashamed to say that on looking at my earliest pictures I have been overcome with chagrin that I failed to fulfil the forecast of my youth."'

* * *

At this time I think it might be appropriate to speak of a painting which Millais completed and sold in 1872, but which, because it was not publicly exhibited until after his death, I did not mention earlier.

(The owner of the picture had refused permission for it to be shown.) The picture was inspired by the fourth chapter of the first volume of Thomas Babington Macaulay's *History of England*, wherein Macaulay begins his analysis of the reign of James II. He takes up King James's brutal persecution of Dissenters, especially the Scottish Covenanters, citing a blatant example that took place three months after the start of James's reign:

> Two women, Margaret Maclachlan and Margaret Wilson, the former an aged widow, the latter a maiden of eighteen, suffered death for their religion. They were offered their lives if they would consent to abjure the cause of the insurgent Covenanters, and to attend the Episcopal worship. They refused and were sentenced to be drowned. They were carried to a spot which the Solway over-flows twice a day and were fastened to stakes fixed in the sand between high and low water mark. The elder sufferer was placed near the advancing flood, in the hope that her last agonies might terrify the younger into submission. The sight was dreadful. But the courage of the survivor was sustained by an enthusiasm as lofty as any that is recorded in martyrology. She saw the sea draw nearer and nearer, but gave no sign of alarm. She prayed and sang verses of psalms till the waves choked her voice.
>
> After she had tasted the bitterness of death, she was, by a cruel mercy, unbound and restored to life. When she came to herself, pitying friends and neighbours implored her to yield. 'Dear Margaret, only say God save the King!' The poor girl, true to her stern theology, gasped out, 'May God save him, if it be God's will!' Her friends crowded round the presiding officer. 'She has said it. Indeed, sir, she has said it.' 'Will she take the abjuration?' he demanded. 'Never!' she exclaimed. 'I am Christ's! Let me go!' And the waters closed over for the last time.

There are numerous possibilities here for a painting. Millais, characteristically, settled on a three-quarter-length portrait of the younger Margaret standing alone, tied at the stake. Macaulay said nothing about her physical appearance, but Millais's Margaret Wilson was one of the most beautiful women ever to come forth from his studio. With her long black hair hanging over her shoulders, her full red lips, her perfect facial features, her short-sleeved, tight-fitting blouse, open at the neck, she is perhaps his sexiest portrait.

As with all of his best work, Millais felt a close kinship with his subject. Indeed, in the sixties he had done two drawings of Margaret Wilson, one of which appeared in a July 1862 issue of *Once a Week*. She was a person who, with a full life ahead of her, had preferred to die rather than relinquish her principles. What if he, like young Margaret, had been willing to risk everything by refusing to compromise with his basic principles? Would he then instead of becoming a very good artist have achieved greatness? This, I intuitively feel, was on his mind when he painted *The Martyr of the Solway*.

CHAPTER 24

1886–91

AFTER Millais's Grosvenor Gallery show closed, at the end of January 1886, a new painting of his went on exhibit, which in one form or another would be seen by more people than any other picture by a British artist. It was called *Bubbles*. One day he saw his five-year-old grandson Willie, the son of Effie, blowing bubbles. On an impulse he painted the boy 'bubbles and all.' A little blond boy dressed in green velvet is looking up at a large soap bubble.

The picture was sold to a Bond Street dealer, Arthur Tooth, who hung it in his gallery, where it could not but attract attention, favourable and unfavourable. Whistler loved Millais's earlier work, but he called *Bubbles* 'the apotheosis of pot-boiling'. Whistler's friends and eventual biographers Joseph and Elizabeth Pennell said that the picture suffered from 'that excess of sentiment and tendency to haste to which Millais yielded in response to the public demand'. For that very reason it was sold to the publisher of the *Illustrated London News*, who reproduced it on a full page of his Christmas number. It was seen by several million people, but that wasn't the end of it. The *Illustrated London News* resold *Bubbles* to the Pears soap company which used it in advertisements all over the nation and in Europe.

Millais was reproached for the commercialisation of his picture, but he didn't apologise. Nor should he have done so. It wasn't inherently wrong for *Bubbles* to appear in advertising. Just think of the countless commercial reproductions of Whistler's *Mother*, of Grant Wood's *Old Gothic*, and, most particularly, of Leonardo's *Mona Lisa*. If

Bubbles was objectionable, it was not because of the advertising but because of the maudlin picture itself, not comparable to the fine earlier portraits of children.

* * *

When the 1886 Exhibition opened, it seemed as if Millais had meant it when he said that he was thinking of retiring. For the first time since 1860, when he had been preoccupied with illustrations, he had only one entry at the Summer Show, a full-length portrait of his favourite engraver, Thomas Barlow.

While the Exhibition was on, a series of three articles, nominally by Holman Hunt, appeared in the monthly *Contemporary Review*. (Although Hunt provided the material for the pieces, they were written by Harry Quilter.) Entitled 'The Pre-Raphaelite Brotherhood: A Fight for Art', they covered the early years of the movement. After the last had come out, Millais wrote to Hunt, 'I have just finished your articles in the Contemporary. They are quite *charming* and *most interesting*, albeit very sad reading.'

He was saddened for the same reason that he had nearly wept at his one-man show. He could only think of what he might have done had he uncompromisingly followed up on his early triumphs. In the words of John Greenleaf Whittier:

> For of all sad words of tongue or pen,
> The saddest are these: 'It might have been!'

In more ways than one, I think, Millais was affected by the articles, coming so soon after the Grosvenor show. When he next wrote to Hunt, early in 1887, he said, 'I am awfully hard at work. Just going at it.' The Exhibition of that year demonstrated just how hard he had been working. After submitting only one picture in 1886, he now had five entries. There were two male portraits, neither of which was among his best, and also two pictures of children. *The Nest* showed a young mother holding up her little daughter to see a bird in its nest. *Lilacs* presented a seven-year-old girl spreading out an apron to catch flowers dropped from a lilac tree.

The most intriguing of the works of 1887 was the fifth and largest one, which, I suggest, was a response to the *Contemporary Review*. It was called *'Mercy', St Bartholomew's Day, 1572*.

St Bartholomew's Day, of course, takes us back to Millais's most highly praised picture, *A Huguenot*, which aroused renewed enthusiasm at the Grosvenor retrospective, and was extolled in the *Contemporary*. This revival of interest in a picture painted thirty-five years earlier, I believe, gave Millais an idea. He would focus on the other side of the massacre.

His setting is the entrance of the house of a Roman Catholic man, just before the start of the slaughter. The head of the household, wearing a protective arm band, is about to take part in the carnage, summoned by a brown-frocked monk in the background. The 'Mercy' in the title refers to a Franciscan nun who has thrown herself at his feet, beseeching him not to go. Millais has cleverly reversed the motive of the earlier picture. Whereas the Huguenot's girlfriend was saying 'Don't be a victim,' the nun's message is 'Don't be an executioner.' The man has been affected by the plea, but, like the Huguenot, he will probably not yield.

It was a master stroke to present a contrasting glimpse of the same event. The picture moreover is effective and shows that great care had gone into it. But the emotional impact does not approach that of its predecessor. It was not for want of trying. It was just that in his declining years John Millais could not do what he had done in his youth. He painted *A Huguenot* when he was twenty-two, *'Mercy'* when he was fifty-seven.

In Wordsworthian terms, there was 'something that is gone'. No longer did he have 'visionary gleam'.

* * *

In 1881, Millais had become the lessee of a large estate twelve miles north of Perth known as Murthly, a sportsman's paradise. There was excellent fishing in the River Tay, flowing through the property. As for shooting, there were pheasants, ducks, partridges, woodcocks, hares, and rabbits. For six years Millais went to Murthly every autumn, but only for the sport. He never even thought about painting.

Then after the disappointing *'Mercy', St Bartholomew's Day, 1572*, in

September 1887 he set up his easel on the estate. He didn't need a 'visionary gleam' to paint a landscape. He had only to observe and reproduce what he saw. He had come to know Murthly intimately. Now he was pleased to preserve a portion of it for posterity. He painted a marshy foreground, trees in the middle distance, and hills farther back. His modus operandi was that of the earlier landscapes. He didn't interpret the scene. He replicated it. He was as careful, he said afterwards, as when he had been copying casts in the Antique School. He called his picture *Murthly Moss*.

Millais enjoyed his return to landscape art. But it was not easy. He told Hunt, 'I find work harder and more difficult as I get older. But I can never get away from it.' Painting was something he had to do. Furthermore, although he was nearly sixty, he still explored new territory. In mid-December he went to Murthly for a fresh challenge, his first snowscape. It wasn't pleasant to stand outside in the midst of a Scottish winter, but he persevered until he finished his picture, *Christmas Eve*, which depicts Murthly Castle on a bright, snowy late afternoon. Back in London, he sold the painting to a dealer named McLean, who, beginning in March, exhibited it in his showroom at the bottom of the Haymarket.

The response to *Christmas Eve* was almost unanimously favourable. The reviewer for *The Times* was ecstatic: 'Mr Millais's snow landscape is a picture about which the gossip of the studios has already said a good deal, and it certainly justifies all that his admirers have been saying. As every artist knows, no landscape is more difficult than landscape in snow. It is rarely done. This picture is a brilliant success, offering more proof of Mr Millais's astonishing power of dealing at will with any of the problems with which art has to grapple. It would be impossible to express more perfectly the face of Winter, seen not in its wrath and fury, but in its more genial aspect. This is the most important picture of the moment and one of the most important of the year.'

Millais's earlier landscape, *Murthly Moss*, was shown a couple of months later at the Royal Academy Summer Exhibition. *The Times'* critic was again enthusiastic: 'Mr Millais's landscape is a work of exceedingly [sic] loveliness, which gave him joy to paint and gives the spectator joy to look upon . . . *Murthly Moss* will divide with *Chill*

October in the favour of those trained in the study of landscape art. It is a faithful rendering of a beautiful subject. The heath, moor, and moss have probably never been so perfectly interpreted as in this picture, in which the chief practitioner of contemporary English art has shown once more that, at his best, it is all the same to him whether he paints the face of outdoor nature or woman or man.'

During the next several years he continued to do landscape and snowscape paintings in Murthly, two a year until 1892. They were never done effortlessly. In August of 1889 he told Hunt, 'I am in pain over my work which I *must* [underlined twice] get out of the studio. I get up every morning at ½ past six and work till six in the evening to accomplish the task.'

He was emphatic about going outside because there he did his best work. His studio efforts in the late 'eighties and early 'nineties were limited to portraits, which weren't outstanding. One of them, in 1890, was painfully bad, Millais's third portrait of Gladstone, which, the *Art Journal* said, 'has not been defended even by his most fervid admirers. It would be difficult to imagine anything more unfortunate in effect than this full-faced presentment of the great radical leader.' In a signed piece in the *Academy*, the highly regarded art critic Claude Phillips wrote, 'It would be unnecessary cruelty to dwell on the too obvious demerits of this portrait of Mr Gladstone. These may be condoned in remembrance of the same master's magnificent earlier profile portrait of the great orator.'

In the 1891 Exhibition, Millais had two portraits of adult women. Phillips wrote tellingly about them: 'It is distressing to find Sir John's portraits so deficient in elegance and artistry of arrangement, so cold and purely external in conception . . . There is a curious impersonality about the presentment, a curiously cold detachment from the individuality which Sir John seeks to characterise; and this, more than any technical shortcoming, disconcerts the beholder.'

Phillips was right on the mark. Millais was not personally committed to his portraits. He was turning them out strictly for money. This wasn't true of his open-air pictures, mostly done in Murthly. Partly because of his associations with the surroundings, his own involvement was clear. One of them, however, the most impressive of the lot, was painted, not in Murthly, but on the outskirts of Perth, a snow-piece of December 1891. Its title is the opening of a familiar song in *As You Like It*:

> Blow, blow, thou winter wind!
> Thou art not so unkind
> As man's ingratitude.

The setting is a bleak, snow-covered footpath. A forlorn, shabbily dressed woman sits on a stone, cradling a baby. In the middle distance a man is walking away, accompanied by a dog that has turned about to look back upon the figures. The baby is presumably the couple's love child, abandoned by the father. Only the dog shows compassion.

This picture is reminiscent of *Effie Deans*. But what a difference there is between them! Despite the situation, *Effie Deans* is not gloomy. Effie is not despondent. Somehow, the spectator feels, she will pull out of it. The current painting, on the contrary, is one of unrelieved desolation. It contains not a glimmer of hope. The bleakness is truly Shakespearean, matching the pessimism of Macbeth's 'Tomorrow and tomorrow' speech. No one could reasonably charge Millais with not being personally concerned with *this* picture. It truly mirrored his feelings at the time of its creation.

The reason he painted it just outside of Perth was that he no longer had access to the Murthly estate. Earlier in the year its ownership had changed hands. The new proprietor would not renew Millais's lease. In late autumn it was terminated. Annually since 1881 he had spent his happiest months at Murthly. He revelled in the outdoors, and upon returning to Palace Gate he always felt re-energised. Now at the age of sixty-three he had it taken away from him. He was no longer welcome there. This explains the appearance of what was without doubt John Millais's most pessimistic picture.

CHAPTER 25

1892–96

Upon returning to London, early in 1892, Millais sought consolation in Tennyson's *In Memoriam*. In poem number 83, a spring song, he found the impulse for a painting in the third stanza:

> Bring orchis, bring the foxglove spire,
> The little speedwells darling blue,
> Deep tulips dash'd with fiery dew
> Laburnums, dropping-wells of fire.

The second line was the title for his picture of a little girl in a meadow on a bright summer day sitting beneath a tree with bright blue flowers covering its branches. It hung at the Academy with '*Blow, blow, thou winter wind!*' It would be difficult to conceive of another artist exhibiting at one show such completely contrasting works.

Before the opening, Millais wrote to his wife, 'I am now at the stage of unbelief in what I am doing and consequently I am not at all happy over my work. However I must trust that my first impressions are the right ones.'

Unfortunately the critics shared Millais's own displeasure with his work. The speedwell picture was regarded as no more than a trifle, and although '*Blow, blow, thou winter wind!*' occupied a place of honour, the response to it was lukewarm. This was an instance where Millais's reputation led reviewers to expect more than he gave them. *The Times* said as much: 'We regret that he has not fulfilled the hopes of his admirers.' As for the principal specific objection to the picture, the *Saturday*

Review complained that it demonstrated 'no appreciation of the grandeur of nature', and the *Academy* lamented that the artist had offered 'a merely prosaic literal reproduction of the scene with no attempt at a personal interpretation'. For many painters this would have been enough, but not for Millais.

Still trusting in his impressions of children, he entered three of them at the 1893 Exhibition. Two were opposing figures. *Merry* depicted a young girl in a red dress smiling spontaneously as she holds a plate with a canary on its edge. In *Pensive* a girl stands in profile with a flower and a dreamy expression. The *Athenaeum*'s reviewer responded to the usual complaint about them: 'Hasty critics gibe at what they call his potboilers, but the real question is what, and how much, thought and skill may be recognised in his works.' As the writer implied, Millais had attended to all of the details. He had neglected nothing.

Standing apart was his third picture, prompted by the opening sentences of George Eliot's prelude to *Middlemarch*: 'Who that cares to know the history of man, and how the mysterious mixture behaves under the varying experiments of Time, has not dwelt, at least briefly, on the life of Saint Theresa, has not smiled with some gentleness at the thought of the little girl walking forth one morning hand-in-hand with her still smaller brother, to go and seek martyrdom in the country of the Moors? Out they toddled from rugged Avila, wide-eyed and helpless-looking as two fawns . . .'

With the towers of Avila in the background, Millais's picture, *The Girlhood of St Theresa*, shows seven-year-old Theresa and her five-year-old brother holding hands as they cross a bridge just after sunrise. As usual, the high point is the central figure's facial expression, one of simple determination.

Millais's fourth picture of 1893 was a portrait of the popular comedian and theatre manager John Hare, later Sir John, currently managing the Garrick Theatre in the Charing Cross Road. He is standing in the Garrick's green room, looking at the spectator. His right hand is behind him, and his left holds an opened text of *A Pair of Spectacles*, the play, by Sydney Grundy, which had provided Hare with his most successful role. He is evidently reading to his company. This was Millais's first superior portrait of an adult since the one, in 1887, of the Earl of Rosebery. Virtually all of the reviewers agreed that it could be compared favourably to the best of his earlier works in the genre.

Most of the critics also liked *The Girlhood of St Theresa*. The *Morning Post*'s appraisal was representative: 'The pathos, simplicity, and spontaneity of the little girl saint are the best possible proofs of Sir John's success. The subject is an exceedingly difficult one, so much so that only a master absorbed by the passion of art would have attempted to depict it, much less succeeded.' It was the girl's resolute expression that particularly captivated viewers, professional and otherwise. But there were a few dissenters from the majority view. Thus the *Academy*, while praising the 'two pretty children', found fault with the picture as a whole. Because, the writer said, Millais had 'failed to penetrate the heart of the subject,' his painting was 'inadequate as an interpretation of the legend'. *The Times'* critic, like everyone else, acknowledged that young Theresa was beautiful, but he could find 'little of the intending martyr in her'.

The *Academy* and *The Times* notwithstanding, this had been a good season for Millais. Reconciled to the fact that he would do no more landscapes, he was hopeful for the future. And yet he had nothing in the 1894 Exhibition nor in any of the minor shows. Not only that, he had, for the first time, gone for a year without painting anything.

While the 1893 show was still on, he had a severe attack of influenza, which persisted for weeks. Additionally, he was stricken in late summer and autumn with other ailments, including rheumatism, and, most ominously, a throat disorder which caused a severe hoarseness in his resonant voice and did not respond to medications.

Week after week he suffered from one affliction after another until finally, early in the spring, he sought relief outside of London. He went to the fashionable Channel resort Bournemouth. He spent eleven days there, in an elite hotel, but the stay wasn't particularly helpful. He wrote to Effie on 15 April: 'I am sorry to say I have gone back a good deal and have had a return of my head disturbance. It was so bad this morning that I thought of telegraphing for you, crying and having to leave the breakfast table. Yesterday I had to recline on a sofa in a private room most of the day, and I am there again this morning. It is most disappointing, and my nerves are quite wretched. I am obliged to dine in the private room adjoining my bedroom . . . My *head was all wrong* when I got up. I am quite incapable of any work at present.'

Three days later he moved from Bournemouth to the nearby town of Christchurch, because, he told Effie, 'I wasn't making any progress. Indeed I felt weaker every day. Here I am much better, the air sharper.' But a couple of days later he wrote, 'My throat has been and is still very troublesome.'

He was troubled most of all by his inability to work. 'This enforced idleness,' he told Effie on 22 April, 'is so wearying to me.'

Effie suggested that he try the famed mineral baths of Aix-la-Chapelle. This consummate Englishman responded, 'All say Aix will not do for me.' Then on 26 April he was guardedly optimistic: 'Indeed with occasional trips out of London I may return to my work, in moderation to start with.' Before the end of the month he was back at Palace Gate, hopeful of exhibiting again in the following year.

* * *

Millais would never again regain his good health, but he did return to work. In light of his physical condition, he was surprisingly active.

'I have worked like fury this week,' he wrote to Hunt in the spring of 1895. Actually he had worked like fury for quite a few weeks. That summer he had three pictures in a minor show, one entry at a recently established exhibition at the New Gallery, in Regent Street, and, finally, four pictures in Burlington House. Eight paintings altogether, all done during the spring, was quite remarkable for a sick man approaching his sixty-sixth birthday.

His reappearance was warmly welcomed by London's art world. As the *Art Journal* said, 'The return of so old and popular an idol, who has been struggling against physical weakness, is a cause of great delight.' It was also a cause of great surprise. He had come up with the most solemn group of pictures he had ever shown. Only two of the eight were in any way cheerful.

There was a reason for both his gravity and his exceptional productivity. It concerned his eldest daughter, Effie.

Effie had made what the Victorians called a 'good' marriage. Her husband was a career army officer, William Christopher James, son of Sir William James, the distinguished barrister who, at the time of his death, in 1881 was a Lord Justice of Appeal. In 1885 William Christopher James was a forty-three-year-old major with the 16th

Lancers, stationed in India, where he lived with his wife and two children. He had had a splendid military career and could look forward to a great future, perhaps even becoming a general.

Then early in the summer of 1894 he was thrown from his horse and suffered a brain concussion. After a few months of sick leave, late in the year he rejoined his regiment. But it wasn't the same as before the accident. He experienced continuing severe headaches. His military career, he realised, was finished. And so on 21 December he did what he apparently thought a dedicated soldier should do under these circumstances. He put a bullet through his head. This in itself was sufficiently shocking for Effie, and for her father, 5000 miles away. But, to compound the agony, just one week later one of Effie's two children, her seven-year-old daughter, became ill and died.

In London, Sir John Millais threw himself into his work. Hence eight notably serious paintings. Of his four Academy pictures only one was not solemn, the least venturesome, *Ada Symon*, a three-quarter-length portrait of a handsome young woman. Two other portraits were notably unlike any of his previous works in the genre. Recently he had told Hunt, 'I feel the remaining sand in the hour glass is running out at express speed.' The picture that would go to the New Gallery was then resting on an easel, *Time the Reaper*, showing a very old man in a robe holding in one hand a scythe, in the other an hour glass. His third portrait was *The Disciple*, showing a young Roman woman in the early days of Christianity. Wearing a black mourning tunic, she sits, hands clasped, listening to a preacher of the new faith. Her facial expression indicates that in thought she is in another world.

Millais's two non-portraits were much talked about, *St Stephen* and *'Speak! Speak!'*. *St Stephen* was based on the account in the book of Acts of the death of the first Christian martyr at the hands of Hellenistic Jews: 'They cried out with a loud voice, and stopped their ears, and rushed upon him with one accord; and they cast him out of the city, and stoned him; and the witnesses laid down their garments at the feet of a young man named Saul. And they stoned Stephen . . . He kneeled down and cried with a loud voice, Lord, lay not this sin to their charge. When he had said this, he fell asleep . . . And devout men buried Stephen, and made great lamentation over him.'

This incident is reminiscent of Millais's earliest paintings, *Pizarro* and *Elgiva*. Again a defenceless person is attacked by a mob. And since the death sentence was handed down by the Sanhedrin, again organised religion comes out badly. (Millais was impartial: the religious figures involved in his scenes of injustice were Catholic, Protestant and Jewish.) But his treatment of the episode differs conspicuously from that of *Pizarro* and *Elgiva*, multi-figure scenes of violence. *St Stephen* might have been that kind of painting. As a young man, Millais would have depicted the actual stoning of Stephen. But, no longer young, he shows us only the denouement: 'He fell asleep.' It is dawn, and the Stephen's body lies unattended. Were it not for the gashed forehead and the blood-stained robe, he might be sleeping. He is not quite alone. In the distance 'devout men' are coming to bury the body.

St Stephen received a lot of attention but not as much as *'Speak! Speak!'*, Millais's crowning work of 1895. The title comes from the opening scene of *Hamlet* when Horatio accosts the ghost. The picture is an imaginative application of these words. The setting is a carefully defined bedroom at night-time of a youngish to early middle-aged man. He has risen suddenly to a sitting position, looking startled. He extends his right arm toward parting curtains which reveal the life-size figure of a beautiful young woman in a bejewelled white dress.

This was Millais's single most ambiguous picture. The only explanation was the two-word title. As in several of his other dramatic pictures, the obscurity was intended. Marion H. Spielmann, the principal commentator on his paintings, recalled asking him about it: 'When I remarked that I could not tell whether the luminous apparition was a real woman or the creation of his tortured imagination, he was pleased: "That's just what I want," he said. "I don't know either, nor," he added, pointing to the picture, "does he."'

Spielmann noted that the woman's figure was 'painted strongly enough to appear a living creature, and shadowy enough to be intended for a ghost.'

We should remember that when Horatio called out 'Speak! Speak!' *he* didn't know what he was seeing. Only later did Hamlet inform him, 'It is an honest ghost, that let me tell you.' And so even the title leaves the issue open.

* * *

Before the 1895 Exhibition had closed, Millais told Hunt, 'I am much better in health, but the voice will never be strong again, I fear.'

Later in the year while visiting Bowerswell, he wrote to Val Prinsep, 'I am voiceless but otherwise in good health, hoping to be back in town the end of this month. Not able to do any work here. I am reading without acquiring any further knowledge as I forget everything a week after I have read the book.'

Soon after returning to London, he wrote unrelated letters to two novelists. One went to that longtime American resident of London, Henry James:

I have been *charmed* by your stories and write to thank you for them. The first book of yours I read was 'The American' and the last 'The Modern Warning'. In both, alas, you make the connections between us [English people and Americans] end disastrously. I know as an Englishman we have *most provoking* ways. Have I not seen him striding down the central aisle of a foreign cathedral between crowds of people devoutly praying without the slightest conception there was an indelicacy in such an interruption, calmly staring up at the architecture and striding up to the altar until stopped by its railing. But I fancy your countrymen have somewhat inherited this inscrutability. At any rate we are too much alike to cut each others' throats. The Irish of course hate us, and I know the Scotch are too jealous of our greater prosperity to feel much affection. Ditto Wales. And yet we have some good parts, and I verily believe are no worse than our neighbours.

On the next day, he sent a very different kind of letter to a very different kind of novelist, a woman known by her pen name, Marie Corelli.

Whereas Henry James was a fastidious writer of quality fiction appealing to a select audience, Marie Corelli wrote romantic melodramas which achieved an immense readership. Indeed for about a dozen years at the turn of the century she was the most widely read novelist in the English language. Millais knew her personally and liked her books. He was a reader who could enjoy both Henry James and Marie Corelli.

Her ninth novel appeared late in the autumn of 1895. Entitled *The Sorrows of Satan*, it had the usual Corelli dosage of melodrama and sentimentality. One thing about this book, however, was unprecedented. Immediately following the title page there was a message from the publisher: 'SPECIAL NOTICE. No copies of this book are sent out for review. Members of the press will therefore obtain it (should they wish to do so) in the usual way with the rest of the public, through the Booksellers and Libraries.' The refusal to send out review copies stemmed from the fact that Corelli's books had been consistently assaulted and insulted by reviewers. This decision did not in the least reduce the demand for *The Sorrows of Satan*. If anything, it may have stimulated interest in the book, which went through forty large paintings. The number of copies sold exceeded that for any novel previously published in Great Britain.

Millais began to read it in December. He was enjoying it until, on Christmas Day, he was unsettled by a passage which he reread several times, containing something said by one of the characters during a discussion on art: 'I am one of those who think the fame of Millais was marred when he degraded himself to the level of painting the little green boy blowing bubbles of Pears' soap. *That was an advertisement*, and that very incident, trifling as it seems, will prevent his ever standing on the dignified height of such masters in Art as Romney, Sir Peter Lely, Gainsborough, and Reynolds.'

Because of Corelli's immense readership, Millais felt that he had to do something. At once he wrote to her, pointing out that he had had nothing to do with selling *Bubbles* to a soap company. He asked, 'What in the name of your "Satan" do you mean by saying what is not true?'

Marie Corelli was in Folkestone, staying at Wampach's Hotel, which, its stationery proclaimed, was the 'only Hotel in Folkestone Lighted by Electric Light'. Immediately she sent this response:

> Your letter has had the effect of a sudden 'bomb' thrown in upon the calm of my present 'sea-side' meditations! – but I have rallied my energies, and I assure you 'in the name of Satan' and all other fallen or risen angels that I meant no harm. It is out of the high and faithful admiration I have for you as a king among English painters that I get inwardly wrathful whenever I think of 'Bubbles' in a soap

advertisement! Gods of Olympus! I have seen and *loved* the *original picture* – the most exquisite and dainty child ever dreamed up, with the air of a baby Poet as well as a small angel – and I look upon all Pears' 'posters' as *gross libels* both of your work and you! . . . Of course it makes me angry, and I confess to being angry with *you* for letting *Pears* have it. 'Bubbles' should hang beside Sir Joshua's 'Age of Innocence' in the National Gallery where people could see it with the veneration that befits all great art.

This did not end the story of *Bubbles* and the soap company. Nearly four years later John G. Millais's biography of his father appeared with an extended commentary on the affair. The younger Millais insisted that his father, 'furious' to learn that the picture would be used in an advertisement, 'protested strongly against this utilisation of his art, but . . . he had no power to prevent their using the picture in any way they liked'.

There are good reasons for rejecting John G. Millais's report. Indeed it was refuted soon after the book appeared in print. The Victoria and Albert Museum Library has a typewritten letter dated 17 November 1899 to one W.H. Keep from Thomas J. Barratt, of A. & F. Pears Ltd., who had spoken to Millais beforehand about using *Bubbles* in advertisements. Barratt noted that John G. Millais had been abroad at the time and deemed the assertion that his father had been 'furious' as 'wholly, entirely, and absolutely at variance with the facts'. On the day that this letter was typed, a more detailed statement by Barratt appeared in *The Times*. He recalled that after seeing a page proof of the advertisement, Millais exclaimed, 'That's magnificent!' When Barratt said that some artists objected to their pictures being used commercially, Millais replied, 'What nonsense! I will paint as many pictures for advertisements as you like to give me money for, and I will write you a letter for publication marking my appreciation of the excellent way in which you have dealt with my picture.' The letter, he later told Barratt, was not written only because it might have appeared to be self-serving.

Five days after the appearance of Barratt's declaration, *The Times* published a letter from Charles W. Deschamps, who had been an official of the 1889 Paris Exhibition, where *Bubbles* was shown.

Deschamps had asked Millais if he took exception to its use in advertising. 'Nonsense!' he replied. 'It was an admirable reproduction and is a credit to Messrs. Pears.'

* * *

Exactly one month after Millais had written to Marie Corelli, the president of the Royal Academy, Frederick Leighton, died. There was no doubt about his replacement. Millais wrote to Rudolf Lehmann (brother of Nina Lehmann, the young subject of the highly acclaimed portrait of 1869): 'The death of our old friend comes more heavily on me than on any other, for it seems I cannot escape being his successor. I had made many vows I would never be President, for many, many reasons, and now duty insists on my breaking them . . . On the 20th the PRA is to be elected, and I tell you sincerely he is more to be pitied than congratulated. If it falls to me, I shall do my best to maintain the dignity of the position.'

His election was almost unanimous. He garnered every vote but his own, which went to Philip Calderon. Five days later, Beatrix Potter wrote in her journal, 'Millais told Mr F— he supposed he had to take the damned thing.' He did take it, he told William Gladstone, because he had had no alternative: 'The death of Leighton was a great shock to the Academy, and I found that it was impossible for me to decline becoming its President, if only for a short time, so that the members may become more in agreement in their next election. Since I accepted it my voice has become worse and the malady has troubled me a great deal.'

It was true that the Academicians could not have agreed on anyone else. As one of them, William Blake Richmond, said to his son just before the election, 'Millais is the right choice as PRA as there can be no jealousy or quarrel about him.'

Soon after he assumed the presidency, his health, perhaps coincidentally, began rapidly to deteriorate. He could not preside over the annual banquet, and only once, briefly on the private view day, did he visit the Exhibition, where he had five entries.

Four were portraits – two men, one woman, and one young boy – and were unexceptional. But the fifth is another matter. It is one of his best paintings, a superb ending to a superb career. Called *A Forerunner*, it shows a nearly nude young man in a leopard skin tying two pieces of wood together to form a cross. He has often been said to represent John the Baptist, but he is 'a', not 'the', forerunner. Millais was non-committal, leaving it an open question. In any event, he stands erect, his resolute expression revealing a man who is buoyantly, self-confidently certain of his beliefs. Painted by a dying man, this is a picture of high hope. The background shows the light of dawn.

Painted with freedom and firmness, there is nothing tentative about *A Forerunner*, nothing to suggest its creator's physical condition. It was extremely well received by virtually everyone. *The Times* saw a demonstration of the artist's 'old mastery and old power of making the brush answer to his thought'. The *Art Journal*'s reviewer found 'no hint of failing vitality' and was reminded 'by its vigour of design and mastery of execution the great achievements of earlier years'. The writer concluded that 'at the fullest tide of his maturity Sir John Millais proves himself to possess still unimpaired the enthusiasms which have made his career and performance unique among those of his contemporaries.'

* * *

On 4 May 1896, the day on which the public was introduced to *A Forerunner*, the following item appeared in a newspaper: 'A telegram from London announces that the disease which has affected Sir John Millais's health so seriously has been diagnosed as cancer of the throat. Sir John's physicians have attributed his disease to his inordinate use of tobacco. His condition is uncertain. He may live for ten days or ten months.' This was printed 6000 miles from Burlington House, in the San Francisco *Chronicle*. John Millais's throat cancer was newsworthy everywhere.

The pronouncement came on 29 April. Within ten days Millais's life almost ended. Three months later, in its lengthy obituary notice, the *Morning Chronicle* reported on what had happened on the evening of Saturday, 9 May:

Sir John's condition suddenly became serious, and Miss [Mary] Millais sent an urgent announcement to Mr G.H. Hames, FRCS [Fellow of the Royal College of Surgeons], very late, asking him to call and see her father. Mr Hames went at once to Palace-gate. Sir John was suffering from dyspnoea – want of air. He was gasping for breath, as one would who had tried to swallow a bone and the bone had stuck in his larynx. When a man is gasping for air he must have it, if he is to live. An operation was necessary – it was tracheotomy. But Sir John insisted upon awaiting the arrival of two other medical attendants before he would have the operation performed. [One of them was Sir Richard Quain, Bart., FRS, President of the General Council of Medical Education and Physician Extraordinary to the Queen. At that moment Millais's portrait of Quain hung at the Exhibition.] He would have died that night if it had not been per-formed. He very nearly did die that night in consequence of it. The operation, which is best performed in the strongest daylight, had to be performed at the earliest moment, at one o'clock in the morning, by the light of a candle. [It was normal practice, before the importance of sterile conditions was understood, to perform surgery in the patient's home. Except for a few private hospitals which resembled luxury hotels, nineteenth-century hospitals were mainly for poor people, often admitted because there was no one to care for them at home.]

The operation was not easy. At first the tubes could not be prop-erly got in. The patient then suffered from septicaemia. Sir John Millais ceased to breathe for ten minutes. It was feared all was over, but artificial respiration was resorted to him, and he was brought round. Subsequently an antiseptic became necessary, and an innovation in medical science, which will doubtless open up an entirely new department of work for the medical profession, was the result. Ozone was for the first time used as an antiseptic. Mr James, and those with him, got it from oxygen, making it in a room adjoining that in which the patient lay, and they got it into the tra-cheotomy tubes. It kept Sir John Millais alive for three months, it relieved him from pain, it made him comfortable, it removed the odour hitherto characteristic of cancer. In the words of Mr Hames, 'In consequence of this success with the ozone no man has ever passed through such a grave illness with such comfort as Sir John Millais. During the three months since the operation and the adop-tion of the ozone, he had practically no narcotics whatever.'

Visitors to Palace Gate saw Millais bolstered up in bed, unable to speak. Sometimes he whispered, sometimes he wrote with chalk on a slate. This was tiring, and after the end of May callers were banned altogether. During his remaining two months, he lived in seclusion, seeing only his immediate family.

On 6 June, Mary Millais wrote to Holman Hunt, 'Papa is just a little better since last week, not in pain, I am thankful to say. The doctors think he may go on like this for some time, some months perhaps. On Thursday last week we did not expect him to live and I must tell you he was thinking of you as he wrote amongst many messages to me – "I wish *Hunt* to be a pall bearer." He rallied in the evening and has been improving since then, but we can't feel hopeful.'

Millais hadn't seen much of Hunt in recent years. This doesn't indicate that their friendship had faltered. It was just that they were leading their own necessarily separate lives. They had families to care for, they were fully engaged in professional work, and although both resided in London, their homes were far apart. At a time when there were no telephones or automobiles, it wasn't easy to socialise. But this final wish of Millais, as conveyed by his daughter Mary, demonstrates his recognition of Holman Hunt as the best personal friend he had ever had and as the person who had exerted the most valuable influence on his art.

Numerous people stopped to ask about Millais. Among them was the man who had become an ARA just ahead of him, with whom he had become quite friendly, Frederick Goodall. Earlier in the year, a couple of months before sending-in day, Millais had asked Goodall for the loan of an Egyptian boy's blue shirt, embroidered with red, which he intended to use in a painting.

'You are not going to get it done in time for the coming Exhibition, are you?' Goodall had asked.

'Oh, dear no,' Millais answered. 'It will be for next year. The subject is "The Child Christ in the Temple".'

Now, in June, Goodall reported, 'After I had called one day to inquire about his health, he told his daughter to "pack up the little blue Egyptian shirt that Mr Goodall had lent him, as he should never paint the picture, and return it with many thanks". I thought it extraordinary that in the midst of his suffering he could think of such a small matter.'

It is intriguing to contemplate this picture with the identical subject of Holman Hunt's most famous painting, the one which Millais had so often disparaged. As he had earlier invited comparison with Sir Joshua Reynolds, did he intend to do the same thing with his old friend?

Among the letters arriving at Palace Gate with inquiries about Millais's health, was one from Windsor Castle. The Queen asked if she could do anything for him. Yes, there was something, he had Mary respond. She could receive his wife at court. The Queen at once consented. Effie dutifully travelled to Windsor, where Princess Louise made the presentation.

John Millais could now die peacefully.

On Wednesday, 12 August, he fell into a state of unconsciousness. That evening G.H. Hames issued his last medical bulletin: 'Sir John Millais is rapidly falling. There is no possible hope of improvement.' Hames stayed at Palace Gate until three in the morning. He left, the *Morning Chronicle* reported, 'with the certain knowledge that the termination of the illness could not for long be delayed. Shortly before five o'clock, however, Sir John rallied, and exhibited signs of returning consciousness. It was the last effort. At half-past eight he was only just alive, and death was momentarily expected. Still he lingered. At one o'clock it was evident the strength had all but gone, and at half-past five in the afternoon he died. Round his bedside at the last were Lady Millais, Mr Everett Millais (who succeeds to the baronetcy), Miss [Mary] Millais, and other members of the family. Sir John was 67 years of age.'

The burial took place one week later. A few minutes after ten on Thursday, 21 August, the funeral procession left Palace Gate and, with one stop along the way, in Piccadilly before the Royal Academy, it proceeded to St Paul's Cathedral.

At noon John Millais's body was laid to rest. One of the pall bearers was Holman Hunt.

Notes and Sources

The following notes give the sources of quotations in the text. Each entry refers to the relevant page number and a salient word or phrase. A published source is represented by the author's name, when known, and an abbreviated form of the title, given fully in the bibliography. For an unpublished source, the citation is the name, shortened, of the library holding the manuscript. 'Morgan' and 'Huntington,' my main sources, refer to the Pierpont Morgan Library and the Huntington Library.

CHAPTER 1

page 7 'A few years ago . . .' Morgan
7 'It amazed me . . .' Hunt, *Pre-Raphaelitism*, 2nd ed., I, 87
8 'a fine, healthy . . .' Morgan
9 'They uttered . . .' Millais, *Life*, I, 10–11

CHAPTER 2

page 13 'I shall never . . .' Millais, *Life*, I, 16–17
14 'the inexorable Sass . . .' Farr, *William Etty*, 56
15 'I feel that . . .' Frith, *My Autobiography*, I, 55
15 'Ah, copies from . . .' Ibid., 35
15 'A huge, white . . .' Ibid., 36
16 'Not having any . . .' Huntington
17 'the students are . . .' Atkinson, 'Art, Politics . . .', 94
17 'wasted time' Leslie, 'The Inner Life . . .', 2
17 'the amusement of . . .' Frith, *My Autobiography*, I, 33

page 18 'the most animated . . .' Goodall, *Reminiscences*, 168
18 'One day . . .' Morgan
19 'When it came . . .' Hunt, *Pre-Raphaelitism*, 1st ed., I, 33

CHAPTER 3

page 20 'set the figures . . .' Hutchison, *History*, 61
20 'One day when . . .' Hunt, *Pre-Raphaelitism*, 1st ed., I, 33–34
21 'We talked . . .' Ibid., I, 66
22 'denunciation of the gods . . .' Ibid., I, 53
22 'Yes, and he got . . .' Ibid., 2nd ed., I, 52
22 'In 1845 Millais . . .' Millais, *Life*, I, 33–34
23 'monotonous street . . .' Cunningham, *Handbook*, 38
25 'when his father . . .' Thomas, *Serjeant Thomas*, 22
25 'I was very . . .' Ibid., 25–26
26 'fills up a couple . . .' Farr, *William Etty*, 56
26 'had the greatest . . .' Goodall, *Reminiscences*, 38
26 'Let your principal . . .' Farr, *William Etty*, 32
26 'I found . . .' Monkhouse, 'William Etty', 911
27 'I accept . . .' Morgan
27 'Of all its . . .' Hunt, *Pre-Raphaelitism*, 1st ed., I, 73
28 'hackneyed . . .' Ibid., 48
28 'Up to that time . . .' Hunt, 'Pre-Raphaelite Brotherhood', 473
29 'No public event . . .' Oliphant, 'The Royal Academy', 753–54

CHAPTER 4

page 32 'Look here . . .' Hunt, *Pre-Raphaelitism*, 1st ed., I, 60–61
33 'perhaps because . . .' Ibid., 67
33 'a condemned cell . . .' *s.n.*, 'Art and the Royal Academy', 229
34 'His habitual . . .' Hunt, *Pre-Raphaelitism*, 1st ed., I, 75–76
36 'As always . . .' Ibid., 80–81
37 'Who's there?' Ibid., 82
37 'Every picture . . .' Morgan
38 'illustrates the sacredness . . .' Hunt, *Pre-Raphaelitism*, 1st ed., I, 85
39 'He cautioned . . .' Ibid., 76

CHAPTER 5

page 40 'The gaunt chamber . . .' Stephens, *Dante Gabriel Rossetti*, 62

41 'Year after year . . .' 'The Royal Academy', the *Scotsman*, 14 May 1852, 7

42 'I never believed . . .' Ruskin, *Works*, vol. 35, p. 45

42 'We did not curb . . .' Hunt, *Pre-Raphaelitism*, 1st ed., I, 133

44 'I have not had time . . .' D.G. Rossetti, *Letters*, I, 40

44 'I just looked . . .' Milnes, *Life of Keats*, I, 255

44 'I can quite . . .' Hunt, *Pre-Raphaelitism*, 1st ed., I, 129

45 'Pre-Raphaelitism is neither . . .' Stephens, *Artists*, 17

46 'Raffaele maintains . . .' 'Conversations in the National Gallery', *New Monthly Gallery*, vol. 13, 536

47 'an artist of the . . .' Hunt, *Pre-Raphaelitism*, 1st ed., I, 135

47 'a picture painted . . .' Morgan

48 'I took *Isabella* . . .' Hunt, *Pre-Raphaelitism*, 1st ed., I, 80

49 'at a peak . . .' Ibid., 170

50 'he was wont . . .' Millais, *Life*, I, 87

50 'excessive fatigue . . .' Huntington

51 'the handsomest . . .' Potter, *Journal*, 418

51 'had the face . . .' Hunt, *Pre-Raphaelitism*, 1st ed., I, 175

51 'a beautiful youth . . .' W.M. Rossetti, *Some Reminiscences*, 70

51 'a young man . . .' Hunt, 'The Pre-Raphaelite Brotherhood', 737

51 'a very genial . . .' Fox, *Journals*, 231

51 'The simplest way . . .' Clement Greenberg, *Collected Essays* (Univ. of Chicago, 1956), I, 153

53 'The line is . . .' 'Our Critic Among the Pictures', *Punch*, 22 (1852), 232

CHAPTER 6

page 54 'I am stunningly . . .' Huntington

55 'Work is the great . . .' Morgan

55 'thoughts of painting . . .' Ibid.

55 'My landscape . . .' Huntington

55 'to paint a copy . . .' W.M. Rossetti, *The PRB Journal*, 8

55 'I have been reading . . .' W.M. Rossetti, *The PRB Journal*, 7

56 'Collinson says . . .' W.M. Rossetti, *The PRB Journal*, 4

57 'I was determined . . .' Hunt, *Pre-Raphaelitism*, 1st ed., I, 202

58 'Rossetti never did . . .' Morgan

page 60 'My dear fellow . . .' Hunt, *Pre-Raphaelitism*, 1st ed., I, 92

60 'Do you know . . .' Ibid.

60 'For prosperity . . .' *Art Journal*, 1841, p. 14

61 'I do not remember . . .' Cooper, *Recollections*, 52

61 'monstrously perverse' *Spectator*

61 'nameless atrocity' *Literary Gazette*

61 'an instance of . . .' *Daily News*

61 'a pictorial blasphemy' *Athenaeum*

61 'a repulsive caricature' *Examiner*

64 'Fashion exercises . . .' Morgan

64 'I hope that . . .' Huntington

CHAPTER 7

page 66 'I cannot help . . .' Huntington

66 'I hold a painter . . .' Ibid.

66 'Above all things . . .' Morgan

67 'Millais's *Isabella* . . .' W.M. Rossetti, *The PRB Journal*, 28

68 'I heard from Patmore . . .' Ibid., 29

70 'He does not care . . .' Huntington

70 'I am delighted . . .' Ibid.

70 'This is such . . .' Ibid.

70 'Collins is . . .' Ibid.

70 'We are both . . .' Ibid.

71 'People better buy . . .' Millais, *Life*, I, 85

71 'acknowledge to be . . .' Huntington

71 'I had to go . . .' Millais, *Life*, I, 88

71 'I truly long . . .' Huntington

71 'I am ashamed . . .' Millais, *Life*, I, 90

71 'I have plenty . . .' Ibid., 99

71 'the dove returning . . .' Ibid., 97

72 'He was flourishing . . .' Champneys, *Memoirs*, I, 184

72 'Such a quantity . . .' Millais, *Life*, I, 101

72 'I figured almost . . .' W.M. Rossetti, *Some Recollections*, 96

73 'The Times has . . .' Millais, *Life*, I, 101

76 'I have dined . . .' Millais, *Life*, I, 116

CHAPTER 8

page 78 'walked along beaten . . .' Hunt, *Pre-Raphaelitism*, 1st ed., I, 263
79 'Our rooms . . .' Millais, *Life*, I, 119
79 'Perhaps the greatest . . .' Ibid., 145
80 'Are those daffodils?' Allingham, *Diary*, 379
80 'A painter cannot . . .' Morgan
80 'You will see . . .' Millais, *Life*, I, 122
81 'I am working . . .' Ibid.
81 'Two lovers standing . . .' Hunt, *Pre-Raphaelitism*, 1st ed., I, 285
81 'My father occasionally . . .' Fenn, 'Millais and Music', 823
83 'It is a scene . . .' Millais, *Life*, I, 135
84 'On our way . . .' Ibid., I, 141
84 'I am very anxious . . .' Huntington
85 'Alas for Miss Ryan!' Millais, *Life*, I, 152
85 'Today I have . . .' Ibid., 151
85 'She is stupendously . . .' Hunt, *Pre-Raphaelitism*, 1st ed., I, 298
86 'Collins wants . . .' Huntington
86 'Crowds stood . . .' Stephens, *Exhibition*, 111

CHAPTER 9

page 89 'All the letters . . .' Woolner, *Thomas Woolner*, 46
89 'I am going . . .' Huntington
89 'We all sat down . . .' University of British Columbia
90 'Altogether the sight . . .' Millais, *Life*, I, 190
90 'Like Macbeth . . .' University of British Columbia
90 'Here I am . . .' Morgan
91 'I leave Saturday . . .' Ibid.
91 'I suppose . . .' Huntington
91 'I have positively . . .' Ibid.
92 'Next Monday . . .' Ibid.
92 'The picture that . . .' Goodall, *Reminiscences*, 218
92 'I have received . . .' Huntington
93 'I openly expressed . . .' Ibid.
93 'I have to paint . . .' Ibid.
93 'I have a headache . . .' Millais, *Life*, I, 186
94 'I think Ophelia . . .' James, *John Ruskin*, 176
94 'I have been sitting . . .' Morgan

page 95 'Mr R . . .' Ibid.

95 'The picture . . .' Ibid.

CHAPTER 10

page 98 'Millais is gifted . . .' Lutyens, *Millais*, 87

98 'He wanted . . .' Ruskin, *Works*, XII, xix

99 'John did nothing . . .' Trevelyan, *A Pre-Raphaelite*, 41

100 'I have worked . . .' Millais, *Life*, I, 199

100 'He is so . . .' Morgan

100 'won all hearts . . .' Thackeray, *Letters*, III, 231

100 'No painter . . .' Morgan

100 'He used to say . . .' Fenn, 'Millais and Music', 824

101 'I was immediately . . .' Ward, *Reminiscences*, 77

101 'he seems quite . . .' Morgan

101 'was regarded . . .' Meeks, *The Railroad Station*, 77

102 'This is the most . . .' Ruskin, *Works*, XII, xix

102 'The country is . . .' Morgan

102 'Millais kept drawing . . .' Trevelyan, *A Pre-Raphaelite*, 79

102 'Mrs Ruskin is . . .' Huntington

103 'awfully bored . . .' Morgan

103 'The shore of Loch . . .' Ruskin, *Works*, XII, xxiv

104 'they had intended . . .' Grieve, 'Ruskin and Millais', 229

104 'You could go . . .' Huntington

105 'Millais has fixed . . .' Ruskin, *Works*, XII, xxiv

105 'Ruskin and I . . .' Morgan

105 'principally to get . . .' Ibid.

106 'They have been . . .' Surtees, *Reflections*, 49

106 'Our new residence . . .' Morgan

106 'Our parlour . . .' Ibid.

106 'I am restless . . .' Huntington

106 'We have purchased . . .' Morgan

106 'I have made . . .' Lutyens, *Millais*, 67

107 'I have been going . . .' Huntington

107 'I think you quite . . .' Morgan

108 'The rain is really . . .' Ibid.

108 'Ruskin and I . . .' Ibid.

108 'You will hear shortly . . .' Ibid.

109 'I am enjoying myself . . .' Millais, *Life*, I, 206

109 'the most delightful . . .' Huntington

page 109 'I am teaching . . .' Ibid.

   109 'My saucy little . . .' Surtees, *Reflections*, 52

   109 'Millais's great delight . . .' Ibid., 49

   110 'I confess . . .' Ibid., 4

   110 'I could not read . . .' Atley, *Acland*, 173–74

   111 'The unremitting rain . . .' Huntington

   111 'amazed, bewildered . . .' Atley, *Acland*, 173

   111 'Ruskin is not . . .' Huntington

   111 'large picture . . .' Surtees, *Reflections*, 51

   111 'I am getting on . . .' Huntington

   111 'There is little . . .' Ruskin, *Works*, XII, xxii

   111 'I get a lesson . . .' Surtees, *Reflections*, 49

   112 'He is the most . . .' Morgan

   112 'They took off . . .' Ibid.

   112 'They were holding . . .' Ibid.

   112 'William is always . . .' Surtees, *Reflections*, 47

   112 'William Millais has . . .' D.G. Rossetti, *Letters*, I, 199

   113 'I have just . . .' Morgan

   113 'It is horribly . . .' Huntington

   113 'I am dreadfully . . .' Ibid.

   113 'You cannot conceive . . .' Morgan

   114 'I cannot help . . .' Trevelyan, *A Pre-Raphaelite*, 86

   114 'I have discovered . . .' Huntington

   114 'If you have no . . .' Ibid.

   114 'The other evening . . .' Morgan

CHAPTER 11

page 117 'After you left . . .' Morgan

   118 'I really must . . .' Ibid.

   118 'I want to express . . .' Ibid.

   118 'Mr Parker says . . .' Ibid.

   119 'Our class . . .' Ibid.

   120 'She contended . . .' Ibid.

   120 'Don't think me . . .' Gaskell, *Letters*, 287

   120 'I think very . . .' Lutyens, *The Ruskins*, 52

   121 'My own Effie . . .' James, *John Ruskin*, 48

   121 'I am happier . . .' Morgan

   122 'We are going . . .' Ibid.

page 122 'We went . . .' Ibid.
122 'I have read . . .' Ibid.
123 'I learned Venice . . .' Ruskin, *Works*, XII, xxvi
123 'I think you should . . .' Morgan
124 'He seemed . . .' Ibid.
124 'My Dear Friend . . .' Ibid.
124 'I married her . . .' Whitehouse, *Vindication*, 15
125 'Mr Ruskin is . . .' Surtees, *Reflections*, 22–23

CHAPTER 12

page 126 'I wish the country . . .' Whitehouse, *Vindication*, 24
126 'I quite hate . . .' Huntington
127 'How can I . . .' Ibid.
127 'so awfully respectable . . .' Huntington
127 'which was too long . . .' Morgan
128 'I feel under . . .' Huntington
128 'an undeniable giant . . .' Morgan
129 'If I had only . . .' Ibid.
130 'Don't come . . .' Ibid.
130 'rushed into . . .' Hunt, *Pre-Raphaelitism*, 1st ed., I, 365
131 'Millais did not . . .' D.G. Rossetti, *Letters*, I, 174
131 'begin a new . . .' Morgan
131 'I shall certainly . . .' Huntington
131 'out of the way . . .' Ibid.
131 'I have been . . .' Ibid.
132 'savage and uncivilised' Millais, *Life*, I, 142
132 'I have been in the country . . .' Huntington
132 'I enjoy the chase . . .' Millais, *Life*, I, 178
132 'Effie is never . . .' Trevelyan, *A Pre-Raphaelite*, 94
132 'Since she returned . . .' Lutyens, *Millais*, 13
133 'It is my belief . . .' Morgan
133 'I have to tell you . . .' Ibid.
134 'Immediately after . . .' Whitehouse, *Vindication*, 12–14
135 'When I think . . .' Morgan
135 'I have no more . . .' Ibid.
135 'I am off to . . .' Ibid.
136 'The Law will let . . .' James, *John Ruskin*, 226–27
136 'I tell the tale . . .' Lutyens, *Millais*, 195

page 136 'Everybody glories . . .' Morgan

137 'I never go . . .' Huntington

137 'That Ruskin row . . .' D.G. Rossetti, *Letters*, I, 200

137 'Effie found my . . .' Surtees, *Reflections*, 274

137 'I am so disgusted . . .' Morgan

137 'You will, I know . . .' Ibid.

138 'We found . . .' James, *John Ruskin*, 236–37

138 'eating heartily . . .' Morgan.

138 'I can prove . . .' Whitehouse, *Vindication*, 107

138 'Should you ever . . .' Drew, *Acton*, 107

CHAPTER 13

page 139 'The only books . . .' Huntington

139 'Mrs Ruskin is . . .' Ibid.

140 'I have been . . .' Morgan

140 'We give ourselves . . .' Ibid.

140 'The world will . . .' Ibid.

140 'People gossip . . .' Ibid.

140 'I am at present . . .' Ibid.

141 'I had rather . . .' D.G. Rossetti, *Letters*, I, 240

141 'I have been . . .' Huntington

142 'We have just . . .' James, *John Ruskin*, 240

143 'Millais is painting . . .' D.G. Rossetti, *Letters*, I, 240

143 'For the life . . .' Morgan

143 'The moment I . . .' Millais, *Life*, I, 248

144 'My dear sir . . .' Davis, *Wilkie Collins*, 167

145 'How he does it . . .' W.M. Rossetti, *PRB Journal*, 56

145 'Millais summoned . . .' W.M. Rossetti, *Pre-Raphaelite Diaries*, 176–77

146 'Mr Gainsborough presents . . .' Hutchison, *History*, 67

146 'Mr Gainsborough's compliments . . .' Ibid., 68

146 'I almost dropped . . .' Huntington

146 'Millais's amusement . . .' Scott, *Autobiographical*, 29

147 'Millais described . . .' W.M. Rossetti, *Pre-Raphaelite Diaries*, 181

147 'the most wonderful . . .' D.G. Rossetti, *Letters*, I, 244

147 'Those children!' Phythian, *Millais*, 57–58

148 'Happy Millais!' Du Maurier, *Young George*, 216

148 'I can scarcely . . .' Huntington

page 148 'Next month . . .' Ibid.

148 'I feel quite . . .' Ibid.

148 'painting sounds . . .' Ibid.

148 'Fancy, my dear . . .' Ibid.

149 'Effie has been . . .' (and all succeeding excerpts from honeymoon letters), Morgan

150 'It was very . . .' Ibid.

151 'I have got . . .' Ibid.

151 'I am not at all . . .' Ibid.

CHAPTER 14

page 152 'I could never . . .' Huntington

152 'I had so fatiguing . . .' Morgan

153 'He wished . . .' Bennett, *Millais*, 41

154 'Here I am . . .' Morgan

154 'Nothing could be . . .' Ibid.

155 'I know every . . .' Ibid.

155 '*Autumn Leaves* is . . .' D.G. Rossetti, *Letters*, I, 300

156 'I never expected . . .' Morgan

156 'Of all Millais's . . .' Stephens, 'The Two . . .', 324

157 'You certainly understand . . .' Bodleian

157 'requires to be . . .' W.M. Rossetti, *Diaries*, 197

158 'I am sanguine . . .' Morgan

158 'Poor Hunt . . .' Ibid.

159 'I sold a little . . .' Ibid.

159 'I made up . . .' Ibid.

160 'An artist should . . .' Ibid.

160 'On the whole . . .' Ibid.

160 'I hope this . . .' Ibid.

161 'The envy . . .' Ibid.

161 'I believe *sincerely* . . .' Ibid.

162 'I think one . . .' Ibid.

162 'I have great . . .' Ibid.

162 'I am already . . .' Ibid.

162 'I am really . . .' Ibid.

163 'I had a little . . .' Ibid.

163 'We went for . . .' Ibid.

164 'Just a line . . .' Huntington

CHAPTER 15

page 165 'My baby robs . . .' Huntington
 166 'How can any . . .' Ibid.
 168 'All those whose . . .' Morgan
 169 'JR's pamphlet . . .' Ibid.
 169 'There is no . . .' Ibid.
 170 'He possessed . . .' Pennell, 'John Everett Millais', 443
 170 'disliked having . . .' Martin, *Unquiet Heart*, 444
 170 'Tennyson loathes . . .' D.G. Rossetti, *Letters*, I, 301
 170 'It must be said . . .' W.M. Rossetti, *Ruskin: Rossetti*, 109
 171 'I have been groaning . . .' Huntington
 171 'I agree with . . .' Morgan
 172 'The fact is . . .' Huntington
 172 'Whenever Everett . . .' Morgan
 173 'Effie must have . . .' Ibid.

CHAPTER 16

page 174 'I think withdrawing . . .' Huntington
 174 'My poor dear . . .' Ibid.
 175 'Shooting partridges . . .' Morgan
 175 'This time . . .' Ibid.
 175 'My pictures . . .' Huntington
 176 'It had long been . . .' Millais, *Life*, I, 329
 177 'I see clearly . . .' Morgan
 177 'I came to get . . .' Ibid.
 177 'A class of . . .' Pictures of the Year, *Saturday Review*, 22 (1867), 141–42
 177 'I am inclined . . .' Morgan
 177 'Oh this isn't . . .' Ibid.
 178 'None of the . . .' Ibid.
 178 'If Combe buys . . .' Ibid.
 178 'The enmity . . .' Ibid.
 178 'At the G . . . .' Ibid.
 178 'Conscientiously . . .' Ibid.
 178 'I am prepared . . .' Ibid.
 180 'Leech and others . . .' Ibid.
 181 'I am convinced . . .' Ibid.
 182 'There is no doubt . . .' Ibid.

page 182 'Why should a man . . .' Ibid.

    182 'Mr Raphael . . .' Ibid.

    182 'If this happens . . .' Ibid.

    183 'How I long . . .' Ibid.

    183 'Yesterday I was . . .' Ibid.

    183 'These pictures . . .' Ibid.

CHAPTER 17

page 184 'A Way to Get On' Morgan

    185 'I have had . . .' Ibid.

    185 'If I was not . . .' Ibid.

    186 'The shops . . .' Ibid.

    186 'I have been . . .' Ibid.

    186 'I never was . . .' Ibid.

    187 'Yesterday I dined . . .' Ibid.

    189 'in low spirits . . .' Ibid.

    190 'Altogether Millais . . .' Trollope, *Autobiography*, 148

    191 'I haven't done . . .' Morgan

    191 'he begged . . .' Gaskell, *Letters*, 661

    192 'When he saw . . .' Ibid.

    192 'The lecture . . .' Collingwood, *Life*, II, 276

    192 'that termagant . . .' Brookfield, *Mrs Brookfield*, 499

    193 'I am sorry . . .' Dalziell, *The Brothers*, 142

    193 'I should have . . .' Ibid.

    193 'I feel rather . . .' Morgan

    194 'I don't agree . . .' Ibid.

    194 'I have your . . .' Ibid.

    194 'I am sorry . . .' Ibid.

    195 'I am obliged . . .' Ibid.

    195 'I am half . . .' Ibid.

    196 'If the mountains . . .' Ibid.

    197 'I fished . . .' Ibid.

    200 'Historical art . . .' Ibid.

    201 'The other day . . .' Du Maurier, *Young George*, 158

    201 'I was fascinated . . .' Ibid., 159

    201 'Yesterday we caught . . .' Morgan

CHAPTER 18

page 204 'If you ask me . . .' Morgan
 205 'Colls has said . . .' Morgan
 206 'It does no good . . .' Ibid.

CHAPTER 19

page 207 'I cannot tell . . .' Morgan
 207 'The children . . .' Ibid.
 207 'The shops are . . .' Ibid.
 209 'I can't help . . .' Ibid.
 210 'I took a long . . .' Ibid.
 211 'It is such . . .' Ibid.
 211 'I don't feel . . .' Ibid.
 211 'a place of . . .' W.M. Rossetti, *Pre-Raphaelite Diaries*, 149
 212 'It is all . . .' Morgan
 213 'I found 50 . . .' Ibid.
 213 'I would rather . . .' Ibid.
 213 'I cannot help . . .' Ibid.
 214 'Mr G.H. Boughton . . .' Monkhouse, 'John Everett Millais', 679
 214 'You are not half . . .' Morgan

CHAPTER 20

page 215 'was one of . . .' Millais, *Life*, II, 107
 215 'I had a delightful . . .' Morgan
 215 'Everything now . . .' (and all succeeding quotations in Chapter
 20), Ibid.

CHAPTER 21

page 222 'I am in receipt . . .' Morgan
 224 'Agnew won't . . .' Ibid.
 224 'The report cards . . .' Ibid.
 225 'Your enduring . . .' Ibid.
 226 'The real happiness . . .' Ibid.
 226 'In Titian's . . .' Ibid.
 228 'I go nearly . . .' Ibid.

page 229 'I was so shocked . . .' Ibid.
229 'my daughter earnestly . . .' Ibid.
229 'When called upon . . .' Ibid.
230 'Mr Ruskin took . . .' Ibid.

CHAPTER 22

page 235 'I wish you . . .' Morgan
235 '"Chill October" was . . .' Millais, *Life*, II, 29
235 'It was at . . .' Jopling, *Twenty Years*, 63
236 'Ours was . . .' Ibid., 67
236 'Unless you return . . .' Morgan
236 'I have not written . . .' Ibid.
237 'It occurs . . .' Ibid.
237 'I hardly know . . .' Ibid.
237 'I am distressed . . .' Ibid.
238 'Injustice to . . .' Ibid.
240 'However strong . . .' Ibid.
240 'In my opinion . . .' Ibid.
241 'I am now . . .' Huntington
241 'My sight . . .' Ibid.
241 'Millais has . . .' D.G. Rossetti, *Letters*, I, 201
243 'I dine with . . .' Morgan
245 'Mr Millais . . .' Oliphant, 'Art in May,' 751–52
245 'Look at him . . .' Ibid., 'The Royal Academy,' 757
246 'I think more . . .' Huntington
246 'he used to say . . .' Jopling, *Twenty Years*, 140
246 'April 6. To Millais'.' Gower, *Reminiscences*, II, 132
247 'I have just . . .' Victoria and Albert
247 'I have long . . .' Huntington
249 'If I were . . .' Du Maurier, *Young George*, 150
249 'My new home . . .' Huntington

CHAPTER 23

page 250 'The face of . . .' Oldcastle, 'Mr Millais' House', 291–95
252 'Sunday is . . .' *New Letters*, II, 333
252 'He seemed . . .' Wilson, *Carlyle*, 405
255 'I have not been . . .' Morgan

[304]

page 255   'He is studying . . .' Huntington

255   'I was profoundly . . .' Morgan

257   'There is plenty . . .' Bodleian

257   'congratulated him . . .' 'Stories of Millais,' 527

258   'I was at once . . .' Spielmann, *Millais*, 125

258   'I am happy . . .' Gower, *Reminiscences*, II, 286

258   'truly a majestic . . .' Ibid.

258   'It was May . . .' Jopling, *Twenty Years*, 49–50

260   'I am a very bad . . .' Monypenny, *Disraeli*, VI, 134

260   'Unfortunately Lord . . .' Morgan

260   'Poor Lord . . .' Ibid.

261   'sat propped . . .' Millais, *Life*, II, 169

262   'I have painted . . .' Huntington

262   'I don't think . . .' Morgan

263   'Australian miners . . .' Millais, *Life*, II, 122

263   'the illustrated . . .' Potter, *Journal*, 122

264   'In the winter . . .' Millais, *Life*, II, 128

264   'Mr Millais . . .' Quilter, *Preferences*, 174

265   'Really my . . .' Morgan

265   'I am just fagged . . .' Ibid.

265   'It is always . . .' Quilter, *Preferences*, 181

266   'The papers . . .' Potter, *Journal*, 153

266   'Retirement is . . .' Huntington

266   'Just one line . . .' Morgan

267   'It is with . . .' Ibid.

267   'Oh, Mary . . .' Ibid.

267   'Mr Millais is . . .' Potter, *Journal*, 153

268   'an ardent appreciator . . .' Hunt, *Pre-Raphaelitism*, II, 392

CHAPTER 24

page 272   'I have just finished . . .' Huntington

272   'I am awfully . . .' Ibid.

274   'I find work . . .' Ibid.

275   'I am in pain . . .' Ibid.

CHAPTER 25

page 277   'I am now . . .' Morgan

279   'I am sorry . . .' Ibid.

page 280 'I have worked . . .' Huntington
    281 'I feel the remaining . . .' Ibid.
    282 'When I remarked . . .' Spielmann, *Millais*, 119
    283 'I am much . . .' Huntington
    283 'I am voiceless . . .' Library of Congress
    283 'I have been . . .' Morgan
    284 'What in the name . . .' Ibid.
    284 'Your letter . . .' Ibid.
    286 'The death of our . . .' Lehmann, *Memories*, 251
    286 'Millais told . . .' Potter, *Journal*, 409
    286 'The death of Leighton . . .' British Library
    286 'Millais is the right . . .' Royal Academy
    289 'Papa is just . . .' Morgan
    289 'You are not . . .' Goodall, *Reminiscences*, 167

Select Bibliography

ALLINGHAM, WILLIAM, *Diary*, London: Macmillan, 1903

ARMSTRONG, WALTER, 'Millais', *National Review*, 6 (1886)

[ATKINSON, J.B.], 'Art, Politics, and Proceedings', *Blackwood's Magazine*, 100 (1886)

ATLEY, J.B., *Henry Wentworth Atkinson*, London: Smith, Elder, 1903

BALDRY, ALFRED, *Sir John Everett Millais*, London: Bell, 1899

BANNER, DELMAR, 'Holman Hunt and Pre-Raphaelitism', *Nineteenth Century*, 102, (1927)

BARRINGTON, EMILIE, 'Why Is Mr Millais Our Most Popular Painter?', *Fortnightly Review*, 38 (1882)

BENNETT, MARY, *Millais*, Liverpool: Walker Art Gallery, 1969

BENNETT, MARY, *William Holman Hunt*, Liverpool: Walker Art Gallery, 1969

BICKLEY, FRANCIS, *The Pre-Raphaelite Comedy*, New York: Holt, 1932

BRIGHTFIELD, MYRON, *Victorian England*, Los Angeles: University of California Library, 1971

BROOKFIELD, CHARLES and FRANCES, *Mrs Brookfield and Her Circle*, London: Pitman, 1906

BURNE-JONES, GEORGIANA, *Memorials of Edward Burne-Jones*, London: Macmillan, 1901

CARR, J. CONYNS, 'Some Memories of Millais', *Living Age*, 224 (1900)

CHAMPLIN, J.D., 'John Everett Millais', *Appleton's Journal* (1874)

CHAMPNEYS, BASIL, *Memoirs and Correspondence of Coventry Patmore*, London: Bell, 1900

COLLINGWOOD, WILLIAM G., *Life and Work of John Ruskin*, London: Methuen, 1893; Boston: Houghton Mifflin, 1900

COLVIN, SIDNEY, 'English Artists of the Present Day. John Everett Millais', *Portfolio*, 2 (1871)

COOK, E.T., *The Life of John Ruskin*, London: Allen, 1900

COOPER, JAMES FENIMORE, *Recollections of Europe*, Paris: Baudry's European Library, 1837

CUNNINGHAM, PETER, *Handbook of London*, London: Murray, 1850

DALZIELL, GEORGE and EDWARD, *The Brothers Dalziell*, London: Methuen, 1901

DAVIES, WILLIAM, 'The State of English Painting', *Quarterly Review*, 13 (1873)

DAVIS, NOEL PHARR, *Life of Wilkie Collins*, University of Illinois Press, 1956

DOUGHTY, OSWALD, *A Victorian Romantic: Dante Gabriel Rossetti*, London: Oxford University Press, 1960

DREW, MARY, *Acton, Gladstone, and Others*, London: Nisbet, 1924

DU MAURIER, DAPHNE, *Young George Du Maurier*, London: Peter Davies, 1951

EVANS, JOAN, 'Millais's Drawings of 1853', *Burlington Magazine*, 92 (1950)

'Expostulation with the Divorce Law', *Fraser's Magazine*, 1 (1830)

FARR, DENNIS, *William Etty*, London: Routledge & Kegan Paul, 1958

FENN, W.W., 'Memories of Millais', *Chambers's Journal*, 6th series, 4 (1901)

FENN, W.W., 'Millais and Music', *Chambers's Journal*, 6th series, 5 (1902)

FOX, CAROLYN, *Journals*, London: Elek, 1902

FREDEMAN, WILLIAM, E., *Pre-Raphaelitism*, Harvard University Press, 1965

FRITH, WILLIAM, *My Autobiography and Reminiscences*, London: Bentley, 1887

GASKELL, ELIZABETH, *Letters*, Oxford: Oxford University Press, 1932; Harvard University Press, 1967

GOODALL, FREDERICK, *Reminiscences*, London: Scott, 1901

GOWER, RONALD, *My Reminiscences*, London: Kegan Paul, 1895

GRAVES, ALGERNON, *The Royal Academy of Art*, London: Graves, 1906

GRIEVE, ALISTER, 'Ruskin and Millais at Glenfinlas', *Burlington Magazine*, 138 (1996)

HODGSON, JOHN E. and EATON, FRED, A., *The Royal Academy and Its Members*, London: Murray, 1905

HUEFFER, FORD MADOX, *Ancient Lights*, London: Chapman & Hall, 1911

HUNT, JOHN DIXON, *The Wider Sea*, New York: Viking, 1982

HUNT, WILLIAM HOLMAN, 'The Pre-Raphaelite Brotherhood', *Contemporary Review*, 49 (1886)

HUNT, WILLIAM HOLMAN, *Pre-Raphaelitism and the Pre-Raphaelite Brotherhood*, London: Macmillan, 1905

HUNT, WILLIAM HOLMAN, *Pre-Raphaelitism and the Pre-Raphaelite Brotherhood*, second edition. London: Chapman & Hall, 1913

HUTCHISON, SIDNEY, *History of the Royal Academy*, London: Chapman & Hall, 1968

JAMES, WILLIAM, *John Ruskin and Effie Gray*, New York: Scribner's, 1947

JOPLING, LOUISE, *Twenty Years of My Life*, London: Lane, 1925

KEARY, C.F., 'John Everett Millais', *Edinburgh Review*, 191 (1900)

LAMB, WALTER, *The Royal Academy*, London: Maclehose, 1935

LAYARD, GEORGE S., *Tennyson and His Pre-Raphaelite Illustrators*, London: Stock, 1894

LEHMANN, R.C., *Memories of Half a Century*, London: Smith, Elder, 1908

LESLIE, GEORGE DUNLOP, *The Inner Life of the Royal Academy*, London: Murray, 1914

LOW, FRANCIS H., 'Some Early Recollections of Sir John Everett Millais', *Strand*, 11 (1896)

LUTYENS, MARY, *Millais and the Ruskins*, London: Murray, 1967; New York: Vanguard, 1967

LUTYENS, MARY, *The Ruskins and the Grays*, London: Murray, 1972

MAAS, JEREMY, *Victorian Painters*, Barrie & Rockcliff, 1969

MARTIN, ROBERT BERNARD, *The Unquiet Heart*, Oxford University Press, 1980

MEEKS, CANOLE, *The Railroad Station*, Yale University Press, 1945

MILLAIS, JOHN GUILLE, *The Life and Letters of Sir John Millais*, London: Methuen, 1899

MONKHOUSE, COSMO, 'John Everett Millais', *Scribner's Magazine*, 20 (1896)

MONKHOUSE, COSMO, 'William Etty', *Dictionary of National Biography*, volume 3

MONYPENNY, WILLIAM, *The Life of Benjamin Disraeli*, London: Murray, 1926

New Letters of Thomas Carlyle, ed. by Alex Carlyle, London: Lane, 1904

OLDCASTLE, JOHN, 'Mr Millais's House at Palace Gate', *Magazine of Art*, 4 (1881)

[OLIPHANT, MARGARET],'Art in May', *Blackwood's Magazine*, 117 (1875)

[OLIPHANT, MARGARET], 'The Royal Academy', *Blackwood's Magazine*, 119 (1876)

'Our Critic Among the Pictures', *Punch*, 22 (1852)

PATTERSON, ALFRED, *A History of Southampton*, Southampton University Press, 1966

PAYNE, J. BERTRAND, *An Armorial of Jersey*, St Helier, Jersey: privately published, 1860

PENNELL, JOSEPH, 'A Golden Decade in English Art', *Savoy*, 1 (1896)

PENNELL, JOSEPH and ELIZABETH, 'John Everett Millais', *Fortnightly Review*, 66 (1896)

PHYTHIAN, JOHN E., *Millais*, London: George Allen, 1911

POTTER, BEATRIX, *Journal*, London: Warne, 1966

'Pre-Raphaelitism', *Irish Quarterly Review*, 1 (1851)

QUILTER, HARRY, *Preferences*, London: Sonnenschein, 1892

REYNOLDS, GRAHAM, *Painters of the Victorian Scene*, London: Batsford, 1953

ROSSETTI, DANTE GABRIEL, *Letters*, ed. by Oswald Doughty and John Robert Wahl, Oxford University Press, 1965

ROSSETTI, WILLIAM MICHAEL, *Fine Art*, London: Macmillan, 1867

ROSSETTI, WILLIAM MICHAEL, *The PRB Journal*, Oxford: Clarendon Press, 1975

ROSSETTI, WILLIAM MICHAEL, *Pre-Raphaelite Diaries and Letters*, London: Hurst & Blackett, 1900

ROSSETTI, WILLIAM MICHAEL, *Ruskin: Rossetti: Pre-Raphaelitism*, London: George Allen, 1899

ROSSETTI, WILLIAM MICHAEL, *Some Reminiscences*, London: Brown Langham, 1906

RUSKIN, JOHN, *Works*, ed. by E.T. Cook and Alexander Weddeburn, London: George Allen, 1901

SCOTT, WILLIAM BELL, *Autobiographical Notes*, London: Osgood, 1892

SHEE, MARTIN ARCHER, *The Life of Sir Martin Archer Shee*, London: Longman, Green, 1860

SPIELMANN, MARION H., *Millais and His Works*, London: Blackwood, 1898

STEPHENS, FREDERIC GEORGE, *Artists at Home*, New York: Appleton, 1888

STEPHENS, FREDERIC GEORGE, *Dante Gabriel Rossetti*, London: George Allen, 1909

STEPHENS, FREDERIC GEORGE, *Exhibition of the Works of Sir John Everett Millais*, London: H. Good & Sons, 1886

STEPHENS, FREDERIC GEORGE, 'The Two Pre-Raphaelitisms,' *Crayon*, 3 (1856) 'Stories of Millais,' *Outlook*, 54 (1896)

SURTEES, VIRGINIA, *Reflections of a Friendship*, London: Allen & Unwin, 1979

THACKERAY, WILLIAM MAKEPEACE, *Letters*, ed. by Gordon Ray, Harvard University Press, 1945

THOMAS, RALPH, *Serjeant Thomas and Sir John Millais*, London: Russell Smith, 1901

TREVELYAN, RALEIGH, *A Pre-Raphaelite Circle*, London: Chatto & Windus, 1978

TROLLOPE, ANTHONY, *Autobiography*, Edinburgh & London: Blackwood, 1883; New York: Harper, 1883

WARD, MRS E.M., *Reminiscences*, London: Pitman, 1911

WATTS, M.F., *George Frederick Watts*, London: Macmillan, 1902

WHITEHOUSE, J. HOWARD, *Vindication of Ruskin*, London: Allen & Unwin, 1950

WILLIAMS-ELLIS, ANABEL, *The Tragedy of John Ruskin*, London: Cape, 1928

WILSON, DAVID ALEC and MACARTHUR, DAVID WILSON, *Carlyle in Old Age*, London: Kegan Paul, 1934

WOOLNER, AMY, *Thomas Woolner*, London: Chapman & Hall, 1907

Index